'Beautifully written, capturing the wonder and personality of each creature, big and small, perfectly. Megan's words make you befriend and root for each of the animals she describes and gives you hope for a better future'

DR AMIR KHAN

'Welcome to frontline conservation, the tough, gritty and real decisions that are protecting our wildlife'

CHRIS PACKHAM

'Packed full of wonderful pictures and deep insights into the lives of the beautiful plants and creatures the planet is in grave danger of losing – don't miss this book!'

DALE VINCE

An Atlas of Endangered Species

An Atlas of Endangered Species

Megan McCubbin

TWO
ROADS

First published in Great Britain in 2023 by Two Roads
An imprint of John Murray Press
An Hachette UK company

2

Copyright © Megan McCubbin 2023

The right of Megan McCubbin to be identified as the Author of the Work
has been asserted by her in accordance with the Copyright, Designs and
Patents Act 1988.

Illustrations © Emily Robertson

A CIP catalogue record for this title is available from the British Library

Hardback ISBN 978-1-529-36953-3
eBook ISBN 978-1-529-36954-0

Typeset in Myriad Pro 11/16pt by Integra Software Services Pvt. Ltd,
Pondicherry, India

Printed and bound in Slovakia by TBB.

John Murray policy is to use papers that are natural, renewable and
recyclable products and made from wood grown in sustainable forests.
The logging and manufacturing processes are expected to conform to
the environmental regulations of the country of origin.

Two Roads
Carmelite House
50 Victoria Embankment
London EC4Y 0DZ

www.tworoadsbooks.com

To the scientists who discover, to the activists who fight and to the teachers who empower – but most importantly, to the species which make this curious world so beautiful. This book is for you.

Contents

Southern Hemisphere 159

Introduction

I have always admired ants; they appear tiny and insignificant, but these robust social insects hatch with such a powerful sense of purpose that almost nothing can sway them from their mission. I have always respected wolves; a powerful apex predator that helps to manage the landscape, but is also capable of sharing intimate social relationships within its pack, caring for the old and the injured while teaching and playing with the young. I have always treasured the daisy; simplicity defined, with a rosette of bright white petals centred around a luminous yellow carpel, yet capable of supporting an entire complex ecosystem of pollinators with only its nectar. When you give yourself a moment to soak in the diversity of life around you, it's impossible to ignore how special it truly is. The Earth is 4.5 billion years old and many species have come and gone in that time, some leaving footprints and others fragments of fossilised bone, giving clues to what came before. There have been meteorites, ice ages, volcanic eruptions and other life-shattering events in the lead-up to today's world – so how lucky are we that we get to exist in the company of ants, wolves and daisies alike?

It feels particularly incredible given that 98 per cent of all species that have ever existed on our precious planet are now extinct. It's a harsh word, isn't it? Extinction. It's final and, often when spoken out loud, filled with dread. But in reality, and at its original rate, extinction is just as natural and important as life itself. However, with the influence of humanity, it has come to represent more than just the gradual loss of another innocent species – with every new fast-tracked elimination comes another mark against us; another heavy weight to bear on our shoulders. It's commonly reported that species are currently going extinct somewhere between 1,000 and 10,000 times faster than the natural baseline extinction rate. Due to anthropogenic activity, we are losing species every single day, including many that we are yet to even discover and appreciate. In October 2022, the World Wildlife Fund (WWF) released their Living Planet Report, which is the most comprehensive study of global biodiversity trends to date. Analysing nearly 32,000 populations of 5,230 species, it detailed how the abundance of wildlife around the world has declined by 69 per cent since the 1970s, South America and the Caribbean being the most severely affected regions with a shocking 94 per cent loss of abundance. And according to the UN Convention on Biological Diversity, an estimated three species vanish every hour, which equals 150 every single day. Each year there could be as many as 55,000 animals and plants that are pushed into extinction. Human activity has led to Earth's sixth mass extinction event, named the anthropocene extinction. We have destroyed, fragmented and polluted habitats. We have burned fossil fuels and pumped unprecedented levels of carbon dioxide into the atmosphere. We have sprayed toxic chemicals on our fields and poisoned rivers. We have first invented plastic and then spat it out into the sea. And we have directly persecuted the species we claim to love.

I realise that I have not started this book with the happiest of thoughts, but don't worry: this is not a book about the end of the world, this is a book about inspiring people doing inspiring things trying to save some incredible and unique species from the brink. It's not an impossible task. Spix's macaw was declared extinct in the wild in 2000 which caused global upset, but today, thanks to a reintroduction project, they represent a huge conservation success and can now be seen flying over the forests of Brazil once more. Przewalski's horse was declared extinct in the wild in 1960, but there is now a self-sustaining population galloping the steppes of Mongolia. And the Antarctic blue whales who were industrially hunted for their oil, causing population collapse, have now made a dramatic recovery. These are all examples of what is possible when we choose to collaborate, raise awareness and, more importantly, act on the science.

But have you ever wondered what it takes to pull a species back from the brink? How would you decide what species or threat to focus on? What methods would you use? How would you determine if your efforts were working? Or perhaps more importantly, where would you even begin? These are all questions that I have asked myself hundreds of times, so I thought it was about time that I found out the answers and wrote them down on behalf of all other curious minds out there.

Throughout the twenty chapters in this book, I'll take you around the world so we can get to know nineteen remarkable species on the knife-edge of extinction… and one animal that's, well, a little closer to home. From the functionally extinct northern white rhinos and the famous Sumatran orangutans to the lesser-known icons – the sunflower sea stars and the lady slipper orchids – this is an anthology of stories about their fight for survival. It was so challenging choosing only twenty when so many species deserve the spotlight, but I felt that those I selected each had their own important, distinct tale to tell.

Over the past two years, I've reached out to scientists and rangers across the globe who have dedicated their lives to the protection of wildlife. Nobody knows more about these species than the people who live or work alongside them, so I decided to go right to the source. I wanted to know their successes and their struggles, and why they are motivated to do what they do on the frontline of conservation. I conducted all the interviews over Zoom, limiting my carbon footprint, and it's fair to say that I learned a lot. From community conservation to full blown *Jurassic Park*-esque science, I was astounded by the lengths these remarkable humans are going to in their efforts to safeguard the health of the planet. I think diversity of opinion and voice is of the utmost importance since to tackle the challenges of extinction we must collectively put our minds and skillsets together. With that in mind, I have tried my best to speak to as many people as possible on the ground and to recognise their efforts within these pages. However, I have to admit that between language barriers, challenging internet connections and the many biases and privileges that exist within the scientific world, it was not possible for me to find an indigenous voice for every one of these species. I wish I had; it wasn't down to lack of effort as I am aware that indigenous voices are some of the most important in the conversation when it comes to tackling the climate and biodiversity crisis. It's important to remain aware throughout that the landscape and solutions can look very different for the people living within than from the outside.

If we want to make a difference to our world, we need to make conservation as accessible as possible to a wide range of people. I was diagnosed with dyslexia at the age of seven, and at the time I found science, maths and reading three of the scariest things in the world. But as soon as I found ways to learn these subjects on my own terms, I realised that zoology was not only my passion, but somewhere I could make a difference! It took a lot to realise that it wasn't that I couldn't understand science or that I was bad at English, I just needed to learn how I learn best. I didn't fit in with the conventional style of teaching, and that's okay. I am now a science communicator and I always try to discuss complicated topics in a way that I would have understood when I was younger (although if you'd told me then that I would be authoring a book on biology and conservation just twenty years later, I'm not sure whether I would have laughed, or cried and run away…). And so this book has been published with dyslexic readers in mind, both in terms of the communication style and the fonts, layouts and designs used, which have been proven to be helpful for dyslexic thinkers, like me.

Biodiversity is beautiful. It encompasses the diversity of life but also the fascinating interactions between organisms within and between environments – from the soil to the sea, and the air to the forests. It's everything from the genes that code us to the species classifications that define us and the ecosystems that support us. But as we teeter on the brink of climate catastrophe, we are living in a very bizarre moment in time, where we must choose. As it stands, there are too many scientists being ignored, too many species being forgotten and too many people giving up because of the lack of environmental action. There are some days where I feel frustrated and overwhelmed too, but then I remember the species in this book and the exceptional people who are fighting to keep them here. We have the solutions. It is possible to turn this urgently around. And from my perspective, as long as these species walk, fly, slither, hop or swim on the planet, then we still have a lot left worth fighting for.

Northern Hemisphere

Orangutans

Try for a minute to put yourself in the skin of a female orangutan.

She looks down at her chest to see two glistening eyes staring back. He is the most precious thing in the world and she will do anything to protect him. Offspring were not always in her future; you see, she has had a difficult past.

For years, she was kept in a cage by a weird-looking bald ape that she could never really understand. Initially, when she was just a baby herself, she was allowed to play in their house. She swung from the curtains, trying to reach the heights she once lived at in the forest, but they weren't so keen on that. They didn't understand that she just wanted to be free. As she quickly grew bigger and stronger, they locked her up and threw away the key.

When all hope was lost, more people showed up. They broke open her cage and started to repair her wounds and heart. She grew in confidence and one day… she was released back to the forests she once called home. Her own mother was long gone but it was where she belonged.

Today she holds her baby in her arms, trying to teach him to stay away from those other apes that did her wrong. But quite frankly there is almost nowhere left to turn.

The ending of this story is not yet written… and how it plays out is ultimately up to all of us.

As humans we have the ability to recognise and analyse our emotions in such detail that our understanding of our own feelings can be one of the most beautiful things about being alive – although also one of the worst at times. Compassion, love, empathy, humility, anger, frustration, devastation… It's definitely a rollercoaster but it is what makes us who we are as sentient beings.

Sentience is the capacity for any living creature to feel emotions. It involves having awareness and the basic cognitive ability to evaluate the actions of others in relation to yourself, and potentially other parties, as well as assessing the consequences and benefits of a behaviour you may exhibit. For anyone who has ever had an interaction with a non-human animal, it's clear that sentience is widespread. My dogs, Sid and Nancy, can communicate with me with just a look. They feel grumpy when they don't go out for their daily walk on time, sad when I leave them and proud when they think they've got away with digging a massive hole in the back garden. I mean, they never really get away with it – the mud that cakes their noses gives the game away – but it makes me smile to see them trotting around, tails wagging and clearly feeling pretty smug about having 'got away' with their blatant naughtiness. Maybe that says more about me than them! But regardless, it only takes a few seconds in the company of a species separate to our own before you realise that they are capable of feeling and expressing a wide range of comparable emotions.

Categorising sentience is subjective and therefore hard to define. Although after thousands of years of domestication, we know for sure that our canine companions are able to interpret our facial expressions and also manipulate our emotions by adapting theirs. Believe it or not, puppy-dog eyes are a real thing, with dogs purposely exaggerating their eyes when they want something from a person. But what about other species? Well, we are learning more about their levels of emotion every day, so much so that in 2021 in the UK vertebrate animals became formally recognised as sentient beings by law. A bit late to the party if you ask me, but it's a step in the right direction, respecting that domestic and wild animals are more than just 'things' we share our Earth with. I think there's something to be said for looking into the eyes of an animal because, without anthropomorphising, you can sense that there is a lot more going on inside their minds than is usually credited.

Perhaps the most obvious and undeniable example of sentience as we understand it is in the species that are most closely related to ourselves: the great apes. Having walked alongside wild chimpanzees in Uganda, I can say from personal experience that it's a spellbinding encounter that somehow feels both familiar and uncomfortable at the same time as the boundaries of interspecies communication fall away. They are relatable in the way they move; they are simultaneously like us yet unlike us, which is why I think most people either adore great apes or feel unsettled around them. They're almost *too* similar to us; but that's precisely what makes them fascinating. They are our closest living relatives, sharing 97 per cent of our DNA; but what's so remarkable is the difference that 3 per cent can make.

I studied at Liverpool University in the UK and we had an annual visit to Chester Zoo, which is famed for its work in captive breeding and conservation. It's home to a record 35,000 individual animals, and 500 of the world's most endangered species. At the top of that list is a group of critically endangered orangutans.

The zoo houses both Sumatran and Bornean orangutans, two species that diverged from one another approximately 40,000 years ago when the Indonesian islands separated, causing the two to evolve independently. Upon entering the zoo each year, I would make a beeline to go and see them. I knew of a window where they preferred to sit; them watching us, us watching them. Occasionally the dominant male would approach the glass pane and give me the chance to gaze directly into his big chestnut eyes. I remember thinking, 'I need to remember every detail of his face,' because with so much uncertainty about their future in the wild, who knows how long they will be able to exist in their native luscious forests.

Orangutans – meaning 'persons' (orang) of the 'forest' (utan) – are a ghostly presence these days. There are three species in total: the Sumatran, Bornean and the relatively newly described Tapanuli orangutan. In November 2017, it was announced that the Tapanuli would furthermore be classified as a different species, and, with fewer than 800 individuals left in the wild in North Sumatra, it became the most endangered of all the great apes. Initially they were believed to be the same as Sumatran orangutans, but evidence of distinct differences in their genetics and behaviour suggested the two diverged approximately 10,000–20,000 years ago. I find it astonishing that we are still learning such fundamental information about these megafauna groups, which are comparatively so well studied. Sadly, Tapanuli orangutans are confined to an area of just 1,100 square kilometres in the Batang Toru region, which is currently under threat due to plans to build a hydroelectric dam. There are an estimated 104,700 Bornean orangutans left in the wild but scientists are predicting that this figure will drop to a devastating 47,000 by

2025. As for Sumatran orangutans, only 14,000 remain. They are restricted to living mainly in the Leuser Ecosystem, which consists of 2.6 million hectares – only about 1.3 times the size of Wales. It's terrifying to think that collectively orangutans only inhabit 5 per cent of their former ranges. Despite being globally iconic and having approximately £60 million spent on their conservation annually, numbers are still dwindling. So, what is happening to these intelligent giants of the trees?

Ultimately, orangutans are the innocent victims of years of environmental destruction and illegal human activity. Their similarity to us has encouraged a deep fascination with the species, so many of us find them cute or interesting, and this led to (and it sadly continues today) the desire to keep them as 'pets' or for use in the entertainment industry. Despite orangutans being protected by legislation in Indonesia since 1931, the demand for the illegal pet trade is high. A report from the UN Environment Programme (UNEP) suggests that up to 6,000 great apes are either captured or killed annually in the wild for this reason and it's believed that up to 70 per cent of those 6,000 apes are orangutans – including both individuals intended for capture and those fatally injured during the hunting process. Illegal hunters shoot a mother high up in the trees and wait for her and her baby to come crashing to the ground. They then prise the youngster from the mother's warm, bloody fingers to be shipped across the world so it can spend the remainder of its life (some forty years if it's lucky, or unlucky depending on how you look at it) confined to a cage in somebody's garage or garden. This is the bleak reality for many orangutans. It's a grave issue, and is contributing to the demise of the species.

Although the illegal wildlife trade is detrimental, the larger threat to their survival is habitat destruction, in the form of deforestation for the expansion of palm oil plantations, mining, forest and peat fires, and an increase in infrastructure. Palm oil is a type of vegetable oil produced from the kernels of oil palm trees. It's a highly productive crop with a low production cost, and, according to the World Wildlife Fund, it's in nearly 50 per cent of all items sold in supermarkets. It's shocking how much is in the products we buy every day; it's in our food, toiletries and cosmetics, and even clothing. But even for the most eco-conscious of consumers, manufacturers don't make it easy to spot because they label it under many different complex scientific names: elaeis guineensis, glyceryl, octyl palmitate, hydrogenated palm glycerides, palmate, steareth-20, OPKO, stearic acid… the list could go on. It is everywhere, especially in processed products: from soap, lipstick and face wash to bread, pizza, biodiesel, ice cream, and so much more. To feed this insatiable palm oil beast that we've created, by the end of 2020 Indonesia was producing 48.3 million metric tonnes of the oil from plantations covering over 14.6 million hectares of the region. Unsurprisingly, it's the world's largest palm oil producer, and much of that land would have once been home to a biodiverse, low-lying tropical rainforest, filled with orange apes swinging from ancient treetops.

The rainforests in Indonesia are home to between 10 and 15 per cent of all documented species of plants, mammals and birds on Earth. In addition, the habitat stores nearly 300 billion tonnes of carbon – forty times the yearly greenhouse gas emission emitted by fossil fuels. These environments help regulate the climate not only of Indonesia but of the entire globe. We need them to be functional. When the land is deforested to make way for plantations, the carbon-rich peatland soil is drained and becomes highly susceptible to fire. Once on fire, the blaze is hard to control, and it releases so much carbon into our already warming atmosphere that Indonesia now ranks alongside the USA and China as one of the leading emitters of global greenhouse gases; this is all due to deforestation. Researchers at Harvard and Columbia universities detail how the famous giant fires in 2015 that destroyed two million hectares of rainforest may have contributed to 100,000 premature human deaths due to direct and indirect exposure to smoke, not to mention the impacts on wildlife. Despite these devastating impacts, huge areas of prime rainforest are still being both legally and illegally cleared. Estimates vary, but most conservative studies suggest that at least 2.4 million acres are lost every single year. Orangutans are literally clinging to the areas that remain and now experts say that they could be extinct within the next twenty years.

Over 25 million people in Indonesia live below the poverty line. Living alongside orangutans can be difficult if you have limited crops that you and your family rely on, but which these great apes also desire. Orangutans can be persecuted for roaming into the wrong areas looking for food that is no longer in wide supply in the forests. To understand more about this conflict and what it's really like trying to protect these magnificent animals on the ground, I asked veterinarian and former coordinator for Human Orangutan Conflict Response Unit, Ricko Jaya, whether he would be willing to jump on Zoom for a chat. He's currently studying a PhD at the University of Birmingham and he very kindly made some time for me. His stories were both heartbreaking and hopeful at the same time. Ricko became devoted to the conservation of orangutans when volunteering at a rehabilitation centre in North Sumatra. The centre focused on helping seriously injured orangutans, often orphans, to find their confidence before one day being released back into the wild.

'The Human Orangutan Conflict Response Unit was founded by the Orangutan Information Centre and I joined in 2012. We did many confiscation rescues followed by the translocation of orangutans to safe areas and I oversaw 150-something individuals back into the wild,' Ricko explains. 'Focusing on one specific species, I can fill that niche between the conservation needed in Indonesia and medicine. It's outside with people, and it's an ideal job for me!'

I am in awe of anyone in the veterinary world – from the general practice to the more exotic wildlife care. But I have to say – studying orangutans out in the wilderness sounds pretty enticing, doesn't it? Who wants a comfortable office chair anyway when you could be a real-life Tarzan? Of course, it's not quite as easy as that. Rehabilitation is a long, challenging process that requires medical, dietary and emotional support.

Ricko continues, 'The first problem is getting the confiscated orangutan through the trauma to a point where they can be released back into the wild – it takes a lot of time and resources – and the second issue is where they go as the habitat has to be healthy; we can't just release them anywhere. At the moment the numbers aren't going down in our centres. By law, no one is allowed to keep orangutans, so when they are pushed out of the forest – because of deforestation – they come into contact with people that don't know what else to do except capture them and call the rehabilitation centre. In the Sumatra centre, there are about sixty cases and in Borneo maybe around a thousand. Half will never be able to go back to the wild and the rest are waiting until suitable habitat is available. Covid-19 has also made things tricky because we are unable to move around as much.'

Conflict between wildlife and people has always been – and will always be – a huge problem, but it's our perceptions of these species and how we manage that encroachment that is really interesting. Indonesia is home to a wide range of wild animals, so local people are subject to conflict with various species. Elephants, for example, are huge creatures that can weigh over 3,000 kilograms and move in large herds; they can devastate crop fields in just one sitting. This can decimate a family's livelihood. In addition, tigers are apex predators that humans have feared throughout history; they have been known to attack both livestock and humans, which perpetuates the distrust many communities feel towards them. But how do local communities feel about orangutans?

In the UK and much of the western world, orangutans are perceived as gentle giants. I asked Ricko – who usefully for me completed a dissertation on the subject – about this, and he informed me that many of the people who live near them are very fearful of them. They're hairy, 60-kg creatures looming down from the trees; in some villages it's even believed that they can snatch people, lifting them high up into the trees, where they're left to hang. (I'd be fascinated to know the origin of that story…) In a nutshell, they're seen as intimidating, not just because of old stories but also because of the financial destruction that could be caused if they fancy picking your crops.

Every so often, heartbreaking images hit the headlines of orangutans in dire conditions. But being there on the ground facing it head-on must be even more emotionally daunting. Ricko describes a harrowing experience that he and his team witnessed while out on a rescue: 'I remember that back in 2016, there was one orangutan that had been kept as a pet in a cage for more or less twenty years. According to the "owner", they'd kept him since 1998. So roughly the age of the orangutan would have been twenty-two to twenty-four years. Orangutans rarely stand upright on their legs in the wild but even so, the cage he was living in was smaller than his height so he was forced to spend years sitting in the same position. When we confiscated him with the help of the government, we took the orangutan to the rehabilitation centre and he could barely stand up. He couldn't even straighten his legs, you know. And typically orangutans are dependent upon their mothers until they are seven years old, and during that time they learn how to survive, eat and make nests. This guy didn't have that chance. Imagine a 25-year-old man behaving like a four-year-old child – it was very similar. We gave him the best veterinary care and the time to rebuild his strength but whenever he climbs, he doesn't go very far and it's almost like he is afraid of heights. There's no guarantee with rehabilitation that it'll work. Each orangutan is an individual with their own big characters. Some have the drive to make it back and for others, it's just too much. But it's important we can give them that second chance.'

At the Indonesian rehabilitation centre, the orangutans are housed with others of a similar age and skill level. Each individual has a different background and history, so by adopting this method the orangutans are able to pick up skills much faster than if they were learning from a surrogate human 'mum'. 'The best teacher for an orangutan is the orangutan itself,' says Ricko. 'As their caretakers we can provide them with enrichment and the tools they need, but they need to process information and improve skills themselves. They help one another learn the good things and the bad. The earlier they get to us, the more time they have for learning and younger ones can often be released at seven years of age, but when older orangutans come in that have been kept for a long time in bad conditions then it can be more difficult to teach them, so they go through a very soft release. Young orangutans take part in forest schools during the day where they habituate to the surrounding environment. They spend the night in enclosures with all the materials needed so they can build upon their nesting skills. Hard releases are for individuals that have come to the centre directly from the wild and can be returned quickly. They'll be given any veterinary care needed and then released as soon as possible with monitoring in place.'

If all goes well and an individual is released, the team do all they can to support and watch from afar in the early stages, but monitoring post-rehabilitation has its challenges. Firstly, it's difficult to follow them on foot in the dense rainforest and – unlike a tiger or elephant that could be easily radio-collared – this is not possible for orangutans that are moving from branch to branch, tree to tree; the collars break easily and it's a waste. There is the option of surgically implanting a transmitter inside their bodies, which helps track their precise movements for the first three to six months after release, but it's expensive and there isn't enough funding or resource to do it with every individual. That's why rehabilitation is so crucial, because getting it right the first time is critical for the survival of these orangutans.

Thinking back to the orangutans housed in Chester Zoo, I knew that they were also a heavily studied group. I would love nothing more than for those animals to be where they belong in the wild, but it is reassuring to know that they are still playing a meaningful role as ambassadors for their species and are supporting critical research that helps their cousins in Indonesia.

Lelia Bridgeland-Stephens is a scientist working with Ricko at the University of Birmingham, and she's developing some remarkable techniques to aid in the rehabilitation process on the ground. Having witnessed the impacts of illegal hunting and the pet trade of primates in Bolivia, Lelia really wanted to go into research that would make a difference in that area. 'I remember meeting a howler monkey called Baloo who was taken in a similar way to orangutan babies: his mother was shot when he was tiny so that he could be sold as a pet. The poachers broke every single one of his fingers to prise him off his dead mother as he refused to let go. It was the saddest thing I have ever heard and it just shows the lengths people will go to,' she says as she explains why she's so passionate about what she does.

To aid her research into which skills orangutans need to master during rehabilitation, Lelia and her team use a software called the Enclosure Design Tool, which essentially allows them to input data based on simple observations of behaviour. (Sounds sexy, doesn't it? I love a good data spreadsheet!) This can then be compared to wild orangutan populations, highlighting the differences or similarities in locomotion, food processing and social interactions. This helps zoos to encourage more naturally occurring behaviours, as staff can modify enclosures and enrichments based on the results.

'When the orangutans are taken from the wild, they often will have experienced some quite traumatic things,' Lelia explains. 'They can sustain quite severe physical and mental harm, which then has an impact on psychological functioning. And we know that, in humans and other animals, this kind of unavoidable long-term trauma can lead to a phenomenon termed learned helplessness, where you feel that you have no control over that trauma, your own environment and that everything is happening to you and that you don't have any agency to make things better for yourself. It's a really important area to understand because if we can help combat it, it could help give orangutans the flexibility and resilience when they're released back to the wild to face challenges they haven't encountered before. The aim is they will not only bounce back from those challenges, but also learn from them so that they can thrive in the forest rather than just survive.'

Another area of Lelia's study is something called 'cautious exploration'. In the wild orangutans are wary of people and any novel items or experiences that may pose them harm – they'd much rather keep away – but over time living in a rehabilitation centre the fear of engaging with new things can disappear. The orangutans come to trust the centre and their human caretakers – which is a good thing in the short term but not necessarily long-term. Lelia notes, 'Captive orangutans tend to be very curious about new things and although that curiosity is really good for when they're released so that they can try different foods and explore their environment, on the other side there's a worry that they're going to be too comfortable, especially around human settlements, which could lead to dangerous conflicts. One of the things we're trying to do is maintain that balance. When they are young it is very important that there is a human there to look after them – it would be unnatural if not and could cause attachment issues – but as they get older, it's also important that they break away from people. A lot of our research is on social learning, so that's why we put orangutans together so that they learn from one another. It's tricky and we don't have the answers yet, but we are working on it!'

I wish I could say there was someone out there who had the answers, but unfortunately the situation is much too complicated. What we do know is that in order to save orangutans we need to halt destructive deforestation and restore their habitat – saving individuals is only part of the equation. So I have a request for you: go into your food, cleaning and cosmetic cupboards and note down everything that has palm oil in it. It might take you a little while but it'll be worth it as an eye-opening exercise. We are all responsible for the decline of this species and there is a high chance that we could lose them from the wild if we don't move away from these products. Yes – I'm sorry – that does include Nutella, Domino's Pizza and Pepsi #nameandshame. But if we truly care, it's a very small price to pay, and you as an individual do make a difference!

On a larger scale, there is hope to be had too. In recent years there has been a slight decline in recorded deforestation in Indonesia as new initiatives have been put in place to help protect the forest that remains. In 2014 the Indonesian government adopted a community forest management approach that aimed to allocate 12.7 million hectares of primary rainforest to marginalised communities. The hope was to prevent more habitat destruction and reduce wildlife conflict by giving forest ownership back to indigenous people. It has proven to be successful in some regions, and slow in others, but it's an important step forward! Stronger border control and import regulations have also proven successful. Since 2016, Indonesia has only exported verified timber and timber products to the EU. That's not to say some illegal timber doesn't slip through the net, but again we have to celebrate each movement in the right direction. There's a long way to go; the work has only just begun.

But as with all of the species in the book, why should we care about orangutans specifically?

I think Ricko sums it up perfectly:

'Orangutans are a symbol of conservation. By saving the orangutan, we can save the forest and then we can save ourselves. So this is not just about saving one species; they represent the overall effort to save that habitat. It's a habitat that regulates water, pollution and natural disasters. It's those forests that house hundreds of unique, endemic species. There is more than one excuse to save the Indonesian rainforest. People see this effort to save the orangutan like an effort to save our own species. That's how I see it.'

Sentience is a beautiful thing. The vast majority of people really feel the losses when it comes to species decline and extinction. Do you remember the famous footage that went viral in 2018 of an orangutan holding on to a decimated tree trunk as a bulldozer approached? It rightly sparked an outcry. While that sadness can be overwhelming at times, we have to put our faith in the people working tirelessly trying to make a difference. From the orangutan caregivers, rescue teams, vets, scientists and local communities to the people like us in the supermarkets, choosing wisely what goes into our baskets.

Together, we get to decide how the story ends.

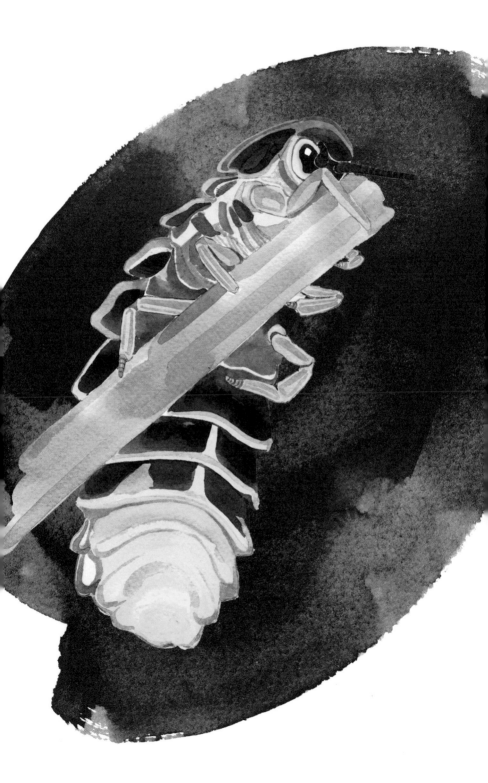

Glow-Worms

Take a second to notice your environment. What can you see – is it bright, is it saturated? What can you feel – the chair you're sitting on and the paper grazing your fingertips? What do you hear – perhaps you're on a train, or reading outside with the breeze and birdsong? What can you smell and what can you taste? It's not often we stop and really focus on the information our senses are providing for us but, when we do, it can be an all-consuming, relaxing moment.

How our five senses function physiologically is a topic that scientists have been trying to crack for centuries. We have a lot of the answers but, like anything, there's always more to understand.

I'm curious – are there some senses you favour above others? If so, how would you rank them in importance? I thought about this for all of five seconds before I conjured an answer, from most valuable to least: sight, sound, touch, taste and, finally, smell. It's not to say I don't appreciate the capacity to taste and smell – as a foodie with an obsession for scented candles and the smell of rain, I truly do treasure those senses – but sight and sound seem to be the senses I rely on the most and it's hard for me to imagine a life without them.

To me, as an able-bodied person raised in the UK, it's hard to imagine anything else, but this sense hierarchy changes depending on both culture and language. In one study, people speaking twenty different languages (including three sign languages) from varying communities were asked to describe a stimulus. For those from a post-industrial society speaking English there were fewer words to describe taste and smell but when asked to describe a picture it was highly detailed, whereas hunter-gatherers from Australia speaking Umpila could interpret smell far more elaborately. In contrast, speakers of Farsi in Iran had more ways to communicate how something tastes. Essentially, we are not only limited by the restrictions of our own senses, but also the languages and culture through which we actualise them.

It gets harder still when we try to understand the world through the perspective of a different species whose senses are beyond our comprehension. For instance, bumblebees are positively charged due to the fast-paced beating of their wings, colliding with molecules in the air. They arrive at negatively charged flowers and, without ever having to land or touch the surface, the static electricity between the two opposing electric fields causes the negatively charged unanchored pollen grains to move up and onto the positive bumblebee. We know that dogs experience much of their world through a strong sense of smell, but recent studies have shown that they are able to detect through scent when their owners are stressed due to increased cortisol levels secreted in sweat; they can *smell* our emotional states. Human eyes have three types of light-detecting cones, red, green and blue, that enable us to see the world in colour. Mantis shrimp have twelve colour receptors, yet scientists have found they do not have great colour vision; instead they see almost different dimensions of movement, which they use to respond quicker. It's as though they can warp time and speed to their advantage. And some snakes, vipers and boas, have pit organs on their snouts with a membrane that can detect infrared radiation for hunting at night. Like thermal cameras, they can detect the warmth of their prey and strike with precision. Will we ever know what it feels like to detect and interpret electromagnetic fields, or hear the low-frequency rumbling within a forest's root system and be able to deduce what it means? There is a whole *Alice in Wonderland*-esque dimension constantly buzzing around us and, for the most part, it goes completely and beautifully undetected.

Humans are mesmerised by light, whether naturally produced from the sun and other stars or artificially emitted from fireworks and screens. It establishes night and day and its different hues and intensities can alter our mood and emotions. Traditionally, the contrast of light and dark symbolises good and evil. Fairies, unicorns and angels often beam light, whereas gremlins and demons are depicted as creatures of darkness. So, it's no wonder that displays of natural light are cloaked in supernatural folklore. The northern lights, also known as the aurora borealis, were believed by the Cree, indigenous North Americans, to be the spirits of friends and family trying to communicate with loved ones left behind, whereas in Scotland the lights are referred to as 'Na Fir Chlis' or 'Mirrie Dancers' and were believed to be the sky-warriors engaged in battle. In the Philippines, fireflies were thought to be parts of a shattered star, while in Amazonia they were said to be bringing light from the gods to provide hope and guidance.

Now I don't mean to burst the mystical bubble but we now know that the northern lights are caused by electrons colliding with oxygen and nitrogen molecules in the atmosphere's upper surface and that light from a firefly is created by a chemical reaction known as bioluminescence. And every year, many more species are being added onto the 'glowing' list, emphasising just how important light is in biology for communication, camouflage, prey location and mating.

Most prevalent in marine organisms (or so we think currently), bioluminescence is adopted by sharks, jellyfish, dinoflagellates (a type of plankton), anglerfish, algae and squid among others. On land, there are some insects that have mastered the adaptation too. This is not to be confused with biofluorescence, which is the ability some animals have to reflect sunlight in another wavelength and glow (as platypus and puffins do under UV); bioluminescent species *generate* their own light.

Glow-worms are one such species. Not actually a worm like their name suggests, these are beetles that have the ability to shine from their bums (or lower abdomen, if you want to be professional). It's a remarkable spectacle that almost has to be seen to be believed, but you're most likely to catch a glimpse during peak mating season in June or July. But the big question remains: what is this chemical reaction that creates such beauty?

A specialised organ called a photophore, in glow-worms' abdomens, produces light when the substrate luciferin is oxidised by the luciferase enzyme to make oxy-luciferin molecules, the product of which is carbon dioxide and photons of light. But where my inner nerdiness gets really excited is when I think about the heat and energy efficiency of this process. Old-fashioned incandescent light bulbs give out 3 per cent light and 97 per cent heat, which is wasteful; modern fluorescent light bulbs give out

70 per cent light and only 30 per cent heat, a big improvement; but that is nothing on nature's own bioluminescent beetles, which produce no heat whatsoever, just 100 per cent light!

The word 'glow-worm' is the generic term for many species belonging to the Lampyridae family, of which there are 2,000. The most common species across Europe is the nocturnal *Lampyris noctiluca*, which can grow to up to 25 millimetres. They display strong sexual dimorphism as adults, as it's only the females that can shine. Wingless females light up to attract a mate; leaving the males, who do have wings, to approach. Once the eggs hatch, they remain as larvae for up to three years and are impressive predators, injecting poison into slugs and snails that slowly paralyses their bodies and liquefies their insides. While this happens, the larvae will hitch a ride on its prey's back until it is completely turned to mulch. (I know what you're thinking: de-lish-ous!) In their short-lived adult form they'll only survive for a maximum of two weeks, reliant upon energy reserves built up during their larval phase; their sole purpose is to reproduce the next generation.

In the UK the species can be found in grasslands, hedgerows, heathlands, clifftops and rides predominantly across the south of England and Wales with occasional rare sightings in Scotland. They are believed to be absent from Northern Ireland. People living in close proximity to these beetles have noticed that their once shimmering habitats have been slowly fading each year, and, while this decline was originally anecdotal, more evidence is emerging to explain the species' worrying disappearance. Assessments are done by counting the female glow-worms, for the obvious reason: the glimmering yellow/green bioluminescence is a good indication of their whereabouts. A study in 2020 recognised that they've been declining annually by 3.5 per cent across the south-east of the UK, resulting in a staggering three-quarter population loss since 2001. Glow-worms have not been officially classified as an endangered species by the International Union for Conservation of Nature (IUCN) but regardless, their diminishing populations are extremely concerning, and they play an important role in our interconnected ecosystems. One man investigating the situation and lending them a helping hand, and home, is Peter Cooper.

Peter is a British ecologist and self-confessed 'lifelong nature nerd' (my kind of person) and has been investigating this worrying trend, alongside Derek Gow. In my opinion, Derek is one of the greatest conservationists in the UK; he has been largely responsible for the successful reintroduction of water voles, white storks and beavers. Peter has followed suit, working closely with Derek on projects supporting harvest mice and even endangered Scottish wildcats. But, in 2020, they turned their attention to glow-worms.

'I'd only seen a glow-worm once in the wild before, but in 2020, Derek set me the task of developing a reintroduction project for them,' Peter starts reflecting.

There are two main reasons that their project is important. Firstly, conservation. As Peter explains, 'There have been nationwide declines, especially in the south-east of England, and they are potentially suited for reintroductions elsewhere to good habitat. Glow-worms aren't the best at dispersing naturally. The females can't fly at all and although the males can, they aren't brilliant at it as they'll only fly very short distances. So at the moment, if there's a patch of great habitat for them they have no way of getting there.'

It's well known that insect populations are in serious trouble. The combined pressures from climate change and intensive agriculture are responsible for what is now being called the 'insect apocalypse.' Farming practices have changed significantly in the last eighty years, moving from a delicate sustainable patchwork of fields to harsh monocultures sprayed with pesticides and fertilisers that harbour little life. And with a change in climatic conditions, insects don't stand much of a chance. The effects of this are being reported all over the world. In the UK, a recent citizen science project detailed how flying insect numbers have declined by 60 per cent since 2004. If figures continue to dwindle, the knock-on effect will be catastrophic: food shortages across the world, the mass extinction of a wide range of plants, loss of animal and human life, the complete breakdown of functioning soil and, potentially, full-scale environmental collapse. These scenarios must be acknowledged and acted upon with urgency but, in order to do that, we need to start looking at insects differently.

This is the other aspect of Peter's project: social engagement. Glow-worms aren't globally threatened but they are a species that can significantly engage the 99 per cent of the general public who might not be aware of British wildlife, other than some pigeons and a few foxes. In Peter's words, 'I always found nature to be magical and I could look at a smooth newt and feel excitement, but that's not the same for everyone. Whereas no matter who you are, if you see a little glow-worm glowing in the dark, you'll be fascinated! Having a light in the dark can be a powerful story and motivator.'

If you can get people to love a small insect with a superpower, then it's an opportunity to be harnessed for the environment; our ecosystems hang in a very delicate balance and all Earth's creatures play a part in that. Peter dotingly refers to them as a gateway drug into the natural world, and that's true for more than one reason!

In the UK, people have donated millions to save the panda, the elephants and the big cats. Yet, we lay damaging artificial lawn like there's no tomorrow and relentlessly mow what natural lawn we do have to within an inch of its life. We tend to focus on the species far away, without a second thought for the ones on our own doorsteps. But wouldn't it be wonderful to see our gardens and local parks return to the glowing, buzzing insect metropolises they were always meant to be? We can each help cultivate a more conservation-conscious society by making sure what space we have is as eco-friendly as possible. 'The great thing about glow-worms is that you can still have a nice, manicured lawn as long as you have some *mess* too,' Peter continues. 'During the larvae stage, they need scrub and long grass, but after they pupate into their adult form, the vegetation needs to be short enough that the female can travel upward, giving out her glow to catch the attention of the flying males. A female will not move more than about a metre for the rest of her life so if the grass is too long and scrubby, they may be concealed and they may lose out on the chance of mating. People are less likely to hack away all their wild space if they think glow-worms are present, as we have found with many of our release site landowners,' he goes on, addressing my question of how to challenge our stubborn mindset on tidiness.

But before I get onto the release of glow-worms back into prime habitat, we should discuss the captive breeding process, which takes place in specially designed enclosures at a state-of-the-art facility. I'm just kidding! All the magic happens in Peter's home, inside plastic takeaway containers. (I mean, that is one way to recycle!) On Zoom, he held up one of his pots, but there was nothing to see other than some compost. 'At the moment, they're in semi diapause,' he begins. Diapause refers to the inactive state some invertebrates enter during the colder winter months, often tucking themselves away under leaf litter or inside dead wood. 'What we're trying to do,' he continues, 'is boost numbers for release, by reducing these captive individuals' lifespan by half. It seems counterintuitive but it will speed up the number of generations and the big-picture recovery. Normally the larvae would go through two winters in diapause and then pupate in their second summer, whereas we are trying to get them to pupate in their first summer. It has been a bit of a trial-and-error investigation as this type of project is completely new and we are learning as we go. We initially had housing problems as we didn't realise how important humidity is, so while we hatched six hundred larvae last year we also had big die-offs. One of the key things for any captive breeding programme, especially new ones, is to not be afraid of mistakes as long as you don't make them twice. I sought advice from a wonderful German glow-worm enthusiast and we have found a good technique now.'

All organisms have a strategic life cycle that works specifically for them in the wild, and one of the benefits of captive glow-worm conservation is that you can speed up the reproduction by slightly altering their patterns. This doesn't cause any harm to the tiny beetles and for a species on a local knife-edge, it's a valuable method. Peter and the team get the best results from keeping the glow-worm larvae in a semi-diapause state throughout the winter, as opposed to being fully inactive. They are kept at the lower end of room temperature, approximately 18 °C, and are fed a juicy mollusc every two weeks. This helps keep them awake and well fed, so they have enough reserve to pupate and reproduce earlier. Inside their tubs is coco-fibre substrate and a 100 per cent cellulose sponge cloth to retain moisture, keeping the habitat from becoming too humid. And one single takeaway tub, which can hold between 500 and 650 milligrams, is suitable to house thirty or forty glow-worms!

Captive breeding in this capacity is only done when things are bad enough to warrant concerns that the species won't recover on its own. In the long term, things will only improve if the root of the problem is corrected. There is no point in putting so much effort into reintroduction if, after release, there is no suitable habitat for them to thrive in.

'We're having increasingly milder, drier winters here,' Peter says, 'therefore, a big concern isn't moisture and humidity, it's desiccation. They could be drying out, which is a problem especially for the young larvae in the undergrowth. The best thing we can do is to increase the resilience of the populations. If you've got these glow-worms in low densities, or numbers, then they are very vulnerable and the impact of just one particularly mild winter will be extremely severe. By increasing their numbers you can increase the odds and we are able to select habitats suitable for their release.'

There is another way we can help support our local glow-worms. Nocturnal insects, bioluminescent and non-bioluminescent alike, respond to and are governed by light. Sadly, the intensity of night-time anthropogenic light pollution is on the rise and has been for some time; year on year it increases by an average 6 per cent. As a result of this, an estimated 85 per cent of the UK population has never seen a truly dark sky before. The problem is clearly visible if you have ever taken a flight and looked out of the window at night as you come in to land in a fully lit city. It may be quite mesmerising for us to see from above but, for insects that rely on light for communication and breeding, it's confusing. A paper in the *Journal of Insect Conservation* identified that LED lights that are typically used in street lighting impacted the ability of male fireflies to locate a displaying female, even at low light before sunset. Unsurprisingly, therefore, there is a correlation between artificial light and a decline in population. Some measures are being taken to reduce light pollution, such as hoods on lights, which prevent light being directed above. This has worked well for some species but whether it could be an effective strategy for glow-worms, only time will tell.

There is always some opposition to the idea of reintroduction and intervention when it comes to wildlife. 'Wildlife reintroductions are unfamiliar to a lot of people in the UK, particularly those in nature conservation and academia actually. There's a lot of knee-jerk opposition to the idea of introducing something. It's partly down to unfamiliarity with the idea of it, but also philosophy. I think there's often an essence of "just let nature be, and it'll come back by itself", Peter explained. And I agree, people are nervous of the unknown even with native species, thanks to shifting baseline syndrome (the change in accepted environmental norms over generations). It's also true that sometimes the best thing you can do for wildlife is to leave it alone, but that's only the case if it's not at a tipping point. At the end of the day, as natural as extinctions are, these human-driven declines are, I feel, our responsibility to make right.

Southern
Resident Orca

The ocean waves act as a gateway into another dimension, a portal into another world if you will. There's hope to be found when you submerge yourself into the big blue below; personally, I think it's the best form of escapism when life on land becomes too intense and overpowering. I find my mind drifting there often. All I have to do is close my eyes to be transported back into the sea – my happy place – where the sound of crashing waves, the feeling of salt on my skin and the sunbeams racing down into the deep navy abyss brings me a sense of calm and

tranquillity that I can't seem to find anywhere else. In part, I imagine it's due to the mysterious and inaccessible nature of the environment and my unwavering need to discover its deepest secrets. It's alluring and addictive, drawing you in further with every exploration.

Home to the most bizarre and unexpected creatures on Earth, oceans are the perfect example of how life can survive almost anywhere when given the chance. It's a concept I find comforting and like to remind myself of, as our own species' trajectory of blind destruction catapults us closer and closer to an unknown oblivion. Whether it's a giant tubeworm living on sulphur-rich hydrothermal vents that expel water at temperatures up to 400 °C, Antarctic fish containing antifreeze-like proteins to survive the freezing polar temperatures, or immortal jellyfish that could – in theory – live for ever, life is relentlessly adaptable. It's impossible not to marvel at its ingenuity! Most of these tantalising animals with remarkable adaptations live on an evolutionary branch so far away from our own that they are near impossible to relate to. But that's not the case for everything; some species bridge the gap between the marine and the terrestrial, capturing the curiosity of us land-based mammals with their pure charismatic magnetism and depth of behaviour, not so different from our own.

Whales, dolphins and porpoises are aquatic mammals belonging to the order Cetacea. They evolved from a common ancestor approximately fifty million years ago. When it came to classification, historically cetaceans have caused quite the uproar within the zoological community, and it wasn't until the early nineteenth century that scientists finally agreed they were not fish but mammals. Unlike fish, cetaceans birth live young, produce milk, are endothermic (warm-blooded), and have three ear bones, a blowhole and lungs for respiration and a horizontal caudal tail that moves up and down as opposed to side to side. Up until the early 1990s there was very little evidence about how these mammals came to be in the water, but in the last two decades the origin of cetaceans has become one of the most well-documented cases of macroevolution in the world. Macroevolution refers to evolution above the species level, i.e. the formation of a new group of organisms, like cetaceans. A fascinating area of science! So, how did it happen?

Fossils of the extinct Pakicetus were reportedly first discovered in 1983, embedded within a river delta in present-day Pakistan. Pakicetus was one of the earliest cetaceans – an ancient whale – that had four functional legs and feet best suited for life on land. Its skeleton held further clues to an earlier heritage: unique ear structures and a specialised ankle bone that is only found in even-toed ungulates like pigs, camels, giraffes and hippos, the last of which we now know is the closest living relative to modern-day cetaceans. While all life began deep within the oceans, billions of years of evolution has led to species developing adaptations needed to colonise land and thrive terrestrially. The ancestors of cetaceans were no different – they simply (although there's nothing simple about it) returned to the sea. Pakicetus is the first evidence of this macroevolutionary transition. Scientists hypothesise that there could have been such an abundance of food and lack of competition that over time, it just made sense to occupy that open oceanic niche. Pakicetus lived predominantly on land at the edge of rivers and lakes within Pakistan and India, feeding on fish as well as other terrestrial land mammals. Over a period of approximately ten million years, the Pakicetus and other early cetaceans evolved to live a fully aquatic lifestyle and developed the necessary adaptations, such as streamlined bodies, flippers, a two-lobed tail (aka the fluke), a blowhole and a respiratory system that enabled them to hold their breath underwater. Fast-forward to modern-day cetaceans and their diversity is astonishing, with approximately ninety different species. They are so successful that they inhabit every ocean around the globe.

Whales are the oldest cetacean in evolutionary terms and can be split into two groups: the odontocetes (meaning toothed whales, e.g. sperm whales, porpoises and dolphins) and the mysticetes (referring to the baleen species that filter-feed, e.g. blue whales and humpback whales). This divergence between the two occurred approximately 35 million years ago, and further divergence of the odontocetes gave rise to porpoises and dolphins. In the time that we have shared the planet with these beautiful, intelligent creatures, we have hunted them industrially and are changing their home to such an extent that many species were – and are – teetering on the brink of extinction. Statistics from December 2020 have shown that 25 per cent of all cetaceans are classified as threatened, with their status varying between vulnerable and critical, and a further 10 per cent are identified as 'data deficient', meaning there is not enough information to provide an official status designation. Reading between the lines, there's probably many more species at risk than we realise or can officially determine. Like many other animals in this book, the causes of their impending extinction are numerous and extensive; for whales specifically, this includes commercial whaling, both historically and present-day, the global death toll of which has amounted to an estimated three million over the past century; by-catch, where they are the unintentional victims of the fishing industry getting caught in nets and fishing wire; pollution, including chemical, sewage and plastic waste; toxic algae blooms, which have seen hundreds of whales washed up dead on shores; unethical tourism that disrupts the natural habitat and causes noise pollution; and the many consequences of climate change.

Orcas are one of the species that is currently listed as 'data deficient' due to the possibility that, within the group, there could be two diverging species, but this is unconfirmed until a full taxonomic review takes place. However, a 2006 consensus concluded that there were possibly as many as 50,000 individuals, but as with any other oceanic megafauna, their numbers are remarkably challenging to monitor precisely due to their remoteness and vast range. That being said, as a group they are comparatively well studied due to their preference for coastal waters and their massive geographic range, with pods living in every ocean and in almost all temperatures, from the freezing seas of Antarctica to the crystal-clear warm waters of Mexico and California.

Orcas have a fearsome reputation as they have often been observed demonstrating highly specialised apex predatory behaviour, targeting species larger than themselves. This stigma is reinforced by their colloquial nickname, 'killer whale.' This contributes to the widespread misconception that orcas are whales, but they are not; orcas are the largest species of dolphin in the world. The name 'killer whale' has an interesting western history.

Spanish sailors in the eighteenth century would encounter orcas on their voyages, and reportedly observed them hunting large whale species, which led to them being named 'asesina ballenas', or 'whale killer'. Over time this evolved to the term as we understand it today, with its various connotations. Even their scientific name, *Orcinus orca*, alludes to the fear some humans once had of them. The etymology of the word 'Orcinus' means 'in the kingdom of the dead'; Orcus was the Roman god of death and was known as the punisher of the underworld. Quite the intimidating image. Yet, reputation and preconceptions can change with accrued knowledge, especially if the media is on side. Over time we began to admire and respect orcas for the enchanting species they truly are, despite their nickname, which still prominently lingers on.

Elsewhere around the world, orcas are celebrated in the purest and most meaningful sense of the word. Along the Pacific north-west coastline of North America, First Nation cultures have long recognised orcas as the guardians of the sea and symbols of luck, compassion, family, protection and longevity. They are the primary focus of many native legends too: for example, legends commonly depict the idea that when a person drowns at sea, orcas carefully retrieve the lifeless body and take it down into the deep before transforming it into one of their own species. Orcas are believed to be the spirits of their human ancestors, hugging the coastal waters to communicate and stay close to their old lives. A legend almost as beautiful as the species itself!

Orcas live in social pods of up to thirty individuals and their bonds with one another are so tight that they rival our own.

There are many parallels that can be drawn between orca and human behaviour, which is one possible reason we are so captivated by them. I grew up with such a love of orcas, which is probably a testament to the patience of my nan and grandad, who would indulge me when I insisted on watching *Free Willy* for the hundredth time in the space of one week. Just in case you're unfamiliar with the 1993 movie, it's a heartfelt story about a twelve-year-old orphaned boy named Jesse, and his bond with an orca named Willy who he rescued from captivity and released back home to the wild. Highly emotive and wonderful – or at least it was at the time through the eyes of a small girl; I would dream of one day saving orcas like Jesse. A passion that has only grown stronger, especially since the release of the famous documentary *Blackfish*, which exposed the cruelty of places like SeaWorld, who imprison these intelligent creatures in swimming pools that have frequently been compared to bathtubs. Orcas in the wild travel up to 140 miles per day and have been known to dive to depths of over 1,000 metres; this alongside their social requirements means that the only place an orca truly belongs is in the open ocean.

In comparison to the other species in this book, numbers of orca are far greater; considering they are not officially listed as endangered, you might be wondering why I have chosen to include them. It is because of their relationship to individual ecotypes. In ecological terms, an ecotype is a genetically distinct, isolated population of a species that has adapted to a very specific habitat or niche over time, and so far ten ecotypes of orca in which multiple pods exist have been identified. Scientists are now considering whether some are distinct enough to qualify as their own species or subspecies. Each group can be distinguished by their behaviour, vocalisations, colouration, body type, diet and social structures. It's essentially evolution in action, and these ecotypes vary so much that losing one is a huge loss of specialist culture, behaviour and genetics. When conserving orca we must delve down into the conservation of their specific ecotypes; and in the Pacific north-west there are three:

1. The offshore orca: the smallest of the three ecotypes, which lives the furthest from land over the outer continental shelf between southern California and the Bering Sea. They are very rarely encountered, so little is known about them, but they live in very large pods of over fifty individuals and prey on sharks and smaller fish. Their population density is unknown, although a rough estimate of 300 has been suggested.
2. The transient orca: always on the move with very large home ranges anywhere between southern California and the Arctic Circle. They live in smaller pods but maintain very strong relationships with their relatives. Transient orcas feed almost exclusively on marine mammals, with different pods utilising different behaviours to feed on specialist prey, which could be anything from sea lions or harbour seals to minke whales, grey whale calves and even sometimes sea otters. In the last decade their numbers have increased by roughly 4 per cent each year, which collectively totals up to 400 individuals today. (Finally, some good news!)
3. The resident orca: consists of two genetically distinct populations, the northern and the southern Pacific residents. Both are fish specialists that live within small home ranges and eat almost exclusively salmon, although northern residents have been found to be more generalist in their diets, seeking

out other prey species. They're also distinct in their dialects and behavioural traits: for example, the northern residents engage in beach-rubbing activities whereas the southern residents do not. Both live in large pods that occasionally come together to form greater communities. They live very close to the coastline, in close proximity to people, and are therefore widely studied. The population of northern residents consists of 240–260 animals and the number is increasing, whereas the number of southern residents is quickly decreasing, with only seventy-four documented individuals as of September 2020.

All orcas are protected under the Marine Mammal Protection Act, but only the southern resident (SR) population are listed as endangered by the Endangered Species Act. The first significant decline in their population came as a direct result of living close to people. Through the unbelievably stressful process of live capture, to export these mammals into captivity in the developing marine park sector during the 1960s and 1970s, populations of SR orcas dropped by 40 per cent. All for our own greed and entertainment. And the population is yet to bounce back, as new threats keep pushing them further and further to that dreaded brink. To understand these threats, and their parallel solutions, more, I approached orca researcher and fellow science communicator, Connel Bradwell, who completed a degree in wildlife conservation at Nottingham Trent University in the UK and then moved to British Columbia, Canada, to study orca and work as wildlife education manager for the Northwest Wildlife Preservation Society.

'The southern resident orcas' home range is mostly in the Salish Sea, which is a marginal inland sea between Vancouver, Seattle and West Vancouver Island stretching out towards the Pacific Ocean,' he explains. 'When I started working with them in 2011, ten years ago, there were ninety individuals so the population had declined by twenty in that time, which for a species that is so long-lived is quite the significant drop. As a specific ecotype, they are unique in almost everything that they do and they never interbreed with other ecotypes. This is a group that is so well studied that we know every individual – we know their family tree, their ages, their genetics. The reason that I am so passionate about their conservation is because when you lose a population like that, you are losing a culture; it's not just a declining number or a loss of individual dolphins.'

The SR orcas are split into three different pods, J, K and L, which each occupy a different range within the Salish Sea and move around according to the migration of Chinook salmon, their primary food source. Each pod has its own distinct language and traditions. These behaviours are passed down the family through the generations, from one individual to another, and it impacts how they eat, their mating choices and what activities they do – seemingly just for the fun of it. The first evidence of cultural differences in orcas came from a study looking at their vocalisations, and, despite overlapping ranges between pods living close together, the scientists found through auditory analysis that the sounds between pods are as different as the Greek and Russian languages. Some pods even have dialects or regional accents. It's so astounding but when you think about it, it's so obvious; it's harder to think of a reason why they wouldn't have those differences!

The average lifespan of a female is forty-six years and males average around thirty years, so the younger calves have a lot of time to learn pod-specific behaviours. Resident orcas live in strong matriarchal societies where offspring stay close to their mothers throughout the course of their lives. Family units like these are known as matrilines and pods can consist of multiple units who travel and interact closely with one another, sharing some degree of relatedness. They are highly dependent upon their societies, especially when the going gets tough. They're able to communicate the know-how of surviving in new environments with new resources, which goes a long way to explaining how ecotypes arise in the first place, and results in behavioural flexibility. Orcas are one of the only other species, other than ourselves, with evidence to show how culture drives not only fascinating behaviour but also genetic evolution.

You could assume that this type of resilience and flexibility would put them in a strong position in an ever-changing environment; this may well be the case for the offshore and transient ecotypes, but for the southern residents, which live so closely to the major cities of Vancouver, Seattle and Victoria, the anthropogenic threats leave them exposed and vulnerable. Talking about the driving forces of their decline, Connel adds: 'We know exactly what the problem is. It is multifaceted but there are three main drivers: food loss, pollution and shipping noise disturbance. Northern residents live in a less densely populated region along the northern coast of British Columbia and Alaska, and they will eat a variety of fish species so that's why their population is healthy, but the southern residents are struggling. They are Chinook salmon specialists, and they eat little else, depending on the time of year. It's like a panda that needs bamboo; it will feed on other items but they only make up a tiny percentage of their diet. Estimates show Chinook makes up 80 per cent of SR orca diets and historically, this was no big deal as we would have healthy, reliable Chinook runs, but salmon populations have decreased in all major river systems. This means the SR orcas are losing their food supply. Even though they are an ocean species, their fate is so connected with the terrestrial environment. The Chinook spawn within the river system around North America but because of the pollution, we've seen massive losses. There's a lot of politics but if you ask someone here in B.C. what they're worried about, they'll probably answer the economy, Covid-19 and the salmon. It's the salmon that drives our ecosystem.'

Chinook salmon are anadromous, meaning that they hatch from eggs laid in freshwater rivers and migrate towards the saltwater oceans to feed and grow. It could be anywhere between three and eight years before they return to their freshwater natal grounds to spawn as adults. These animals are incredibly hardy, going through the energy-intensive process of smoltification, a developmental, physiological and behavioural transformation that occurs during the transition from young freshwater salmon to fully grown, saltwater salmonids. It's a remarkable life cycle but also one that leaves them vulnerable as they're dependent on the health of not one but two habitats, and as it currently stands neither are particularly healthy. If we continue along the same trajectory, 77 per cent of all marine life could be decimated in the coming years, according to the Changing Oceans Research Unit, and scientists think that half of the salmon in British Columbia could disappear as early as 2050. This would obviously be a disaster for many reasons, but particularly for the survival of SR orca pods. Salmon are reliant on clear, cool and oxygenated river systems with enough prey for them to establish energy reserves for the big migration, which can be over 3,000 kilometres in some areas.

Since 1984, Chinook salmon populations have declined by 60 per cent; some are considered endangered and others threatened depending on the area. It's becoming increasingly challenging for them to migrate and reach their spawning grounds due to the presence of impenetrable man-made obstacles like dams, as well as battling the impacts of warmer waters, a product of climate change. A single SR orca needs to eat somewhere between eighteen and twenty-five adult salmon every single day to meet their energy and nutritional requirements, which equates to approximately half a million a year based on the current population statistics. But it's not just the orca that benefit from a healthy salmon population: commercial and recreational fishing in the Salish Sea bring hundreds of millions of dollars into the Canadian economy. Chinook salmon are also a keystone species in the food chain, providing food for bears, coastal wolves and scavenging birds as well as for cetaceans. They even sustain the Great Bear Rainforest; their bodies decompose on the riverbanks, leaving nutrients that are absorbed into the soils. This is both a fantastic example of how all species are interlinked and a sad case study of what can go wrong when this network becomes imbalanced.

In the early 1900s, First Nation communities and anglers could catch adult Chinook the size of a small human during their main migratory run from May to July. They are the largest Pacific salmon species, as their nickname 'king salmon' suggests. These giant fish would have easily weighed in at 80 pounds, although the largest on record was caught in Petersburg, Alaska in 1949, weighing 126 pounds and over 4.9 feet long! Their size is almost unimaginable in today's world; these giant fish are confined to history, their average weight today being a meagre 30 pounds, but nevertheless they're still packed full of an unusually high concentration of omega-3 fatty acids that makes them highly desirable to any hungry predators. Orcas born post-1990, after salmon began to decline, are found to be shorter in body length in comparison to older individuals. Populations only evolve in places where they can thrive – it's as simple as that – but we humans tend to get in the way and force environmental changes at such a pace that species cannot evolve the adaptations needed to survive under these new conditions. Not only is the orcas' food supply continuing to decrease in abundance, but the pods might be facing an additional problem: catching their food once they've found it.

Connel has studied the relationship between the number of boats surrounding pods and the orcas' behaviour. 'The resident orcas are incredibly vocal. I mean, they're consistently chatty. Sound is so important to them because they're constantly using echolocation to find, hunt and catch their prey,' he explains. An evolutionary characteristic of odontocetes, including both whales and dolphins, is their ability to echolocate for the purposes of communication, navigation and locating food. Sound travels about four and a half times faster underwater, whereas light does not, so echolocation enables these cetaceans to 'see' their environment through the emission of high-frequency clicks that bounce off objects, returning to them and providing a picture of their immediate environment. Orcas send out a 'click train': multiple clicks in fast succession that act like an auditory torch; this enables them to locate prey up to 500 feet away. 'They have the most amazing ability to distinguish between different species of prey using only sound because of how the echoes return after hitting the swim bladders of their targets,' Connel says. 'The various species of salmon have very unique-sounding swim bladders.'

Shipping is one of the most prolific generators of underwater noise pollution. Sound is primarily produced by the propellers, as well as by on-board machinery and the engine. With a dramatic increase of vessels since World War Two, ambient shipping noise has been on the rise, with some areas of the ocean increasing up to 3 decibels (dB) every decade. In the north Pacific Ocean, this noise has been doubling in its intensity every decade for the last sixty years. That might not seem like a dramatic number but, just like our aim to stop temperatures rising over 1.5 °C, per pre-industrial levels, every increase makes a huge difference. 'When I put my hydrophone in the water,' Connel says, 'the tankers' sound would often drown out the orcas almost completely. It is the most awful noise even for my ears, and they're dealing with this constantly.'

Oceanic sound pollution is a consequence of how our global economies function, relying heavily on fossil fuels and international trade. The ports of Vancouver and Prince Rupert, located near the orcas' territories, are two of Canada's largest. They facilitate approximately 3,160 vessels every year and trade in over $200 billion annually from 170 other economies around the world. This means that the three SR pods who once lived in one of the most pristine and well-suited habitats on Earth now find themselves living right in the centre of one of the world's busiest shipping lanes and ferry routes. It becomes especially hard to fight for a reduction in sound pollution when the direct cause is our system of trade, which so many countries are so heavily dependent upon. To quieten the pollution would mean a complete and utter reshape of our international consumption.

One study looking at the effects of shipping noise on SR orcas found that while the sound emitted by ships can vary, the average produced is 173 dB – equating to 111 dB in the air, which is roughly the same volume as when attending a concert by your favourite rock band. I don't know about you, but when I go to a concert I'm always at the front, and my ears are left buzzing for hours after the event. Orcas rarely position themselves right alongside the ships (unlike me and those concert speakers – sorry eardrums), but based on the geography of the shallow channels in the enclosed Salish Sea, the orcas could be subjected to approximately 60 to 90 dB per ship. This is the equivalent of a lawnmower right next to your ear – but tenfold because there are multiple ships, multiple times a day. The intensity of the sound does vary by water temperature and salinity levels, but nonetheless, imagine how much stress the constant noise would cause day in day out. It would be enough to drive anyone insane – especially if it was affecting your ability to feed and speak.

The anthropogenic soundscape of the Salish Sea keeps getting louder, with more and more traffic from oil tankers, ferries, cruise liners, commercial and private ships, naval sonar, drilling exploration and underwater construction projects. In some oceanic regions, this type of pollution has reduced the area cetaceans are able to communicate in effectively by 90 per cent. And while it's hard to definitively judge how much of a negative effect this is having on their hunting, researchers have concluded that each individual orca could be losing anywhere between 4.9 and 5.5 hours of foraging time each day. That is a significant period of time where it is too loud for their echolocation to be effective in locating prey, and could have severe repercussions on their precious energy stores. And it's only predicted to get worse. The expansion of the Kinder Morgan pipeline, which carries crude and refined oil from Alberta to the coastline of British Columbia, is predicted to increase the number of oil tankers from sixty a year to over 420 in the orcas' habitat, with some saying that this project is a 'death certificate.' If it continues, which is highly likely at this point, then there is over a 50 per cent chance that this ecotype of orca will decline to such a low density that the damage will be irreversible and they could be lost for ever within this next century. Not only is it a problem for sound but also for the occurrence of fatal collisions and major oil spills.

So what is currently being done to save the orcas from extinction?

According to Connel, 'There are a few things happening: the government is closing off key hunting areas, for example the west coast of San Juan Islands and Saturna Island. These are little islands with big cliff faces that are great for orca as they push the salmon against them. They've always been historically really important for the pods so new regulations are shutting down fishing and stopping a lot of close proximity boat traffic, which is not a bad thing. But as we know, just because you have a marine protected area doesn't mean that the sound from further away can't get in. It is really tricky, but the Port of Vancouver actually does a really amazing job with a scheme that rewards boats and ships that create less noise.' The port authority launched an Enhancing Cetacean Habitat and Observation (ECHO) Program back in 2014 to better understand the cumulative effects of shipping on orcas and other cetaceans around the coastline of British Columbia. In addition, their scheme encouraged ships to reduce their speed in sensitive areas to 11 knots or less, adjust their routes according to orca movements and clean their hulls and propellers to reduce sound. 'If you show up to the port with your tanker and prove to them that you avoided key areas, travelled a good route, have a nice clean vessel and moved slower, then they will reward you by giving you half-price on your mooring,' Connel says.

According to a paper published in 2017, if noise disturbance was reduced by 50 per cent and Chinook salmon stocks rose by 15 per cent then the declining population of SR orcas would start to show signs of growth (Lacy, R. C. et al. 2017). The Port of Vancouver has released figures from 2020 detailing that underwater sound intensity on one of their busiest passes was reduced to nearly 50 per cent, with nearly 90 per cent of all ships volunteering to take part in their slow-down scheme. These figures are set to increase from 2021 and beyond. Great work by the port! But as ever, it's one piece of a rather large puzzle.

One of the main issues is bringing the salmon back. 'When you're dealing with this,' Connel explains, 'you have to look at major industries and major polluters alongside climate change and urbanisation. Those are big issues to take on and it's whether there's the political will to really deal with it. Salmon simply need a nice clean river and I don't think that's too much to ask for!' With the addition of salmon-friendly drains, hatcheries and quotas, the community around British Columbia are busy trying to find a long-term sustainable solution but it's a work in progress.

To lose the SR orca ecotype wouldn't just be losing a singular family or individual group of animals; it would be condemning a unique culture and genetic diversity to oblivion – their language, behaviours, ecosystem services and, of course, their spiritual connection to the communities that live alongside them. There are so many similarities between orcas and humans, not just their brains and degree of intelligence but their close, complex relationships towards one another. I asked Connel if there is anything that still surprises him about their behaviour and he noted, 'One of the most amazing traditions is that this ecotype love a party. The three pods meet up in one massive super-pod.

They'll come together once or twice in the spring and summer seasons and they just go crazy. They communicate. They jump. They flip around. They rub their penises together. It's a proper party like they are catching up after not seeing one another for a while. They don't just bump into each other either. They somehow communicate exactly where to meet and wait until each pod is present before they start behaving in a way that can only really be described as them having a really great time. When you understand their behaviour and personalities, then you can better understand how to protect them.' If these fascinating, intelligent creatures become extinct before we have mastered the technology that will enable us to decode their complex social behaviour, we will lose the chance of discovering a deeper understanding of life itself and, perhaps, the opportunity to learn a bit more about ourselves too in the process. If that's not enough motivation to save them, then I don't know what else is!

Asian Elephant

In the depths of Myanmar's evergreen jungle is a herd of Asian elephants. Despite their humungous size, they could almost go unnoticed as they peacefully browse on the irresistible vegetation that surrounds them. Their textured grey skin perfectly camouflages them against the contrasted patches of light and shade that litter the forest's floor. As the sun begins to set on their long day of munching, the birdsong begins to quiet and the cicadas begin to buzz. It's a tranquil sight.

Suddenly, catching the family off guard, a loud, high-pitched squeak echoes through the trees as a young calf accidently tumbles into her mother's legs. Greeted by a rumble through the ground that only an elephant can discern, the adults of the herd look down at the baby before continuing to eat. The young elephant picks herself back up and tries again… she, too, is attempting to browse, but hasn't quite worked out what the long, dangly thing on the end of her face is supposed to do. She is one month old, weighing just over 100 kilograms. Stable(ish) on her legs, she's enjoying building lifelong relationships with other herd members as she mimics their behaviour, trying desperately to pick up the techniques needed for life in the jungle. She flexes the muscles in her trunk, causing it to sway back and forth and back and forth over a cluster of sedges. She desperately attempts to grasp the fragile stems of vegetation using the flexible tip of her trunk, her mouth slightly open in anticipation, but she hasn't yet mastered the precise skill of grasping. Her ears wave as she lets out another squeak, seemingly in frustration. It will be another couple of months of practice before she is ready to feed on plants to any degree of significance. For now, and for the next couple of years, she can always rely on the fatty milk provided by Mum.

She retreats to her mother's legs as the herd moves on further into the jungle.

If you haven't seen a newly born elephant calf learning how to use its trunk, well, all I can suggest is that you immediately tear yourself away from this page (tricky I know) and have a quick google to seriously swoon over one of nature's greatest creations – and then hurry right back…

The desk where I'm writing is against a window with a gorgeous backdrop of the Cairngorms National Park in Scotland; a pine forest and an overgrown field that's teeming with wildlife. It's a source of both inspiration and distraction, as my gaze is occasionally pulled away from my screen and the mission at hand towards whatever mysterious creature is lurking within its edges. In recent days I've watched red deer, bullfinches and an amusingly relentless pigeon attempting (and failing) to mount our small window-suction bird feeder. While the UK is one of the most nature-depleted countries in the world, with 40 per cent of its native wildlife in decline, this little Cairngorm bubble – although still far from what it should be – is our largest national park and home to a quarter of Scotland's rare and endangered species. For some, like red squirrels, snow buntings and ptarmigans, it's a final stronghold; so it's no wonder this place has quickly become my wild sanctuary and refuge too. But as I unintentionally look up this time, I see something new stalking through the cow parsley opposite. A domestic black cat with a button white nose. And my gut reaction isn't exactly positive.

I personally have nothing against individual cats, but a 2021 report from Cats Protection detailed that 26 per cent of households in Britain have at least one cat and each individual can kill up to ten times more wildlife than wild predators of a similar size. It's understandably an emotive topic for any wildlife lover, and I'd be heartbroken to see one of the bullfinches mentioned earlier being caught by a cat.

Living alongside these cats is as close as I get to human/ wildlife conflict, as it's probably the only animal I would actively discourage from my garden. We eradicated all native apex predators, such as bears, wolves and lynx, over 1,000, 250 and 1,300 years ago respectively, and all major megafauna herbivores, like elk and bison, even further back – over 8,000 and 6,000 years ago. I am grateful that my biggest conflict is not one that threatens my life or my livelihood, but, as someone who fights to promote and protect biodiversity, I am also saddened that we have wounded our ecological equilibrium by removing these key apex players. What would it be like to live among a functioning ecosystem that had no need for intensive management due to the presence of the animals mentioned above? Things would be different – certainly for the better in terms of our environment, although measures would be needed to help farmers protect livestock and to make people feel safe during the transition.

One species that is plagued by human/wildlife conflict is the Asian elephant. This species of elephant has declined by 50 per cent in the last seventy-five years and estimates suggest no more than 50,000 remain in the wild. Very sadly, over 70 per cent of their historical native habitat has been destroyed, and those who have clung on are now confined to small pockets in thirteen countries across Asia. Generally speaking, elephants are the largest land mammal on our globe, although Asian elephants are the smallest of the three subspecies, weighing between 2.2 and 5.5 tons. The other two, the African savannah elephant and African forest elephant, live (as their name suggests) on the African continent and are larger in size with bigger, rounded ears, whereas Asian elephants have smaller, slightly narrower ears that some say resemble the shape of India. Asian elephants also have only one 'finger' on the outer side tip of their trunk (whereas African elephants have two, one on each side). There's also a difference in the number of ribs, but unless you're involved in a post-mortem or some kind of skeletal reconstruction, that's not necessarily the most helpful means of identification. But now you're wondering, Asian elephants have twenty pairs of ribs and their African cousins have twenty-one. (If that question comes up on your next pub quiz… you're welcome!)

There is no other species that captures people's hearts in the same way as elephants, and the more we know about them, the

more there is to love! They have 40,000 muscles and 2-metre-long
sensory nerve fibres in their trunk, making it possibly the most
sensitive organ in the mammalian kingdom. They communicate
through low-frequency vibrations, or seismic waves, sent
through the ground and picked up through their large feet.
But, most importantly, elephants are self-aware, tightly bonded,
highly intelligent animals. They mimic sounds, use tools, display
empathetic behaviour and have impressive spatial memories,
used to find the most direct path to watering holes or floodplains,
even at distances over 50 kilometres away. They've been observed
grieving and mourning members of their families through
ritualistic behaviours, such as touching and smelling the body of
the deceased.

Despite how intelligent and sacred elephants are, they
often clash with humans as they pursue food sources in local
communities. Imagine waking in the middle of the night to the
sound of a herd of Asian elephants next to the house, grazing and
trampling every rice, pulse, bean and groundnut crop you have
spent months cultivating to feed your family – only for them to be
gobbled in the space of a few hours. I can't pretend to know what
that would feel like, but I bet measures would be taken in order
to prevent it happening again. Human/wildlife conflict can be
described as a reciprocal negative relationship; it can come in many
forms and with many different species, big or small. From a human
perspective, these clashes occur in the form of damage to crops
or a threat towards people and/or their domesticated animals; but
on the other hand, from the animals' perspective, you can't blame
herbivores for crop-raiding or predators for predating – it's in their
instinct to eat. This problem is a sad consequence of agricultural
and human expansion, deforestation and overgrazing, all of which

force wild species – once settled in undisturbed habitats – to venture into new areas in the hope of finding sufficient resources to survive. Essentially, due to loss of land, what is left of our wildlife is spilling out over its edges. That redistribution often forces animals towards communities and their fields of crops and livestock.
It becomes a greater problem in developing countries, where social and economic losses can threaten a family's livelihood and overall stability.

At the time I'm writing this, the total human population is 7.97 billion, and is predicted to increase by 1.1 per cent each year. That doesn't sound like much but it's actually an additional 81 million tiny human mouths, wants and desires to satisfy every 365 days! And as a result, it's hardly a surprise that conflicts between people and wildlife continue to grow in intensity. It's a conservation issue that's widespread but not evenly distributed. Typically, in rural areas there is a higher level of food insecurity and poverty, and less access to education and healthcare than for those living in cities. The perception of conservation and wildlife can vary massively within a country too; rural populations live in areas with greater biodiversity, where more conflict occurs, but they are also forced to live with conservation restrictions and specific policies limiting their access to nearby natural resources. It's an incredibly complex issue. To understand it further, I spoke to Christie Sampson, an American ecologist with over ten years of experience who has lived in the villages around Myanmar attempting to conserve the endangered Asian elephant.

Christie was looking for graduate programmes while working as a geographic information system (GIS) intern for the Smithsonian Conservation Biology Institute. A GIS is a computer-based method of mapping, logging and visualising forms of location data. During the search for the next step in her career, Christie was approached by her boss, Peter Leimgruber, who wanted to gauge her interest in a new project. 'Peter said to me, hey, we think we have scored funding for a study on elephants that may be based in Kenya, or maybe Sri Lanka, would you like to jump on it?,' she told me. 'So I said sure and eventually I ended up working in Sri Lanka, looking at the effects fire or livestock grazing were having on Asian elephants inside protected areas. I spent a lot of time in areas within national parks on foot, which was so lucky as tourists generally are not allowed to get out of their vehicles. People would drive by as I was measuring elephant dung balls and it was great. My study naturally progressed to Myanmar, but after some time, I began focusing on the conflicts. I lived in the villages and spent my days collaring and mapping Asian elephant movement patterns,' she recounted.

Myanmar is a beautiful country that is very under-studied from a conservation perspective, due to the nation's political and civil instability. From the remote snow-capped Himalayas to the tropical and subtropical forests, wetlands, savannahs and coastal ecosystems, there is so much biodiversity. Despite the 160,000 square miles of forest, numbers of Asian elephants have continued to fall, plummeting from 10,000 individuals to just 2,000 in the space of seventy years. These animals are being forced to forage in the space between primary forests and the growing human settlements. This was precisely why Christie was drawn to the region. 'Originally only a very small proportion of my research was working with the communities, but that quickly grew to 95 per cent of my work. I would visit and spend time living in various villages that are very remote. I would usually stay at the headman's house and sleep on the family's floor under a mosquito net but it was a great way to create those close relationships, especially going back year after year. It didn't matter how poor the area was, when you'd show up you would always be welcomed with tea and cookies,' she recalled with a smile on her face.

To firstly understand how the elephants were using the habitat, Christie and her team needed to fit some satellite collars. To minimise stress they were on the lookout for healthy elephants without any young. If successful the vet would approach first, getting into the right position to tranquillise the elephant, before the rest of the team would move in to fix the collar. Each one contained a battery with enough power to last for five years. 'The first way to track collared elephants is with the VHF frequency, which means we can track them on the ground using a device with bleeps when we point it in the right direction. I wanted to test this before placing it on a wild elephant, so one of my first experiences was trying it on one of the captive individuals that were kept in the camp outside the village. These elephants were allowed to free-roam every night, were checked in the morning by the mahouts for any injuries and then released back to the forest again. The collar was fitted on a fifty-year-old bull called Shwe Do Win who was super-sweet and gentle, and he led us on a merry chase through the jungle at 6 a.m. through bees' nests and the thickest mud, but at least it worked! The second way to use the collar is through the satellite, which transmits a GPS location every hour, day and night. It was great because every couple of days I would open my emails to see all these locations from wild animals. I began to understand where these elephants were going and how they used their landscape. I ended up collaring fifteen in total throughout the project, but seven of those individuals ended up disappearing never to be seen again,' Christie said.

Now, it's common for a scientist to be surprised by the results of their study – it's the mysteries that make it such an appealing field, after all – but what Christie helped uncover was something no one could have predicted, mainly because you'd never want to believe another human being capable of such cruelty.

Most stories about elephant poaching refer to the killing of African elephants to satisfy the demands of the ivory trade. We've all seen the photos and the reports of this brutal practice; but this isn't the story I am referring to. Asian elephants have been facing a new, quiet threat driven by a small number of misinformed and deluded consumers, but it has nothing to do with a desire for ivory.

Unlike their African cousins, who have tusks whatever their sex, only male Asian elephants have tusks and over time, through generations, they have been selectively bred out of the population by humans. Historically, males with large tusks were removed from the wild to be used in labour or for ceremonial purposes, so only a tiny percentage of males today have tusks and even these have very small ones that are hardly worth the poaching effort.

'I would watch the elephants roam over large distances, but all of a sudden they would move in a very small area in a random pattern, going back and forth. Instead of moving a couple of kilometres a day, they'd stay within a hundred metres and then I would stop getting points. It was like they would blink out of existence,' Christie continued. 'I didn't know if the collar had stopped working, if they were sick or if they had been poached.

The mahouts at the elephant camps would go out with officials from the Myanmar government to check and that was how we found out poaching was such a huge problem in Bago Yoma, in central Myanmar. Most of the time when that would happen, the elephant would be found dead and sometimes skinned.' It was clear from Christie's professionalism that she had told this story a hundred times before, but I was floored hearing it for the first time. My heart broke that little bit more.

Elephant skin was first documented at markets in the early 2000s, although it likely appeared before then. The industry has grown from small-scale to a commercial trade since 2014 as traffickers have advertised and glamorised the product known as 'blood beads', chunky ruby-coloured marbles sold as bracelets and necklaces. The process of making these beads is unimaginably horrific. The red colouration comes from the blood of the elephant, which is taken by poachers while the animal is still alive. According to a report by the international NGO Elephant Family, each bead takes a day to make and is then threaded into a piece of jewellery. One bracelet costs approximately £300. It is marketed as a gemstone for traditional wenwan jewellery, although there is no evidence that jewellery was historically made in this way. The skin is also ground up into a powder and sold to traditional medicine markets in China as a remedy for stomach illnesses, from ulcers to cancer. There is no medical evidence to support the claims that this 'treatment' works. These products are a just marketing scam.

In their investigation, Elephant Family found traffickers discussing their actions online and a woman named 'Jaz' openly selling her 'exclusive knowledge as the inventor' of the skin beads to users of the popular social media platforms, WeChat and QQ.

She was the first, and continues to be the most active, trader online who uses multiple profiles, consistently posting evidence of the manufacturing, sourcing and selling of elephant products, regardless of social media rules and guidelines. There are photos of her at the Myanmar–China border claiming she even prefers to collect the 'material' herself. This helped identify 'Jaz' as a leading criminal responsible for creating the demand for this horror show. The sad thing is, she prides herself on it.

Since 2013, there have been 101 reports of elephants being skinned and Myanmar has been named as the main source. In 2017, there was a new case every week in the region Christie was working in. These elephants were only located thanks to tracking tags and a few chance encounters, so imagine the numbers that have died and remained undiscovered within the dense forests. For endangered species living at such a low density, every loss is a huge detriment to conservation efforts and to the health of that environment.

Christie described her first encounter with a victim as incredibly disturbing and heart-wrenching. 'I knew that elephant, I had followed his movements and then to see what eventually happened to him was…' She paused, unable to think of the right word. There are some situations where there are no expressions that do an emotion justice. 'Once we realised what was happening, we started to find other examples,' she went on. 'I was away at the time but my collaborators found a mass grave of a herd just piled up in a creek bed. It had only just happened and there were body parts lying everywhere covered in flies, they had even killed the baby. Thankfully, not that it would have mattered at this point, they didn't skin him or her. Sheets of the adult skins were hanging up to dry so they could be easily transported by the poachers once they returned. I was grateful not to see that first-hand.'

The people killing these elephants are highly experienced with skills specific to the job; it's challenging to remove thick elephant skin and not something you just do on a whim.

In the face of such heartbreaking destruction, it is easy to feel anger and frustration and to lose hope. I'm not immune to these emotions, especially after listening to stories like these. But conservation is about people, so we must look to each other for the solutions. In areas where there is a high-level elephant/human conflict due to crop-raiding, it is reported that there can be a greater degree of poaching, as community members often do not see a way out of the situation. Pointing poachers in the right direction, for some, might be a simple solution to protect your livelihood while earning some quick money for your family.

'I was very aware that I was a westerner in these villages and when the elephants were poached, I knew I had to turn to the communities to figure out what they wanted. Too often scientists come into these remote locations telling people how to fix their problems, but I wanted to support local knowledge and ideas,' Christie said. 'I developed questionnaires with social scientists and spent time getting to know members in the villages, trying to understand how they feel about human/elephant conflict and coexistence as well as their conservation beliefs. I also worked on some education outreach projects with local schools, where I translated books about elephant ecology into Burmese for the children. Overall, we found a huge desire to conserve the elephants. Some people wanted to preserve them for their children and for their work as ecosystem engineers, but another common response was, "we want elephants in Myanmar, but just not in our backyard". Christie explained this in an understanding tone. 'I worked with the village headman and religious leaders, talking to those who had their crops raided by elephants, to estimate the damage and ask what they thought would reduce the conflicts. There was one monk who had giant speakers and he'd be called any time an elephant appeared to broadcast to the whole village to keep people away for their protection. Another person tried playing his guitar to scare them off, which didn't work, but it's important to listen. We ended up sourcing electric fences and generators that are normally used for livestock, which helped. It was only because of the community input that it was so successful and we saw a decline in crop raiding.'

The Myanmar government supported Christie and the team after this discovery. With collaboration from the World Wildlife Fund and Friends of Wildlife, it was announced in 2020 that there had been no poaching incidents reported in the Yangon and Bago regions of Myanmar since 2018, though unfortunately we have been unable to get much of an update since.

These projects are possible thanks to people trying to make a difference in the world, but they are subject to funding. The process is lengthy and stressful but if you are lucky, your study might be chosen to receive enough financial support to proceed. The length of time these grants cover generally gives you enough time to gather enough data for your qualification, at whatever level that may be, usually between three and five years. After Christie's PhD funding ran out, she had to leave Myanmar. I asked her how she felt about leaving, and she replied, 'There are local people continuing the work, which I am so happy about, but I do wish I could still be part of it. Conservation funding leans towards the shiny, new ideas and not necessarily towards sustaining a programme that is ongoing. You're less likely to get approved if it's just a continuation rather than saying, "Hey, this is my new idea, and in the first year I can get all this new information and have this impact."' Christie's point speaks to a problem in academia, where funding and access do not always correspond to action.

So, how do we pull the Asian elephant species from the brink of extinction?

We must consider local communities and their priorities when creating conservation plans. Christie concludes, 'It's not realistic to say we have thousands of acres of land that no one is allowed to touch except for the elephants. There has to be a compromise making it worthwhile for people who share the landscape with these giants. Stop imposing western views on other cultures. There is conflict and it won't always be perfect on either side, but given the chance we will learn a lot from indigenous knowledge. Traditionally in Sri Lanka, villages have a fantastic land-sharing programme where buildings are at the centre, surrounded by a livestock buffer zone, which is further surrounded by crops, and then the forest boundary. They move their active crop sites after each harvest around the system, which has proven a good strategy in coexistence. Hopefully, we are swinging towards a side of conservation that aims to protect rather than restore after a population or landscape is decimated.'

New technology can be so exciting and opens the door to new discoveries. But sometimes the most effective conservation method is communication. You don't always need the latest kit to make a difference. You can support local communities and, if appropriate, share knowledge back and forth. It could be as simple as reporting illegal wildlife crime items that crop up on social media platforms, or even talking to your neighbours about installing hedgehog highways or wildflower meadows in your gardens.

Just remember, we are all in this together.

Sunflower Sea Star

I have always had a fascination with stars. I can't begin to tell you how many hours I have spent gazing up at the sky, 'night-dreaming' of all the possibilities. Parallel universes, black holes and alien life forms – which I am certain are out there somewhere, awaiting discovery. When looking at the images of space, the great expanse of the universe really puts everything into perspective. I find that there's great comfort in being so insignificant in the grand scheme of things. We are nothing but a speck on a speck in the history of space. No matter what decisions we make today and the worries we carry, whether that's on a small or a large scale, the Earth will still be spinning and the stars will be shining for billions of years to come.

However, back down on Earth at this critical point in time we are anything but insignificant. You, as an individual, are important. And you have a decision to make, as your actions (and mine) will decide the fate of biodiversity on this planet going forward. Stars are magical – spheroids of plasma held together by their own gravity. But their beauty is certainly rivalled, if not topped, by the stars closer to home. The ones that lie on every ocean floor, mirroring the sky above, and adding to the richness of life on Earth – sea stars, also known as starfish.

And there is one species in particular that needs our appreciation more: the sunflower sea star.

Thinking back to all the underwater experiences I have been fortunate enough to have had, whenever the seabed was visible there were always sea stars present too. Any time you dip your head below the waves or peer into a rockpool, you're never too far from one. There are an estimated 2,000 different species, varying in shape, size and pigmentation. They are incredibly successful animals, inhabiting all of the planet's oceans and habitats, from the polar regions to the tropics, from shallow tidal pools to seagrass meadows, coral reefs and even the deep sea. They've been observed as deep as 6,000 metres below sea level, although the greatest diversity of stars is always found in shallower water near the coast. I was brought up referring to them as starfish, but in recent years scientists have been trying to make this name redundant as it leads to the misconception that they are fish, when the only similarity that sea stars have to fish is that they live underwater. They have no gills, scales or fins and are in fact marine invertebrates belonging to the phylum Echinodermata. Closely related to sea dollars and urchins, they have radial symmetry, which essentially means that their arms are arranged around a central point. The most extraterrestrial part of their physiology is how they are able to move around their environment. I can remember being at Bournemouth aquarium in the UK as a child and a small sea star was moving along the inside of a glass tank. I pressed my nose into the glass panel as if getting my eyes closer to the sea star would suddenly make its movements and unusual appendages make sense. But it just perplexed me further. Now I know that on each arm, hundreds of tube feet were rippling across the glass, peeling each 'foot' off, moving it and then suctioning it again back onto the glass. Tube feet align along grooves under each arm and are essentially made from sacs of seawater and muscular protrusions. These unusual appendages operate via hydraulic pressure and allow them to move across the ocean floor, hunker down in strong currents and manipulate food, and are also critical for respiration. It's weird and wonderful, and I love it.

In September 2013, a dramatic event began to unfold as a species of sea star rapidly vanished in its billions. The sunflower sea star has an arm span of 1 metre, making it the largest star species known to science. But size isn't its only surprising and impressive attribute. Most people typically envision sea stars with five arms – the stereotypical star shape – but individuals of this species have somewhere between sixteen and twenty-five arms! They really do resemble the many-petalled sunflower. They vary in colouration from bright yellow and orange to brown and purple. For these reasons, and the fact that they prefer low sub-tidal environments rich in seaweed and kelp, they are a firm favourite among divers and ocean enthusiasts. I've never seen one myself, but they often make appearances in nature documentaries – have you seen those sped-up clips of the seafloor where the urchins and sea stars move around like a living game of Tetris? Actually, even without the fast-forward the sunflower sea star can move surprisingly fast, at a rate of 1 metre per minute, though perhaps that's not surprising given its 15,000 tube feet. As a top predator, they hoover up smaller sea stars, sea urchins, clams and snails, etc, and therefore play a vital role in managing those populations and the ecological integrity of their environment. When filmed and played in fast-forward, it is mind-blowing to see how their prey creates this moving carpet over the seafloor as they scarper away from these giant alien-like creatures.

Sunflower sea stars were once very widespread across the north-east Pacific, along its 3,000-kilometre-plus coastline from Alaska to Mexico. In fact, they were once so common that people suggested they were the robins of the sea. But as of 2020, they were relisted as critically endangered because since 2013 an estimated 5.75 billion of them have disappeared from the oceans, equating to a 90.6 per cent population collapse. This is an extreme percentage – although sadly one that is not too uncommon in this book – but the surprising element is how quickly it occurred. The majority of the loss happened within just three years. It's highly unusual for a species that was once so common to just vanish, but sightings became a rarity and it initially caused quite the confusion. They're not the obvious species that jumps to mind when thinking about megafauna – or at least they certainly weren't for me; until now, that is. They're one of those organisms that you grow to love the more you understand about them. Their unusual and unique appearance has made divers across the Pacific treasure them and even compare being in their presence to that of being up close to an elephant or grizzly bear. Therefore, it comes as no surprise that their disappearance has been a huge loss for people and the environment. But despite this devastation, very few people around the world are even aware of the events that unfolded below the waves.

Sea star wasting syndrome (SSWS) is a condition that was first described in 1896 off the east coast of the USA, but historically has always persisted at low levels. Small white lesions initially appear on their bodies and spread rapidly to the surrounding tissue until it begins to decay. Sadly, at this point sea stars are unable to maintain their internal hydrostatic pressure, which causes them to go limp and lose their ability to grasp the seabed substrate. As their water vascular system shuts down and their lesions spread, the body begins to fragment and their arms fall off, eventually leading to the death of the animal. This process can happen very quickly – over the space of just a few days. Towards the end they barely keep their characteristic sea star shape and appear instead as though they have simply 'melted' away into the seafloor. SSWS has been noted in a total of forty different species, all of which have a larger than average body size. Originally the disease was believed to be a virus; however, recently evidence has come to light that shows that it could be a bacterial infection caused by an imbalance of microorganisms on the sea stars themselves. This change in bacteria might lead to reduced oxygen uptake, causing the animal to suffocate, although this theory is hotly contested by marine epidemiologists.

Looking back at the history books, there are records of large scale 'die-offs' caused by SSWS between the 1970s and 1990s, but never an epidemic like this one. The size of the outbreak and the spread over such a huge geographical area was unheard of. It had an impact on at least twenty sea star species in the region, but the sunflower sea star bore the brunt of it. The first signs began in June 2013 when ochre sea stars, or purple sea stars, off the coast of Washington state were noted to be suffering. By August, after a massive monitoring survey conducted by marine

researchers and citizen science participants, the sunflower sea star
in British Columbia was found to be wasting away, and the disease
continued to spread until it reached southern California, Oregon
and Mexico in 2014 and 2015.

To find out exactly why this catastrophic event occurred, I
spoke to Dr Sara Hamilton, a marine biologist who has devoted
her time to helping this ocean giant. Growing up landlocked
in the mountains of West Virginia in the USA, Sara never really
experienced the sea, but after a trip to the coral reefs at the
Florida Keys she became hooked. 'I had never been snorkelling in
the ocean before, and it was just absolutely stunning,' she says. 'I
came face to face with a sea turtle but there were also barracuda,
corals and jellyfish. I remember coming up to the surface and
I just knew I had to get scuba-certified. It blew my mind.' Sara's
later career and primary research revolved around the ecology
of kelp forests, and how people and communities are intimately
connected to these habitats. Sara adds, 'I had never actually studied
sea stars specifically before, but my lab got a call from the Nature
Conservancy, who were offering me a grant to help conduct an
IUCN Red List assessment for the sunflower sea star. It was funny
timing because at that point I was working on my kelp thesis and I
had promised myself that I wouldn't take on anything new. I didn't
want to stretch myself too thinly and burn out, but then I thought
about what my younger self would do and why I got into science
in the first place; it was ultimately to conserve marine life, like that
sea turtle that got me fascinated with the oceans to begin with, and
helping a species become internationally recognised as critically
endangered felt important. So, I said yes.'

This was a common theme among the scientists and rangers
I spoke to for this book, and it's a thought that I am familiar

with personally too. No matter your area of expertise, the one thing everyone has in common is that they devote their lives to their research and protection of animals due to a fundamental love for life.

Kelp forests play a key role in maintaining and protecting our atmosphere by boosting oceanic oxygen levels through photosynthesis, providing protection to many rare species and protecting coastal communities from erosion and oncoming storms. An ocean without kelp is like land without trees. At the beginning of 2013, the north-east Pacific Ocean experienced a record-breaking marine heatwave. The sea surface was on average 2.5 °C warmer than 'normal' and this rise persisted for 226 days – the longest duration for any heatwave ever recorded in such an environment. This forced severe and well-documented declines in population numbers and shifted ecosystem functions as harmful algae bloomed, increasing concentrations of a neurotoxin acid that resulted in the closure of fisheries and an unprecedented number of marine mammal strandings. The water became very low in nutrients and so further up the food chain many birds and whales were left starving and eventually died en masse. A 2.5 °C rise may not sound like much, but it is the difference between a healthy and a dying ecosystem. Since this marine heatwave, Northern California has seen a 95 per cent drop in kelp forest cover. A 60-fold increase in sea urchin numbers makes restoration very challenging as they munch through the forest without the threat of predation from sunflower sea stars, their top predator, which were declared functionally extinct in the region since the start of their decline.

The SSWS epidemic began at the start of the marine heatwave, so it's no wonder that scientists started looking for a connection between SSWS and temperature. Unsurprisingly, there was a positive correlation between the two: high temperatures were found to exacerbate the disease, killing the sea stars much faster than in colder waters. Despite the species being able to withstand quite harsh intertidal environments with crashing waves, storms and everything in between, climate change is making them much more susceptible to this deadly disease. The loss of sea star species from fragile balanced ecosystems, like kelp forests, has proven to cause significant reductions in biodiversity, so much so that in 1966 the term 'keystone predator' was created and used to describe the purple star. They influence community composition and can therefore be blamed for huge ecological shifts in population dynamics. This influx of urchins that are decimating kelp cannot be solely attributed to the decline in sunflower sea stars but it's likely to have had an impact. Sara says, 'If twenty identical guns are shooting at someone, how do you tell which bullet is responsible for the fatal shot? I call it the "firing squad problem" because there are so many threats coming at our marine ecosystems causing epic collapses and it's hard to blame a decline on one specific reason. These are complicated stories.'

We – humans – like to blame events on one specific reason but the reality of it is that these threats act like a chain reaction and aren't mutually exclusive of one another.

Looking towards the future, there is a big push to try to save the sunflower sea star through captive breeding. A relatively new initiative at the Friday Harbor Labs at the University of Washington and the Nature Conservancy hopes to re-establish populations back to their former range for the benefit of the species, and the kelp forests that we are all so dependent upon. However, that may be many years away, and rearing sea stars in captivity, especially those associated with SWSS, is very difficult. Sara explains, 'They previously didn't survive well in captivity, especially species as large as the sunflower, so it's challenging to raise them in aquariums and historically that has prevented a lot of research into basic physiology, like how they reproduce and how long they live for. To observe in the wild you must be a good diver but there is another big challenge in that you can't tag individuals and get reliable data from the same sea stars.' This is because of another widely known remarkable adaptation – sea stars have the ability to 'drop' an arm if under attack, distracting the predator trying to take a nibble while allowing the rest of the sea star to escape to safety. A new arm is then regenerated, which takes approximately a year. This amazing strategy has served them well, but for scientists trying to understand them it's quite a pain, as the sea stars just expel the arms with the tag attached. For these reasons, there is very little information on sea stars; and if studying the stars impacted by the epidemic wasn't tricky enough, Sara continues, 'It is really hard to find "clean" stars that haven't been infected or exposed. You need these individuals in a lab setting because then you're able to control the environment and determine what exactly causes the syndrome by exposing the animals to varying conditions. But while the epidemic was happening, you'd bring the stars into the lab and they would just start disintegrating and dying before your eyes. It's frustrating because we were given the funding to conduct the research when it was already too late. Money in conservation is limited, and the governing bodies show bias towards the "cute and cuddly" animals, and only act on a reactionary basis to the rest. We need proactive thinking so that funding is given before it reaches this point.'

However, there was a huge breakthrough in 2021 because dozens of captively bred young sunflower sea stars, apparently no larger than a poppy seed, had metamorphosed from floating larvae into miniature stars. This was the very first attempt at rearing sunflower sea stars through the early larvae stages in captivity – and what a success! To establish a breeding population, the research team, led by Jason Hodin, spent six months collecting thirty healthy adults from the Salish Sea. Each was named for their physical appearance – e.g. 'Clooney' had silver colouration and 'Prince', you guessed it, was bright purple. There aren't any plans for a reintroduction just yet as the project is still developing and learning new things about their life cycle. But eventually, if agreed to be beneficial by wildlife agencies, scientists could embark on a scheme to return captive-bred individuals back to the wild.

One of the questions I have been posing to all the scientists I've spoken to is, 'Are you hopeful?' Sara's response hit home for me. She said, 'I generally try to avoid thinking about whether I feel optimistic or not, because there's so much bad news about the species we're losing and there's so many problems that if I thought about it on a daily basis, I wouldn't be able to do the work that I do. I compartmentalise. A funny fact is that while I'm one of the leading experts on the sunflower sea star – I know where they live, where they don't live, everything that we know and don't know about them – I have only ever seen one sunflower star in the wild, and that was by accident before I started working with them. I wish I had spent more time with it and appreciated that moment more. We have generations of scientists growing up now studying species that they'll probably never encounter. There's just something very wild about that.' It is difficult remaining hopeful at times but, despite this, Sara did end on a positive note. 'While I don't know if we will ever be able to save this species, I do what I do because I get to engage with a lot of people who treasure the ocean and are involved in making decisions about it for the future. I value being in the position where I can bridge science and public policy by informing the audiences and talking to those who want to find solutions as much as I do. For me, I love these ecosystems but it always comes back to the people trying to save them,' she concludes.

I am part of a generation of scientists who increasingly research species that they may never get to see, if the climate crisis and extinction rates continue along the same trajectory. It's a sobering thought but it makes me even more determined to use my voice for their protection in the hope that I can make a small difference, but also selfishly so that I get to observe them in their natural environments. I'll never take encounters with wildlife for granted. I love using my imagination to think about the stars up in the sky, but I'd hate to one day be using it to picture what the seafloor would have looked like with sunflower sea stars. I don't want to have to imagine a kelp forest brimming with sea horses and sea otters. I want to be able actually see it, explore it and enjoy its beauty for years to come, and for the generations following me to have that same opportunity. With projects like this, we do have reasons to be hopeful. One small step for sea star conservation, one giant leap for ecological restoration.

Exquisite Spike-Thumb Frog

The age of dinosaurs lasted 165 million years. During that time species survived ice ages, volcanic eruptions and extreme temperature changes, but the secondary impacts of an asteroid that hit the Earth 66 million years ago abruptly ended their almighty reign, ultimately rerouting the course of evolution. This mass extinction event saw the demise of 75 per cent of species. But what if things had happened differently? If those species had survived, what might the world have looked like? Well, fossil evidence shows that Triceratops was one of the last remaining non-bird species, and scientists believe that if the asteroid had hit just minutes later and fallen into deeper waters, then descendants of this species and other large reptilian dinosaurs could still be alive today. This might seem irrelevant, but we are currently staring down the barrel of the sixth extinction crisis that might one day have people dreaming of bumping into beavers, barn owls and butterflies...

Anyway, what of the 25 per cent that did survive the asteroid impact? Most famous are the birds, the only true living dinosaurs. Ancient crocodiles, sharks and snakes also survived and perhaps it's clear why: they're all tough by reputation, with strong defences, able to withstand severe conditions in their respective habitats. But, it's amphibians that are perhaps the most surprising and intriguing group to have evolved from the dinosaur age: frogs, toads, salamanders, newts and caecilians. These small, amazing creatures have been around for 350 million years, proving their hardiness and resilience.

Originating from the Greek word 'amphibios', *amphi* translating to 'of both kinds' and *bios* translating to 'life', the word 'amphibian' means living a double life. This alludes to their impressive life-cycle strategy: after hatching from eggs they begin their aquatic lives completely submerged in fresh water and breathe through gills, before metamorphosing into adults with functioning limbs, lungs and gas-permeable skin suited to respiration above the surface, on land. This is a characteristic adapted by most species, with the exception of axolotls and some salamanders. There are about 8,000 different amphibian species worldwide, and nearly 90 per cent of them are frogs!

I'd happily bet that most people have a memory associated with frogspawn, whether that was during a biology class at school or a visit to your local pond. They're one of those animals that people are naturally drawn to, regardless of age. I got just as much joy and excitement a few days ago walking through a wildflower meadow with young, newly emerged, common frogs jumping on my walking boots as I did as a child watching tadpoles develop, sprouting legs as if from nowhere. Even though I now understand scientifically how they transform, my inner childlike fascination still tingles and buzzes. It's nuts, and beautifully bizarre!

Frogs can be found all over the world, on every continent except Antarctica. They inhabit a wide range of climates, from frozen tundra and deserts to temperate regions and the tropics, and are remarkably diverse. Some are dull in colour, others are vivid with striking patterns; some are excellent swimmers, others climb trees; some can jump up to distances of over a metre and others just a few centimetres.

Despite their large distribution as a taxonomic group and their prosperity over millions of years, frogs and other amphibians face a collective threat. During the late 1980s and early 1990s, herpetologists noticed a sudden drop in amphibian populations, and a 2004 global assessment confirmed that 32.5 per cent of all species were declining, a greater percentage than birds and mammals at that time. Today, 14 per cent of species are listed as endangered by the IUCN and a further 8.9 per cent are considered critically endangered. What is more concerning is that global data is insufficient, so some species may have already been lost for ever; some we knew of and others that we were not lucky enough to discover in time.

As always, climate change, habitat destruction and invasive species are among the usual suspects putting on the pressure, but in this chapter I'd like to focus on another culprit: *Batrachochytrium dendrobatidis*, also known as Bd or chytrid. This species of chytrid is a waterborne, highly infectious skin-eating fungus that targets the porous skin of its amphibian host. National Geographic Explorer Dr Jonathan Kolby is a policy expert specialising in the illegal wildlife trade, with a PhD on the spread of chytrid throughout the world by the trading of frogs. His work led him to Cusuco National Park, a small cloud forest in the Merendón Mountains, close to the city of San Pedro

Sula in Honduras, where he found 'Chytrid everywhere. It was a messy situation.'

Microscopic spores of this fungus quickly settle within the layers of a frog's skin. Usually, the skin of any organism functions as a barrier, protecting vital organs from external hazards and potential life-threatening contagions; it helps to prevent injury or infection and aids in the maintenance of body temperature. And while skin is made up of water, lipids, fats and minerals, we humans also have layers of keratin-rich protein cells in the epidermis, or outer layer, called keratinocytes. These are strong, insoluble cells that are our skin's first layer of defence. But the composition of frogs' skin is very different: it is thin, permeable, and protected by a layer of mucus; this allows water and oxygen to be absorbed directly from their aqueous environment. They do have some keratin cells in their skin, but only where natural wear and tear might occur, around their feet or armpits for example. Once chytrid fungus spores have nestled their way into an unsuspecting host's skin, it causes hyperkeratosis, which thickens the layer of keratin, obstructing the skin's permeability, restricting respiration and damaging their nervous system, eventually leading to heart failure and death.

Chytrid likely originated from Asia during the early twentieth century and was spread around the world when amphibian species were imported for medicinal testing or for the pet trade. The fungus may have been unknowingly brought into the USA from infected African clawed frogs in the 1930s, when the frogs were used to research pregnancy testing. It has since spread all over the world; the explanation for this remains a mystery, but it is possible that high winds and meteorological events accelerates its global distribution. According to a report published in the journal

Science in 2019, chytrid has caused the extinction of ninety frog species and a further 501 are threatened; 124 species' populations have plummeted by over 90 per cent. This is the most severe disease-related biodiversity decimator in known history.

Established in 1987 and covering 58,000 acres, the Cusuco National Park holds within it a richness of endemic rare and endangered animals. Cloud forests account for only 1 per cent of the world's woodland and can be found in tropical mountainous regions between 500 and 2,500 metres above sea level. These geological features give way to a pretty dramatic climate, as warm lowland air currents are forced upwards where they cool and condense, creating a persistent cloud cover that blankets the vegetation. It's that type of tropical rainforest that goes beyond 'green and luscious'; the depth and variety of colours produced by the mosses, lichens, ferns and epiphytes dangling from the tall trees with moisture coating every surface creates a mystical image. It's a habitat that has inspired scenes in *Lord of the Rings* and *Avatar*, but in real life it's not an easy environment for humans to settle in; it's cold, wet, and on the side of a steep mountain range. But that being said, it's the perfect environment for frogs. Or at least, it would be, as of the thirty amphibian species that live in this national park, half are listed as threatened with extinction.

Instead of spreading himself out across the world documenting species and their distributions, Jonathan made the decision to focus all his work in Honduras to try to make a difference to that one area. 'I decided to stay because while chytrid was a hot topic of research, there still weren't enough people studying it relative to the level of crisis it was. Most people I knew would go from place to place, do a sample survey, find chytrid, publish a paper and go on to the next location and repeat. But that never explained much, so

I wanted to have a stab at a long-term study to understand how it works and whether we can try to turn it around,' he explains.

'The biggest challenge with chytrid fungus, in a nutshell, is that once it embeds itself into a new environment, you can't get rid of it,' Jonathan goes on. 'There's been so many attempts and there's so much research but the question remains, how do we target and kill this microscopic-fungus without damaging other species that exist in the same environment? It's really not something that we can feasibly do or even hope to do. So what that means is that it will continue to spread from the seventy or eighty countries that it's in now and we're running out of time to stop it from killing more species. We also don't yet have a long-term cure or a vaccine, although there are ways of mitigating it in very controlled environments. We are able to rescue captive assurance populations from the wild, clean them up and keep them alive, but the main problem is how do we put them back? And where do we put them back? And can we ever put them back? There's no simple answer,' he states matter-of-factly. Having just gone through a pandemic ourselves, it's easy to understand how catastrophic and fast-moving these types of diseases or viruses can be. Sadly, when it comes to protecting a non-human species, purses are pinched and people with the power to allocate funding to find a solution play on ignorance, forgetting that one day soon the fall of biodiversity will turn around to bite us – hard; likely much harder than any virus could.

'It blows my mind how little we are really talking about this in the media, you know, it seems the worse it gets, the less we talk about it,' Jonathan says. 'In itself, that's quite a fascinating physiological response. But what's happening around the world at the moment is a scattering of small and large rescue efforts. Our intention in Honduras is to set up a facility where a handful of species can be brought into captivity in large enough numbers to support for a long enough time until a solution is found. We are limited by resources as to how many species we can help but, based on their rarity and chances for success, we've selected three species so far. Two are endemic and critically endangered, the exquisite spike-thumb frog and the Cusuco spike-thumb frog, and the third is a type of red-eyed tree frog that isn't endemic but lives in very fragmented populations,' he goes on.

The way this aquatic disease works is that it most often infects the animals as tadpoles. At this stage of life, tadpoles only have keratin tissues in their mouths, so the damage isn't life-threatening to the individual but of course, the more tadpoles carrying it are swimming around, the more chytrid is spread to others. And what scientists are finding is that the peak of the infection happens when they metamorphose into adults. It's the perfect time to hit; the young frog's immune system is naturally low as all its energy is being used to grow new organs for life above the water's surface. But this is where things get interesting: in areas of high infection in Honduras, there are surviving adults without traces of chytrid at all. This is bizarre given all we know about how prevalent this fungus is! So, either all the susceptible young frogs are dying straight away, leaving only adults with natural immunity, or there are some genetically distinct, special individuals that can 'self-cure', to use Jonathan's expression.

Regardless of how these individuals have managed to survive, they give hope that if chytrid-infected tadpoles can survive to become fully developed adults with a strong, functioning immune system then these species might just be in with a chance against extinction. A hands-on, intensive plan has been put into action. Jonathan says, 'We call it "head starting", where we plan to take out hundreds, if not more, of each of these three species every year at that stage of transition between a tadpole and a metamorph. We'll rush them to our facility where we can keep them in very controlled conditions, trying to replicate their wild environment as closely as we can to do whatever is necessary to reduce the burden of their infections. We don't need to cure it completely but we need to help them to survive through that really weak stage. That might mean something as simple as warming the water slightly as we know chytrid doesn't survive well at higher temperatures, or giving the tadpoles better nutrition, so they're not as stressed about finding enough food as they might be in the wild. There are also chemicals that are effective in controlling the infection but they can sometimes be harmful to certain amphibian species at certain life stages, so we prefer to adopt more natural methods whenever possible. Once their immune systems are strong enough, we can start putting them back into the wild en masse. And then we start over again with the next generation and keep going for as long as we need to until the population stabilises or ideally starts to increase. At that point, we can walk away and leave them to it while we start on another three species that need similar help.'

There are always unknowns that need to be accepted with these projects, but the ambition of Jonathan's project is to help the slow-motion process of natural selection to do its thing without these small populations going extinct in the meantime. When we think back to Covid, some people were more resilient than others, in terms of both catching it and exhibiting symptoms. It's exactly the same with the frogs, but the proportion of the population that is more resilient to chytrid is unknown so there is little room for error. 'We hope to get more adults in their natural habitat so they can mate and create tons more tadpoles. Yes, most will still be hammered by chytrid, but we are buying more time for natural selection to select for the resilient individuals. We want them to find their own solution but at the moment, they need our help,' Jonathan says.

The exquisite spike-thumb frog might just be one frog species of thousands, but this charismatic amphibian is one that the ecosystem can't afford to lose. Admittedly, their rarity and their remote existence high up in the misty mountains of Honduras means the specifics of their biology is largely under-studied, but they deserve just as much protection as any other endangered species.

Freshwater Pearl Mussel

I t goes without saying that for every organism whose reproduction is dependent on finding and seducing a mate, it's beneficial to be as attractive as possible. You want to stand out from the crowd and be noticed by the opposite sex so you can eventually pass on your genetic material to the next generation. Each species, population or even individual has their own unique ways of doing so. It could be something artificial like a rock gifted between penguins, or a naturally occurring adaptation (known as a biological ornament) that becomes increasingly prevalent over time through evolution. The concept is called sexual selection and it helps communicate your personal 'fitness' to a potential mate. For example, the colourful tail feathers of a male peacock or the impressive antlers of a red deer. In these cases, the bigger and the more complex these ornaments are, the better, as they signal, 'Hey, check me out, I'm the best of the bunch, fancy making a baby with me because they'd be the best and most impressive too… wink wink?'

For humans, there is a long list of desirable qualities, but voice pitch, face shape, height, muscle tone, proportions of hips and size of bum are listed as some of the most important factors that determine whether we find someone attractive. In today's world, we attempt to manipulate sexual selection through the way we present ourselves on social media, using filters or Photoshop to look more attractive, and by modifying our physical bodies with plastic surgery, Botox and implants. Yet, changing our appearance and trying to enhance our desirability is nothing new; humans have been doing this since the beginning of civilisation, with clothing, jewellery, face painting and body piercing, gifts, theatrical and musical performances, and visual art. As a child I once visited the 'Valley of the Kings' in Egypt, where lie sixty-two underground tombs holding priceless ancient Egyptian treasures and mummified corpses. There was one female mummy on display, clearly of royal descent. I peered down at her peaceful face in shock. I wasn't fazed by looking at her near-perfect preserved body; instead I was surprised that her electric blue eyeshadow was still perfectly intact on her eyelids after thousands of years. It was beautiful. She died a long time ago but a part of her personality had been preserved with her, still visible in her make-up.

Beauty trends come and go, but the practice of making ourselves feel more beautiful and attractive remains. Wearing jewellery is decorative, and has traditionally been used to showcase status and power. Some pieces of jewellery are considered timeless, never diminishing in value or public admiration. I used to watch lots of old Hollywood movies where gorgeous actresses would enter the scene bearing strings of shining pearls around their necks. I thought that was the most glamorous thing in the world. And for the longest time, they were. As Coco Chanel once said, 'A woman needs ropes and ropes of pearls.'

Pearls have long been called the 'queen of gems' and anyone wearing them associated with beauty, wealth and high status. The first evidence of pearl jewellery dates all the way back to 420 BC and a necklace worn by an unidentified Persian princess or queen, found in her sarcophagus. The ancient jewellery originally had approximately 216 pearls on it but many crumbled when touched during its excavation; the remainder are now on display in the Louvre Museum in Paris. Wearing pearls has always been a statement. From the last queen of Egypt, Cleopatra, who reportedly dissolved one of the largest pearls in the world into her glass of wine before drinking it as a way to impress representatives from the Roman Empire, to Lady Sarah Churchill, Duchess of Marlborough, who exclaimed, 'I feel undressed if I don't have my pearls on. My pearls are my security blanket,' they have been adored for centuries.

Most of the world's precious gemstones, like rubies, jade and diamonds, are formed under the Earth's surface as layers of deposited minerals are compressed over time. Pearls are completely different. They are made by aquatic bivalve molluscs – freshwater mussels or marine oysters, to be precise. Ironically, they are not made to be beautiful and have nothing to do with attracting a mate. Their reproduction method is called spermcast mating, a strategy often used by sessile marine organisms. Males release sperm into the water that is then drawn up by the females using a tube-like structure called a siphon to fertilise her eggs. During this process, the eggs move from the gonads to a specialised chamber inside the gills of the female, known as a marsupia, until the microscopic larvae are developed enough to continue their lives on their own. So you see, pearls really have nothing to do with it. In fact, these bivalves only create pearls when under threat of invasion, as a natural defence mechanism. Bivalves are called bivalves because they are just that – two calcium carbonate mantles (or shells) held together by an elastic ligament. These valves can open and close to filter-feed and reproduce but, of course, that does leave the animal occasionally vulnerable to an irritant, like a piece of organic matter or a parasite, entering its soft tissue body. When this happens, these invertebrates start to secrete layers of aragonite and conchiolin, the same calcium-rich minerals that make up its valve, to engulf the invader. Multiple layers of these substances make up the nacre – mother-of-pearl – material. We tend to think of pearls as perfectly uniform in size and shape but natural ones actually come in all different shapes and sizes.

Freshwater pearl mussels are pearl-producing species, as their name suggests, and are widely distributed across Russia, Europe and the north-east of North America, but studies have indicated a massive decline across their range. In some cases, in central and southern Europe, between 95 and 100 per cent have disappeared and they are now one of the most endangered invertebrate species alive today. In the UK, they were once a common sight, but they are now a rarity. They are virtually extinct in a lot of their former range, but a handful of strongholds remain. Scotland is home to most of the viable, functioning populations, whereas England only has one healthy one left, in Cumbria. For *Springwatch* in 2022, I was lucky to go and film a smaller population on the River Tyne in Northumberland. It was the first time seeing the species and I couldn't wait.

We headed to a lay-by in a secret location and put on our waders and waterproofs. The mussels were on the other side of the river so we took our time walking across, carefully placing our feet on the slippery, rocky surface of the river bed. The water was about waist-deep in the middle, which was where I lost my balance and fell straight in causing freezing cold water to fill my waders! But, it was totally worth it when I got to the other side. Hunkered down in between the rocks, these remarkable animals, which can live to over 100 years old and reach up to 17 centimetres long, were perfectly camouflaged in their freshwater home.

Historically, pearl hunting was a huge problem for these mussels, which were somewhat easier to find and harvest than other pearl-producing species in the sea. In the 1850s, they quickly became overharvested when demand for pearl jewellery skyrocketed. A natural pearl produced by a mollusc in the wild takes years to form and only 1 in every 1,000 individuals will ever create one. It's akin to finding a needle in a haystack. But, thankfully for these bivalves, a Japanese entrepreneur, Kōkichi Mikimoto, successfully founded the cultured pearl industry, which took off in the early 1900s, relieving the pressure on wild populations. He was able to reliably produce perfectly spherical pearls, which now satisfy 95 per cent of the world's demand, from mussels in captivity. Today wild freshwater pearl mussels are a protected species by law but face other, perhaps even more severe, dangers.

Dr Louise Lavictoire is the head of science at the Freshwater Biological Association (FBA) in the UK. She got involved with mussel conservation after realising she wanted to get hands-on to make a practical difference to a species on the brink. 'A lot of people ask me why I work with freshwater pearl mussels. Most people have never seen one so they ask: "would we miss them if they weren't there?" Biodiversity loss is massive and I'd argue that every species has an intrinsic value and a right to be there, but mussels in particular because they are more important to the ecosystem than people realise,' she explains. 'Each mussel can filter fifty litres of water every single day and that helps to improve the water quality of our rivers; all this particulate matter is removed from the water and sequestered in the sediments around them. Not only does that create clearer waters for people, but it helps create better habitats and microhabitats for all kinds of invertebrates, fish, plants, eels and even mammals, like otters, too. In the areas where the numbers of mussels are strong, you'll see excellent fish-spawning habitats. They are one of the ultimate keystone and indicator species for this environment; the only issue is that they need relatively good water and substrate quality to survive. They need fast-flowing, clear, well-oxygenated rivers.'

It's a catch-22 situation where mussels can have a role in maintaining these important river ecosystems but can only survive if the habitats are healthy enough to begin with. And at the moment, they're far from it. Since 1970, freshwater species around the world have declined by a devastating 83 per cent. And in the UK specifically, 10 per cent of all species that live in fresh water are threatened with extinction. (When I say fresh water I am referring to ponds, lakes, streams, rivers, canals, ditches, wetlands and springs, etc.) Many of these habitats have been polluted or modified to a degree that makes life hard to survive in them. There are roughly 90,000 kilometres of rivers around our nation but reports show that only 14 per cent of English rivers meet a good ecological status – although even they have some level of chemical contamination. This isn't a new statistic. In fact, in 2019 the government announced plans to revive and protect 75 per cent of the UK's waterways by 2027. It's something they clearly haven't taken seriously; as I write this, in 2022, people are being told not to swim in UK waterways as untreated raw sewage is being dumped into them, causing human health risks. It's grotesque in more ways than one.

The two main pollution sources are the untreated sewage, which accounts for 35 per cent of the problem and is released by water companies, and the agricultural run-off from pesticides and fertilisers, which is responsible for 40 per cent. Spraying fields with toxic fertilisers and pesticides is dangerous since not only does it have devastating consequences for the soil, pollinators and local wildlife, but as it rains these chemicals contaminate freshwater bodies. Over time these toxins exceed levels considered safe, building up to damaging or deadly concentrations. Eutrophication occurs as sewage and livestock waste accumulates, leading to an influx of nutrients; as a result, algae blooms start to emerge. This stops the sunlight from penetrating the water and reduces levels of photosynthesis. The plants and algae begin to die as a result, which then reduces oxygen levels in the water, killing off any inhabitants that remain.

Since their environments are becoming increasingly inhospitable, one of the main concerns is the success, of lack thereof, of their reproduction cycle. Every year in the summer, the females will each eject somewhere between one and four million microscopic larvae, known as glochidia, into the water in a highly synchronised event over the space of one or two days. They produce such huge numbers to compensate for the fact that the vast majority will be swept away by the water; but a few of the lucky ones will be inhaled by juveniles of salmonid fish species, like salmon or brown trout. Within a few hours the glochidia attach themselves onto the gills of the fish, where they grow and develop until the following spring. By hitching a ride in the fish's gills they develop in hyper-oxygenated water before detaching themselves further downstream. It's a clever means of dispersal for an organism that is otherwise immobile. They spend their first few independent years buried under the sediment until they have grown large enough to be lodged between the stones on the riverbed. This life cycle means they're dependent not only on the quality of water but on the health of salmonid fish too.

Around the world, there are an estimated 500,000 wild individuals of the freshwater pearl mussel species, which you might expect would be enough of a baseline for them to survive and start increasing in numbers. But sometimes you have to look beyond surface-level statistics. Their population is top-heavy, meaning that it's made up in the main of older mussels, generally over sixty years old. These adults are still successfully reproducing but their young aren't surviving. This undoubtedly means extinction unless a method is found to support and stabilise the next generation. So that's where Louise and her team step in with specialised facilities at the FBA's species recovery centre.

'At the moment we have five populations of mussels from rivers around the UK that we are actively breeding,' she says. 'Four are English populations, where we are seeing the harshest declines, and the other is a Welsh population we are breeding on behalf of Natural Resources Wales. It has been a case of trial and error to get the rearing conditions right for the juveniles, including the complex relationship each population has with its host fish species. Some will only reproduce successfully on salmon while others need trout so it's quite a resource intensive programme.'

The FBA species recovery centre is located on the shores of Windermere in the Lake District and is the first of its kind in the UK. It has been breeding mussels since 2007. I asked Louise to take me through the life of a mussel produced at the hatchery.

'I'll use one population as an example,' she replied. 'We collected some adults from one Cumbrian river in March of 2007, right at the beginning of the captive breeding project. We focused on this location to help reinforce the population as this particular site had declined from hundreds of thousands of mussels to around three hundred aging adults. The water temperature in March is low and while the mussels don't hibernate, it's not their active growth period. They were safely moved to the hatchery, where the adults began breeding as the temperature of the water started to increase. Their breeding is very temperature-dependent; males release sperm which the female mussels use to fertilise their eggs. They brood them for about six weeks, (again depending upon water temperature) and from that point on we make sure we have some juvenile salmonid fish present to receive the glochidia. We keep the fish for about nine months – again it's very temperature-dependent – until the fully developed young mussels start to drop off.

'We place plankton nets over the outflows of the tanks and check them once a day to collect all of the juvenile mussels. We bring them into a separate building where we have four types of enclosed systems mimicking their prime wild environmental conditions and as the mussels outgrow and graduate from one system, they move on to the next, so to speak. The offspring from the adults we collected in our first year dropped off, or were born I suppose, in 2008. We kept them in the facility for nine years until 2017, and even then they only averaged about an inch in length. We tagged them using vinyl tags, which were superglued onto the outside of their mantle before they were released back to where the adults originally came from in Cumbria. There were about seventy in total for that release.'

I think you can always tell a lot about a person from their study species, and Louise is probably one of the most patient people I have ever interviewed! It's quite remarkable when you think about all that time and resources spent rearing a population of tiny bivalves to the stage where they might have a chance to survive in the wild. And while it might take a long time to raise that young population, it takes even longer to find out whether your efforts have been worthwhile.

After releasing those individuals into to the river, Louise and the team returned in 2019 to see how they were getting on. The release site wasn't large, so they expected to find the mussels relatively quickly, but as they were still very small and mainly hidden under the sediment surface, the team only found about one-third of the numbers they had released two years prior. 'I expect many more were there but we just didn't find them. Now though, we attach PIT tags to our mussel releases,' she continues. PIT stands for Passive Integrated Transponder, which is essentially a microchip that contains a unique code. If you have a dog or a cat you'll be familiar with how they work. In the case of the mussels, these tags can be glued using dental cement onto the shell without causing any harm to the animal. Even when they're buried under the sediment, all Louise needs to do is run a waterproof reader over the riverbed to find out which individuals are nestled away safely.

Louise rounds off: 'Pearl hunting is more of an issue in Scotland than England currently because numbers are higher there, but the main solution that we need to see right now for the freshwater pearl mussels is the restoration of natural processes. We should be taking out structures that force the river to stay within pre-defined channels so that rivers can behave in a normal, natural way – enabling them to move, change, spread and flood when necessary – to take the pressure off these habitats. We should be removing pollution and focusing on restoring the habitats where there are populations of adult mussels and salmonid fish so that one day we don't have to do captive breeding.'

It's easy to blame historical pearl hunting for the demise of this underappreciated species, but it is our damaging pesticides and pollution that is the true cause. Companies releasing literal shit into our rivers need to take accountability and change, otherwise we will continue to see drastic declines. Captive breeding is a safety net for these mussels, a net that many others don't have, and they deserve and need clean water just as much as we require clean air. It shouldn't be a big ask. We will always think pearls are beautiful, but maybe we could learn to appreciate and respect their creators more. Imagine if we held freshwater pearl mussels in the same regard as we do some of the most talented artists in history – Leonardo da Vinci or Vincent van Gogh, perhaps. Maybe then they'd be in with a chance.

Hammerhead Shark

I t was 2 a.m. when my alarm rang out; I hastily switched it off as to not wake the others. I quietly grabbed my head torch, jumpers and hat that I had left in a pile by the door just a few hours before, and walked over to the dock, trying not to trip on the unfamiliar path. It was my first day volunteering at the Shark Lab – a research station on the island of Bimini in the

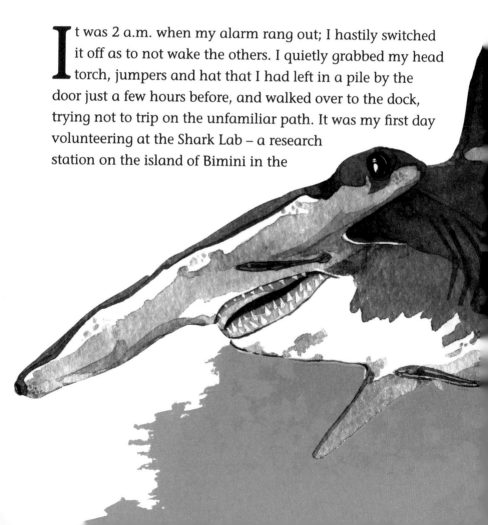

Bahamas. I didn't know what to expect but I was full of excitement and anticipation at the possibility of seeing my very first shark. I was struck by the stars, which shone so brightly in this remote part of the world untouched by light pollution, and, as we sped out to sea, the intense electric blue of the bioluminescence produced

by the microscopic plankton, bacteria and ctenophores in the water exploded like a performance under the waves. I'd never seen anything like it – it was peaceful and dramatically spellbinding at the same time. As we made our way out into deeper waters on the small power boat, we used our torches to search for the bright yellow and orange buoys bobbing on the water's surface that had been set the afternoon before. Below the buoys were longlines – a series of hooks with bait set out across the water column. The hooks used by the lab are shark-friendly circle hooks and the lines are checked every two to three hours to minimise any potential stress. They are set by staff and volunteers once a month as a way to monitor the shark populations around the island. Depending on the research that is going on, the sharks are 'worked up', meaning they have their measurements, DNA and isotope samples taken. They may even be tagged too.

On the boat, we drove slowly in parallel down the first longline. It was pitch black at this point and eerily quiet, with the exception of an occasional wave crashing against the bow. We were looking for a buoy submerged under the water, but all the buoys on the first longline were floating – there were no sharks. The second longline – all floating – no sharks. I was beginning to think that this wasn't going to be the night. But as we reached the end of the third line, there she was. A female tiger shark. I froze, not wanting to get in the way of the experienced team as they brought her up alongside the boat and started to take measurements so she could be released. She was young, only 1 metre in length, and had the most striking dappled pattern on her side, which gives the species their name. I was called to help: 'Can you hold on to her dorsal fin?' someone asked. I was so transfixed on her that I didn't look up to see who was speaking to me, but I followed their instructions without hesitation; I leaned over the side and held the dorsal fin on her back. The roughness of her skin, composed of dermal denticles, was an entirely new texture to me. I was trying to soak in every second of the moment – getting to work with a species I had only previously dreamed of – while also learning how and what to do. Within a matter of minutes, she was free to go. I let go of her fin and stepped back with the rest of the team to watch her disappear into the dark water. I didn't say one word on the ride back home. I just smiled, not wanting to forget a thing.

It was one of the most extraordinary wildlife encounters of my life. In the months that followed, I got lots of experience working with all kinds of species, from lemon sharks to the big bull sharks. I was driving the boats, setting up the longlines and helping to lead the 'work-ups'. But there was always one that I was desperate to see: a hammerhead...

Gaining practical experience in the field of conservation is fundamental to achieving your academic and career goals. It opens doors in a way that the books don't – not that the books aren't important; they are – but having hands-on experience can't be overlooked. I am a visual learner with dyslexia, so I was always drawn to improving my skills practically. It suited me so much better than any written exam and it helped boost my confidence when I didn't quite understand how to calculate complicated models or convey statistical analyses that my friends would seemingly breeze through. So, each and every summer from the age of fourteen I took on an internship, some based in the UK and some a little further afield. I was drawn to understanding predators, especially those which were largely misunderstood, so I became fascinated by everything from tigers to praying mantids. It was the diversity in their behaviour, and the combination of stealth, power, agility and intellect, that left a lasting impression on me. By the time I was eighteen I had already worked with a number of the apex predators, but there was still one that I hadn't yet seen.

At this stage I had hardly dipped my toes into the ocean – my mum was scared of open water and my stepdad would only get in if it was warm and there was something he deemed interesting enough to see. My dad, however, took me swimming every other weekend at the local pool in Southampton, where I would play mermaids and race down the flumes. I loved the water but it never really occurred to me that I could study it. That was until I heard about Bimini Biological Field Station in the Bahamas. I mean, I couldn't very well continue saying I wanted to study predators without having worked with one of the most beautiful of them all – sharks. So, I applied to their programme, packed a bag and flew away to join the Shark Lab.

The Shark Lab is a world-renowned research station located on the southern island of Bimini, and volunteers travel from all over to gain experience and follow in the footsteps of its founder, the late Dr Samuel Gruber, aka 'Doc'. The mangrove-dominated island is a unique one, situated only fifty miles off the coast of Miami, USA, and next to the Gulf Stream. It's essentially a nursery ground for young sharks, as the larger adults travelling in from the Gulf Stream find their way to the shallow flats of the island to give birth. The mangroves provide a refuge for the young pups of various species as they grow, hiding them from both predators (predominantly larger sharks) and harsh storms. The precise number of species that visit the island throughout the year isn't known because of the varying habitats and depth of water, but they are numerous! It's a hotspot for some very special elasmobranchs (sharks and rays) – from the manta rays and southern stingrays to the tiger, bull and reef sharks. The time I spent in Bimini started a lifelong love and admiration for these misunderstood animals. Over the years, I have tried my best to support worldwide shark campaigns for their protection and filmed a CBBC documentary, *Planet Defenders*, detailing their plight in UK waters. It's safe to say I'm a self-confessed shark fanatic.

But today it is not simply enough to love sharks; we have to act now to protect them. It's hard to believe that a group of animals that are so well designed that they have largely remained unchanged for over 450 million years are in so much trouble. They have survived five previous mass extinctions involving ice ages, asteroids and sea-level depletion, yet they may not survive humans, and we've only been around 300,000 years. To put that into perspective in terms of Earth's history, has only existed for 0.067 per cent of the time that sharks have. They swam in the oceans long before dinosaurs roamed the land 230–240 million years ago, and even before trees took root just under 400 million years ago. Across the globe, there are over 520 different species in all shapes and sizes, from the 18-metre whale shark to the 20-centimetre dwarf lantern shark. While their diversity as a group is reason enough to admire them, it's their fundamental role within the ecosystem that we really can't live without. As apex predators they hold the top spot on the trophic level, helping to maintain the balance and health of the ecosystem. They keep their prey from becoming too numerous and encourage them to evolve and grow stronger at a speciation level by feeding on the weak and injured. But other than simply impacting prey numbers, sharks also affect their distribution – for example, in the presence of tiger sharks, green sea turtles continuously move around their habitat, preventing them from overgrazing on seagrass, which stores huge volumes of carbon. And as animals, they also store carbon; large fish, like sharks, tuna and swordfish, consist of 10–15 per cent carbon. When they die of natural causes and fall to the ocean floor, something termed 'carcass deadfall', their bodies are buried and sequestered by the sediment, locking the carbon away. In addition, because sharks tend to migrate, this nutrient cycle is distributed between locations and varying depths, which is so important for the ecosystem. The bottom line is that we, as a species, need the ocean, and the ocean needs sharks.

It's truly heartbreaking seeing and hearing the latest science on shark abundances, as the picture seemingly grows bleaker and bleaker by the day. In the last fifty years we have decimated a terrifying 71 per cent of them. Three-quarters of all documented species are threatened with extinction, so for every ten sharks that would have been swimming in the open water during the 1970s, on average today there would only be three. I use the word 'decimated' and not 'lost' because to lose something is passive, but in the case of sharks we have previously and continue to actively kill them off. An estimated 100 million sharks are taken from the oceans every single year. The threat to them that receives the most media coverage and always makes headlines is shark-finning: a form of fishing whereby sharks are caught, their fins slashed off with knives and their bodies (often still alive) discarded in the water, where they suffocate to death as they fall to the seafloor. Unable to swim and bleeding profusely, they struggle to breathe without the constant flow of oxygenated water over their gills. This is to satisfy the demand for shark fin soup, considered a delicacy in China and parts of Taiwan and South East Asia. Their fin is made solely of cartilage with no nutritional value and no flavour, so the soup has additional stock ingredients added to make it taste palatable to consumers. Another misconception that has made the soup grow in popularity is the belief that sharks do not get cancer and their fins have medicinal properties. This is simply not true. I have seen sharks with large tumours and there is no science to suggest eating them has any benefit to human health… if anything, it is quite the opposite. A study from the University of Miami found that sharks contain high levels of mercury and have a neurotoxin called BMAA in their cartilage, which is linked to neurological diseases, like Alzheimer's and amyotrophic lateral sclerosis (ALS). So far so grim; but, while finning is undoubtedly having a negative impact on sharks worldwide, blaming solely one dish lets every other industry and causal factor off the hook, so to speak. The other issues are closer than you think. In fact, I'd be willing to bet you have used and potentially are still using shark products and don't even know about it.

To maintain buoyancy in the water, sharks' livers are full of an oil called squalene that can make up 20 per cent of their body weight. Squalene has anti-inflammatory and anti-ageing properties that are moisturising to the skin, so, despite available plant-based alternatives, many cosmetic companies still use shark-derived squalene in their products – in lipsticks, moisturisers, sun creams, eyeshadows, hair conditioners – you name it. Sixty species of shark are directly targeted for their oil and twenty-six of those are on the

IUCN Red List as globally vulnerable. It takes an estimated 3,000 sharks to collect one tonne of squalene. Most of these species live below 300 metres in the deep sea and are specifically sought after as their livers have much higher concentrations of oil. It's an adaptation that helps them maintain neutral buoyancy at those depths. It might be that manufacturers argue the plant-based alternatives are more expensive, but when you consider the cost of the environmental damage, it's a small price to pay. Scientists say that pursuing these sharks is even more damaging to the environment because they are also victims of overfishing.

Overfishing is the unsustainable practice of removing fish from the ocean faster than they are able to reproduce and recover, causing a population collapse. It is thought that 2.7 trillion fish are caught every year using equipment and techniques including long-lines, gillnets and bottom-trawling. Forty per cent of what is caught while fishing is discarded, wasted, thrown back into the sea mostly injured or dead, according to the United Nations Food and Agriculture Organization's report in 2012. This is THE biggest problem for sharks. These commercial fishing methods are non-selective, meaning that any fish, reptile or mammal swimming past can get caught and entangled. Each year, fifty million sharks are thought to die as a result of by-catch or incidental capture. This is something that is getting more attention now, thanks to powerful documentaries like *Sharkwater* and *Seaspiracy* that have sparked public outcry and debate, but nevertheless it remains the shark's biggest threat.

So how can we protect them? Even things that are seemingly designed to help sharks can be problematic. Shark ecotourism has exploded in the last twenty years, with more and more people entering the water to swim alongside them in their oceanic homes. And who could blame them? I always encourage people to get out there and connect with nature in all its forms. Shark tourism has been shown to help reverse their 'ferocious' reputation as depicted in films and media coverage, and helps to secure Marine Protected Areas. It is also a global industry that was estimated in 2011 to be worth a whopping $314 million, with over 10,000 jobs. By 2023, these numbers will have no doubt grown much larger. The island of Bimini – home of the Shark Lab where I interned – is situated within the boundaries of a shark sanctuary. In 2011, the Bahamas declared an exclusive economic zone that stretches for 200 nautical miles across the shoreline, prohibiting any commercial fishing and giving protection to all elasmobranchs. There are very few places in the world to see sharks in the abundance and diversity that they're found here, so it's a hotspot for dive tourism.

And herein lies the potential problem. You see, when it comes to shark diving, guests have paid to encounter certain species so some operators, feeling the pressure to provide close encounters, increase the odds by luring sharks in with chunks of fish. Contrary to popular belief, sharks are incredibly cautious and will generally move away from human activity given the chance. This practice, then, has sparked some serious debate as it could have more detrimental impacts than positives. The concerns are that it may alter shark movement patterns, conditioning resident individuals to favour ecotourism sites and ultimately changing their metabolisms, energy expenditures and reproduction. For example, one study looking at the impact of daily food provisioning of resident sicklefin lemon sharks in French Polynesia found that the population is experiencing inbreeding due to a reduction in gene dispersal. These individuals spend more time grouped in one area expecting food than they do moving on to new locations. Evidence also suggests that this feeding might shift nocturnal species into a more diurnal rhythm, which has implications for the food chain. There are a lot of pros and cons, but what's certain is that we have still got a lot to learn on the subject.

This brings me back to the predator I have always longed to meet: hammerhead sharks. They are seasonal visitors to Bimini, coming to the island in the winter between December and April, and I just missed out on their arrival. I was boarding the plane home when I got a message from a friend who told me that they had finally returned. I was gutted to say the least, but it does give me a good excuse to return one day.

Alongside the great whites, hammerheads have to be one of the most well-known species. Their distinctive elongated, flattened head, the term for which is 'cephalofoil', is what makes them so recognisable; and there's a good reason for it. Sharks have a sixth sense; they are able to detect electromagnetic fields in the ocean which helps them navigate and locate food. Packed along their lateral line (which runs along each side of their body) and their nose are jelly-filled pores known as the ampullae of Lorenzini. These are specialised electroreceptors that are able to pick up the faintest of electrical pulses produced by prey. While this trait is something that all elasmobranchs share, the hammerheads have taken it a step further. The evolution of their head shape was most likely caused by the drive to enhance their electro-sensory prey detection; a larger head means more pores and a greater searching area. It's helpful considering they favour stingrays and other benthic (floor-dwelling) species as their main source of prey that often hide themselves away under the sand. So, a large hammer-shaped head can essentially act like a metal detector, scanning the floor for their next meal. Their wide-set eyes, positioned on either side of their head, are also a great benefit; they afford the hammerhead a 360-degree view of its environment, with excellent binocular vision and depth perception. Evolution at its best!

One person who knows hammerheads better than most is Vital Heim. He is a scientist studying for a PhD with the University of Basel in Switzerland, and is an expert on the impact of shark diving on greater hammerheads around the island of Bimini. He knows virtually all the hammerheads who visit the island and has spent countless hours trying to understand their behaviour. Collaborating with a local dive site, Vital focused on answering questions like, 'How much are the greater hammerheads eating during provisioning events?' and, 'How long do they spend at the site?' in order to create a model that would estimate how much they would need to eat for their body weight to meet their energetic needs. 'For my PhD the first chapter is about long-term monitoring of the local hammerheads,' Vital explains. 'We have data at the lab of what I call "control" sharks that have been tagged but have never visited the dive site before. They provide baseline data about how an unprovisioned shark should move and behave in Bimini. This gives me a chance to compare to sharks who more often visit the dive sites and do receive food.' An individual great hammerhead could consume up to 4.75 kilograms of bait on average per dive and, using complex bioenergetic modelling techniques, Vital found that some were able to fulfil their daily energy requirements based on the food given by the tour operator.

I asked Vital if, as someone with a wealth of experience around these charismatic giants, he believes that shark diving is more positive or negative. Vital took a second to think before responding. 'Shark diving uses these individuals as a reusable resource, it sounds very odd, but it's true. If a country decided to allow shark fisheries then once an individual is removed from the population, that's it, it's gone, and you have to hope the population will recover. But there are greater hammerhead sharks in Bimini, like the female named Medusa, who are known all over the world within the diving communities. She generates money for conservation every day, which is crazy to think of. Having good shark tourism also encourages other countries to create sanctuaries and protected areas as they begin to see the value economically. These dives, if done responsibly and safely, are an opportunity to educate people. I was out on the boats every day with divers, talking about my work and how endangered hammerheads are… most people had no idea. I do see too, often, operators conducting tours badly, where they compromise safety by touching and getting too close to the animals. This does need to be sorted but in general, I think it's important.'

So shark diving is not in and of itself a massive issue, but it's an important link in the story. As these greater hammerheads migrate away from the protected waters around Bimini, they make their way west to the coast of the eastern USA, where recreational fishing from the shore is quickly emerging as the latest conservation issue for the species and others, like the critically endangered scalloped hammerhead. Recreational fishers are simply those who fish for the fun of it. Authorities in Florida have given protection to these two species of hammerhead, saying that the sharks must be 'immediately returned to the water free, alive and unharmed' if they are caught by recreational fishermen using a line and hook from the beach. Ninety per cent of anglers in the USA reportedly practise a catch-and-release method to minimise the stress to the animal and protect their populations – but, before release, they often take a quick selfie or two with the fish if it's an impressive size or is a rarity. Catching a greater hammerhead is deemed a huge success among the community. Why you would want to haul a big shark out of water for a selfie, I don't know. It must be an ego thing. For some species of shark, the catch-and-release method, if done quickly by experienced anglers, can be successful, but for sensitive greater hammerheads, it can end in fatalities.

I wanted to understand more about this problem and I knew exactly the person to go to. Dr David Shiffman is a bit of a legend when it comes to promoting shark science, and was one of the first people to notice how much of a problem this really is. 'Everyone thought it wasn't a problem because no one was really looking. With recreational fishing, there's this emerging body of evidence all over the world that it's becoming a conservation issue in a lot of ways,' he says. 'There's a few reasons for that. One is just the scale of it. You see these horrifying videos of the supertrawlers and how much they can catch in a day. And you think to yourself, *going fishing with your family or friends in the lake near your house and you catch maybe three fish all day and you wonder, well, how can I possibly have an impact on that scale?* Well, one person doesn't. But there's a lot more people who go fishing for fun than there are supertrawlers. A lot more. We're talking about hundreds of millions of people who go fishing at least a few times a year, and that adds up. Part of the issue is also the economics, so it's believed that commercial fishing will not ever drive a species extinct because at a certain point, it costs more for boat fuel than you will get from catching and selling the remaining fish. Those populations might be in trouble, but they're not gone. The incentives are different with recreational fishing because you're paying to do it, and going after a rarer species is worth paying more,' he explains. Shocking when it's put like that, isn't it?

Florida is the shark fishing capital of the world, so much so that they even have an unofficial yearly hammerhead-focused fishing tournament. The problem with fishing for hammerheads, even with a catch-and-release method, is that they are incredibly fragile and sensitive creatures. They're a ram-ventilating species, which means they must keep swimming at all times to make sure enough water passes over their gills so that they get enough oxygen. When caught, hammerheads quickly become exhausted and stressed. All sharks build up lactic acid when they are in a stressful situation. We humans also build up this acid when we do a heavy workout, but for sharks, in high concentrations it can become poisonous and deadly. Essentially their circulation breaks down and they die. Shark species that rest at the bottom of the sea and aren't reliant on consistently swimming tend to have a higher stress threshold, but those that do have to keep swimming simply cannot physiologically recover. Hammerheads can die on the hooks if left too long; but, even if it appears you have successfully released one back into the ocean, it's likely that delayed mortality will occur as the acid continues to build, shutting down their system. Research shows with scalloped hammerheads that after they have been released, over 90 per cent will still die later on.

Despite these sharks' protected status, some anglers go after them specifically. 'They love catching hammerheads because it feels like a freight train is trying to run away from you,' David continues. 'They have what anglers call "fight", when the fish is putting every last drop of energy it has into escaping. The science tells us that after about forty minutes of fight time, it'll be a dead hammerhead, even after it's been released. Many anglers say that they are aware and try to reel them in extra fast by doing it within two hours. You don't want to discourage them from being fast but trying to help is not the same thing as helping. It's illegal to purposefully kill a hammerhead in Florida because their numbers are so low, so some of my research looked at how anglers talk about their fishing online. In their own words, they often say, "Oh yeah, if you get caught, say you didn't mean to catch it. It's illegal to target them. But you can say you were fishing for grouper and caught it by accident.'"

I was so surprised listening to David's experiences. It's one thing to be ignorant of the policies and the threat these animals are facing globally, but it's another to be fully aware and still not only engage in illegal activity but brag about it online. David located hundreds of messages from anglers about their unlawful fishing practices and worked with wildlife law enforcement to bring attention to this activity that really needs addressing at the policy level. But it wasn't easy. When bringing evidence to law enforcement originally, their response was literally, 'Well, you weren't there to directly witness it so we cannot do anything.' (David pointed out that this is not how law enforcement works; they wouldn't have given the same response if he were to say, 'My friend has been stabbed.') But I'm pleased to say while there is still a long way to go to protect hammerheads and other sharks, David has made some incredible headway in changing policy and bringing this unspoken issue into the light.

Is there a global solution to shark decline? It's painfully simple. There need to be tighter regulations on by-catch quotas and serious repercussions for those conducting illegal wildlife crime against protected, endangered sharks. But this needs cooperation from countries all over the world. Sharks migrate thousands of miles and have no concept of man-made borders. For us to protect the oceans, we need our leaders to take a stand.

Wild Camels

Camels... I know what you're thinking: why are they included on this list? They're hardly the species that springs to mind when you consider all of the critically endangered mammals around the globe.

If you'd have asked me twelve months ago I would have raised an eyebrow too, but here we are. In a remote area close to the Mongolian and Chinese border lives a small group of a recently recognised species, eking out an existence against the odds. They've survived nuclear fallout, sub-zero temperatures, extreme inhospitable heat and even a total lack of fresh water... Their untold story is one of great conflict and endurance.

Camels belong to the family Camelidae, which includes the true camels and the new world camelids, such as llamas, alpacas, vicuñas and the guanaco. Globally, only three species of true camels roam the world today, but they all originally evolved from a common ancestor in North America 40–50 million years ago, during the Eocene period. Early camelids looked and behaved very differently to those about today. The first known species of that group, called *Protylopus*, was the size of a rabbit and preferred the open woodlands of what is now South Dakota. Over the next few million years, larger species diverged that more closely resembled modern-day camels. They moved away from North America, heading east through what is now Eurasia approximately 7.5–6.5 million years ago, during the late Miocene, and also distributed to South America, where the new world species originated. The later known camel species native to North America was *Camelops hesternus* but that eventually vanished along with other megafauna groups like mammoths, sabretooth cats and short-faced bears some time around 15–11,000 years ago, when humans migrated from Asia during the end of the Pleistocene.

No one has managed to get an accurate count of the number of camels alive today, although estimates suggest that there are over forty million! If current trends continue, research from 2020 suggests there could be as many as sixty million by 2025. That is an indisputably large number of camels. So far, so unendangered. But 94 per cent of the current population is made up of the one-humped Dromedary camel. They're the tallest of the three extant species and can weigh up to 600 kilograms. And almost all of the further 6 per cent are the two-humped Bactrian camels. Both have been fully domesticated. While we can't be sure of the exact date that camels became such a trusty ally to people, archaeologists can estimate the emergence of domestication through markers like artistic representation, reduction in the size of bone remains and increased fossil evidence located next to ancient human settlements. Dromedaries are estimated to have been domesticated on the Arabian peninsula somewhere between 4000 BC and 2000 BC and Bactrians in north-east Afghanistan in approximately 2500 BC. One thing that's for sure is that in comparison to other animals, camel domestication happened rather late in human history; dogs were domesticated around 14,000 years ago, goats around 10,000 years ago, pigs around 9,000 years ago, and horses around 6,000 years ago.

The domestication of these two camel species helped to advance the progression of civilisations, with humans relying upon them then – as they do to this day – for meat, dairy, wool and transportation. Camels are pack animals that are able to carry loads of up to 250 kilograms over thirty miles a day in extreme conditions, and so, as well as being part of nomadic communities, they have been used a lot in overland trading and military warfare. The first example of this was in 547 BC during the Battle of Thymbra when the Achaemenid Persians fought the Lydian Kingdom. The horses were apparently alarmed at the sight and smell of the camels at close range, which made camels an effective anti-cavalry weapon in desert warfare. They were used extensively again by Romanian, Egyptian and Indian corps, among others, during World War One and Two.

Privately owning a camel has historically been a statement of wealth and this idea still lingers today… if you have the right camel, that is. In Saudi Arabia there is the yearly King Abdulaziz Camel Festival, where thousands of camels are judged on the quality of their humps and lips alongside races and milk tasting.

119

It's essentially Crufts for camels. The overall winner could take home the huge sum of £40 million, and owners will stop at nothing to get a shot at winning. In 2021 it was reported that twelve camels were disqualified as their owners had used Botox in the animals' lips and jaws to improve their aesthetics. What a bizarre world we live in!

While most camels are domesticated, there is one species that remains wild. Many resources online and in the media suggest that they are the only two species of camel but that simply isn't true. In 2008, after five years of genetic testing by the University of Veterinary Medicine Vienna, *Camelus ferus* was given official recognition as such; and with only 1,000 individuals remaining, they are the eighth most critically endangered large mammal we have on Planet Earth. (Much rarer than the well-known and beloved panda!) Approximately 600 wild camels live in north-western China and 450 in south-west Mongolia, collectively located deep within the Great Gobi Desert.

They're incredibly elusive animals, so getting a glimpse can be tricky. But from the research that has been done, we understand that they separated from other known species over 700,000 years ago and continued to diverge further in the Gashun Gobi region, somehow avoiding domestication. DNA testing using skin samples showed that there is only a 3 per cent difference between the domestic Bactrian and the wild camel species, which might explain why, in appearance, wild camels more closely resemble the Bactrian, although they have smaller humps, shorter ears, a different tooth structure and a more reddish-brown hue to their coat. But there are some more fundamental differences in their adaptations and behaviour.

Camels are built for living in extreme environments; they are able to withstand brutally high and low temperatures, droughts and altitudes that would be unbearable for any other living creatures. They occupy a unique niche for such a large mammal. Temperatures in the Gobi can reach over 42 °C in the summer and sink to below −38 °C in the winter (while you might solely associate camels with hot environments, they are able to tolerate and thrive below freezing too). Intense sand and dust storms make their habitat even more challenging, and there are often very few food resources and limited water supplies available to sustain them. These wild camels are migratory and research shows they move across the rocky mountain massifs, stony plains and sand dunes in accordance with accessible water reservoirs. They can survive over a week without water but when they do finally drink, they can consume fifteen to thirty gallons of water in just ten minutes. Yet, their most phenomenal adaptation is that when fresh water is scarce, they have the ability to consume salt water. Wild camels are the only species that is able to survive on saline springs with a salt concentration higher than that of the ocean. We don't yet fully understand how the camels are able to absorb and secrete so much salt. It's believed their young only develop this strategy, whatever it may be, after suckling from their mother for up to two years. They can, of course, hydrate through food but this is unreliable, so they've had to evolve perfectly to live life on the edge, making use of every single available molecule of H_2O they can find.

It is astonishing that this small population has clung on for so long, especially considering that in the last 100 years of their existence they have faced so much adversity due to human activity. The wild camels living inside the Chinese border are situated in Lop

Nur, Xinjiang province, which is a former nuclear testing site. They somehow survived forty-three atmospheric nuclear blasts, some of which were far more powerful than Hiroshima. The blasting came to an end in 1996 when a treaty was signed, yet there was still a lot of secrecy around the events in that area and for years no one was allowed inside the province. However, in 1995 the first foreigner, John Hare, who is a former army officer and a fellow of the Royal Geographical Society, was granted access. Over the years he pioneered five successful expeditions to research the camels, and eventually assisted in founding the Lop Nur Wild Camel National Nature Reserve. The reserve still stands and is one of the largest in the world, spreading across 96,000 square miles (twice the size of France!). Amazingly, the camels had not only survived the nuclear testing but were still breeding successfully, with no apparent effects from radiation. This is particularly remarkable considering the science produced by Jun Takada and Enver Tohti, who concluded that 190,000 people living within range likely died due to nuclear-related illnesses and cancer rates skyrocketed 30–35 per cent above the national average. The fact that these camels were so well adapted to living in seemingly impossible conditions most likely gave them the edge to survive. The Lop Nur region is one of the most arid regions in the world and is enclosed by three valleys and the mountain range of Kuruk Tagh. This separates and provides protection from the elements to the camels currently living within the reserve, who almost entirely rely upon salt water. In this region rain might fall once every two to three years, if that, and will average at less than 100 millimetres annually. (Compare that to the UK, which has 1,372 millimetres per year.)

Currently, scientists cannot enter Xinjiang province where the Chinese camel population resides, as another horrifying humanitarian crisis is unfolding. There are 12 million people, part of the predominantly Muslim Uyghur community, who live there, in what is known as the Xinjiang Uyghur Autonomous Region (XUAR). With their own regional language, they view themselves as culturally and ethnically separate to other Central Asian nations. It's been reported in the news very recently that one million Uyghurs are being held against their will in what the state is calling 're-education camps'. In 2020, research from the Australian Strategic Policy Institute indicated that there are likely more than 380 of these 'camps' in the province.

China has been accused of forcing these communities into hard labour and the women into sterilisation. People who have escaped the 'camps' tell horrific stories of torture and rape. It's feared that they will eventually erase the culture and religious beliefs of the Uyghur community. Essentially, all evidence points towards mass genocide happening right now. Today. In 2023. People are being held in what are really concentration camps. Although, China have denied all the allegations of human rights abuse and have said that their re-education camps aim only to tackle Islamist militancy in the area.

So, very understandably, research isn't taking place in the area and the population of Chinese wild camels have been left to their own devices once again. Instead, Mongolia has become the focus point for wild camels for the time being; and breakthroughs can't come soon enough. In 1993 it was suggested that the remaining populations of wild camels would experience a decline of up to 80 per cent in the next thirty years. Thirty years later, while we cannot count them accurately due to their remoteness and the human rights conflicts detailed above, it seems highly probable that declines have been prominent. Trying to understand the species and how to save them has never been more critical than it is right now.

I spoke to Anna Jemmett, who is one of the lead scientists at the Wild Camel Protection Foundation (WCPF). I was curious to know… Why camels?

'I knew I wanted to be a zoologist. I studied at university and was really interested in horses so I thought about researching Przewalski's horses in Mongolia, which are incredibly rare – once extinct in the wild,' she explains. 'But while looking into that, I came across wild camels. I remember thinking, "as if there is one of those!" They drink salt water and travel through nuclear testing zones, which is fascinating. I asked if there were any volunteering opportunities and first went there in 2011 after graduating. I spent a few months with the herders in Mongolia and just fell in love with the animal and the people. The moment a PhD opportunity came up with the WCPF charity, I took it and I feel so lucky to be working with the camels.'

Anna's work fundamentally involves creating a detailed management plan looking at the future for wild camels. With so little known about the species, and so much confusion surrounding them, even very basic data will be a huge step forward in their conservation. Their current focus is estimating a more accurate population figure and assessing their genetic diversity (one of the huge dangers facing wild camels is the hybridisation between them and the closely related domestic Bactrian).

Assessing all of the finer details will help create a long-term strategy for these camels. But getting close enough to assess them has proven challenging, as Anna explains: 'In Mongolia they live in the Great Gobi Strictly Protected Area Park, which is 53,000 square kilometres, so it's vast. No one lives within it and there's a thirty-mile buffer zone around the boundary, but even so very few people ever see the wild camels. There are those who come in to illegally mine gold who might come across them but, other than park rangers, there are infrequent encounters. I've been there four times and have only seen the camels on three separate occasions and that was usually from a distance with them running away. It's such a huge landscape that they're very hard to spot. The best places are around water points, because they have to drink at some point even if it is salty.'

Undertaking research of any kind has its difficulties even with the most bold and abundant of species, but trying to learn about a species you never see is a whole other story. When I go out searching for wildlife or am leading a tour, one of the first things I always say to people is don't only look for the creature itself but also for the evidence they leave behind. So much can be learned from tracks, faeces, secretions and trails, and they have helped advance our knowledge in so many ways. For example, did you know that we can now identify new penguin colonies from space using satellite imagery to search for their poo, or that fossilised footprints can sometimes tell us how fast a dinosaur was moving some 200 million years ago? Looking for clues and piecing together the mystery using evidence is a big part of the picture – and it's no different for wild camels.

'I'm using camera traps to calculate population estimates and microsatellite markers to assess the genome diversity within the small population,' Anna continues. 'I am using old data sets but also collecting new samples in a non-invasive manner, which we collect from the deserts. So, it's either hair that has been caught on vegetation, or their poo. Bags and bags full of poo – the fresher the better – it's very glamorous! If I do find any carcasses, I would take a tissue sample but otherwise I am not taking anything directly from the camels themselves. We're quite lucky in a way because it's dry in the desert and there's a high salt content, which is actually perfect for preserving DNA samples in the poo. I have friends working with tigers in the jungle and it's almost impossible for them to collect faecal samples as it's very wet and just rots away. One technique we use is to find where the camels are sleeping for the night and wait until morning after they have moved on before we go in to collect the samples. That way we know for sure we are collecting the poo as fresh as possible without disturbing the animals. Their faeces dries out so quickly in that habitat that it's very hard to tell what's twelve hours old or months old, and old poo won't have good DNA within it. Essentially, as the food moves through their digestive tract it picks up cells from the gut lining as it travels through the body, and some samples will be better than others in terms of DNA quality. Some can be good, others can be – for want of a better phrase – a bit shit, but so far we have been lucky. We place them into sandwich bags and add some silicon beads to take away any remaining moisture, then I import them back to the UK to the University of Sheffield where I can conduct DNA extraction analysis.'

Imagine trying to get that through customs! But this initial work will help Anna and the team at WCPF to tackle the potential problem of hybridisation with the domestic Bactrians. Some of these domestics are allowed to roam, and, on rare occasions if the female Bactrians are in season, the wild camels venture into the local villages to mate. The big concern here is 'outbreeding depression'. Considering that the wild camel population is already small, losing genes through breeding with a closely related species could be disastrous for the species' survival. 'We don't know how much introgression is currently a problem, if it is at all. It could be like the situation with the wildcats in Scotland where there is a lot of introgression and has been historically for a long time. The lab in Vienna shows there certainly is some hybridisation occurring but at what level, we don't know yet,' Anna says excitedly.

Mongolia is also home to one of the most polluted and coldest capital cities in the world, Ulaanbaatar. It sits at an altitude of 1,350 metres above sea level and during the winter temperatures can reach as low as–24.5 °C, so, during these times, many residents turn to coal fires. Almost half the population of the country live there and on the coldest days, air pollution can hit a deadly daily average of 687 micrograms per cubic metre, which is twenty-seven times the recommended safe level determined by the World Health Organization (WHO). Climate change is the biggest issue we all collectively face, and there isn't a species in this book that isn't directly or indirectly effected by it. The reason why wild camel numbers fell to such low numbers in the first place is largely higher levels of desertification, which is a direct consequence of rising global temperatures. They're losing water sources and vegetation, which is restricting their range to only certain areas within the Gobi. They're built to live in the extremes but, even for the hardiest of mammals, there's a limit. Alongside this there is habitat destruction due to human encroachment as people expand their spaces and bring domestic camels, which causes competition with their wild relatives.

To try to beat the race against extinction, WCPF in 2003 established the first captive breeding centre for wild camels, located in their natural habitat within the buffer zone of the Great

Gobi Strictly Protected Area 'A'. The initial aim was to create an insurance population to mitigate if anything were to go drastically wrong in the wild. The first individuals were rescues or those found within the buffer zone close to people, and they started breeding quickly. Currently forty-two wild camels live within the breeding centre, and plans are under way to apply for funding for a second centre.

There is still so much to learn about these wild creatures that most people barely know exist, and there's a lot of reasons to be concerned for their future. As I learned about them, I became more and more worried about what the Gobi would be like without them. I remain hopeful – not least because it's important for my sanity – but it must be hard for Anna and her team seeing this happen before their very eyes, especially when they're faced with a humanitarian crisis that prevents them from assessing the health of most of the population across the border in China. Despite adversity, Anna is clearly determined to make that difference: 'I hope for a positive outcome every day. WCPF has been running for twenty-four years and in that time have managed to get them a protected-species status on both sides of the border. We, alongside the labs, have proved that they're a separate species and now national parks have been created. These are huge steps but now we desperately need to get on with the scientific analysis that'll allow us to predict what will happen in the next thirty to fifty years. People love camels, so if we can stress that despite there being millions of domesticated camels out there, there is also a critically endangered species that needs our help, then that'll go a long way in improving their situation.'

Over the years, camels have done so much to help grow and sustain human settlements. We domesticated them for their strength, intelligence and ability to combat even the toughest of environmental elements; and it's now time for us to do something for them in return. The fact that there is this 'secret' wild species that's been hiding away for years is astonishing. Let's give them the spotlight they so desperately need, and deserve.

Snow Leopard

Rugged, rocky mountain landscapes are naturally alluring. Their towering zigzagged edges define the horizon, redirecting the sun's beams to create harsh contrasted patterns of light and shadow upon the ancient rocks. With a few exceptions, mountains generally sit within ranges and are formed over millions of years when intense compressional forces move the Earth's tectonic plates towards one another until a collision occurs. This causes the edges of the plates to rise, like a seam connecting the land. These plates which make up the surface of the earth are always on the move, although each at different speeds, shifting annually from 0.4 inches in the North Atlantic to nearly 2 inches in the Pacific. Earthquakes, volcanoes and, of course, mountains, are all the result of this immensely powerful – although slow-motion – process.

Geologists generally define a mountain as a 'landform that rises at least 1,000 feet (or 300 metres) above its surrounding area,' but can vary in steepness, elevation and minerals. You may be familiar with the Alps, the Andes and the Himalayas, which are among the most famous ranges in the world, but what is less known is that there are close to 1.2 million mountains belonging to hundreds of distinct ranges that cover 27 per cent of our planet's land surface. To say they are an important ecosystem would be an understatement. When it comes to biodiversity, mountains act like isolated islands; they are a hotspot for endemism. Often, the richness of unique endemic species is higher on the mountain slopes than on the flat lowlands below. It's important to note here that richness equates to diversity and not necessarily abundance, i.e. number of individual animals. The reason for this explosion of life at high altitudes is the microclimates that exist there. This is because the slopes of each mountain are unique in angle and steepness; they subsequently have varying degrees of temperature, light and weather exposure, creating varied conditions for a wide range of adapted species that occupy a relatively short distance or small area. The further up in altitude you travel, the more specialised, niche-specific species you will find.

I want to transport you to Central Asia, where remote mountain ranges span the continent. It's a habitat important for many reasons, including the production of fresh water, carbon sequestration, soil regeneration, air quality, recreational tourism and biodiversity. This remarkable part of the world is home to between 5,000 and 6,000 vascular plant species, of which 1,500 are endemic, and 140 mammals, including 10–20 endemics, alongside countless bird, amphibian, reptile and invertebrate species. From the rare Ili pika (a small, endangered teddy-bear-like mammal related to rabbits, endemic to north-west China) to the koytendag blind cave fish (a yellowy-orange, small, ray-finned fish found only in one lake in Turkmenistan), the wilderness of this seemingly harsh, isolated landscape promises to be full of the bizarre and wonderful. Unless you live in this region, I am sure many of these endemic species will be as new to you as they are to me. But this is the story of one particular animal who... well... even if you live on top of a mountain, behind some rocks, you will likely be very familiar with. They are a poster species for modern-day conservation, an adorable, heartstring-tugging feline on the brink of extinction. I'm talking, of course, about the snow leopard.

Elusive, agile and powerful, these big cats barely need an introduction. They are medium-sized and live in twelve countries spread across the mountains of Central Asia, where they favour steep cliffs, rocky outcrops and ravines between 3,000 and 4,500 metres in altitude. The environment is dry and cold, often well below sub-zero, a temperature that gives rise to some of evolution's finest adaptations! Snow leopards are known globally for their gorgeous, jaw-dropping fur that can reach up to 5 centimetres in length down their back and sides and up to 12 centimetres under their stomach. It's an adaptation that allows them to remain insulated. But they have adapted in other ways too: round short ears to reduce heat loss, extra-large paws that act as natural snowshoes, wide chest to aid in oxygen absorption and a large, wide nasal cavity that warms the freezing cold air before it's inhaled into the lungs. Unlike most other large cats, they cannot roar. This fact and their unique ecology led some biologists to believe they belonged to an entirely separate genus; however, genetic studies have revealed that they are most closely related to another species:

not African leopards, as you might expect, but the tiger. And while they don't have the throat physiology to allow them to roar, they can purr, hiss, growl, chuff and moan like other big cats.

As apex predators, they are fundamental to the health of the ecosystem, something we have in the past overlooked and ignored (as usual) almost to the point of no return. Despite their remote and hard-to-reach habitat, they've felt the sharp pinch of humanity's actions. The IUCN classify snow leopards as vulnerable to extinction as experts believe there are only between 3,920 and 6,390 individuals in the wild. When you consider the giant expanse of their collective range – two million square kilometres – their population density is low. They've declined by 20 per cent in the last twenty years and numbers are expected to dwindle further. However, in some areas, there is hope.

Kyrgyzstan is a landlocked country in the heart of Asia, bordering Kazakhstan in the north, China in the east, Tajikistan in the south and Uzbekistan to the west. In order to get to the sea, you'd have to travel a minimum of 1,620 miles to the Indian Ocean, making Kyrgyzstan the furthest country away from any ocean. I personally can feel quite closed in when I am not near the ocean but in this case, I think I'd feel differently. Instead of being drawn to the water, my imagination and curiosity would be drawn up and away to the truly rugged and wild mountains that are often absorbed by the clouds. The mountains cover an astonishing 90.7 per cent of the country's surface, making it the third most mountainous country in the world, so it's no wonder that it remains a stronghold for the snow leopard. More than half of the country's landscape, over 105,000 square kilometres, is a potentially suitable habitat for this secretive cat. People on the ground estimate that the snow leopard population hovers at around 300 individuals, but due to the amount of available land, numbers could rise to between 500–600 before reaching carrying capacity.

The Snow Leopard Trust is a charitable organisation who aim to protect the species primarily through community-based conservation. I first heard of their work through a friend, Dan O'Neil, who had the opportunity to go and film at one of their bases (and even meet one of the cats in rehabilitation – the lucky devil!). He kindly put me in contact with the Trust's Kyrgyzstan Country Director, Kubanychbek Zhumbai uulu, also known as Kuban. 'I remember being very young heading into the mountains,' he told me, 'as we often did, with my brother, and asking him whether or not if we were to meet a snow leopard, would it kill us. He replied "Yes, probably." We didn't know that much about them at that time and we grew up hearing myths and legends. But actually, there has never been a case of a snow leopard hurting a human. Whenever they come across a person they don't run away, they just lie down, stay still and rely on their camouflage. They will see you before you see them and they can go unnoticed even if they are lying only a few metres away from you. It's why they're called the "ghosts of the mountains". I've had many trips to the mountains but have only seen them seven times.'

Kuban had always been infatuated with wildlife. His mum was a biology teacher and his grandfather was a highly respected falconer, so it was inevitable that he would follow in their footsteps. Much of his inspiration came from his grandad, who was a conservation pioneer himself. Traditionally in Kyrgyzstan, birds of prey were expertly trained for hunting purposes to catch mammals, like hares and foxes, for meat and fur. There are even records of the birds hunting animals as large as wolves! Of course this would depend on the bird species being used, the most common being the goshawk, sparrowhawk, peregrine falcon, saker falcon and even golden eagle. It's a huge part of the local culture, and, while most people are no longer reliant upon this method for food, there are still a number of hunters with the skillset. Kuban's grandfather was exceptional and was featured in many Soviet films and documentaries hunting with his golden eagles. He also started a successful breeding centre for raptors in the Issik-Kull's Ottuk village of the country and was the first to ever breed saker falcons in captivity. 'I was very young but can remember it all clearly, I am so proud of all he achieved,' Kuban explained. 'After university, at post-graduate school, I wanted to study raptors to continue his work, but in this country we have a lot of ornithologists and not many experts on big mammals. I graduated university in 2000 and did my Masters in Norway studying the seasonal diets of wolves and snow leopards in the Kyrgyz Tian-Shan mountains. I was really interested because there was not much known about this cat in Kyrgyzstan.'

Poaching has always been one of the largest threats facing the species; we humans have sought their luscious fur, fancying it for ourselves, using it for fashion, luxury rugs and even taxidermy. Even basic data on snow leopards is difficult to obtain, and the same goes for monitoring the illegal wildlife trade, but it's been estimated that since 2008 one cat has lost its life every single day due to poaching. It's shocking, especially considering how elusive these animals are and how tough the terrain in their habitat can be. Poachers use a range of techniques to catch them; they shoot, snare and trap them alive. Demand for their coats, however, is not the sole reason for this persecution. A study in 2015 found DNA evidence of snow leopard bones inside tablet capsules of traditional medicines. Supposedly it has 'magical healing powers', and it is often ingested as a substitute for ground-up tiger remnants, also used in traditional medicine.

Since Kyrgyzstan regained independence from the Soviet Union in 1991, the poaching situation there has reportedly improved, although it is still a cause for concern. The concerns for conservationists are complex and multifaceted. The United Nations data indicates that of the 6.7 million people living in the country, over 25 per cent live below the poverty line. Nearly half of the population work in agriculture, where herders and their families earn less than $2 a day, making every individual livestock animal essential for income and food. A single loss is a big knock, so it's lucky that snow leopards usually avoid pastures where people can be found and instead hunt in the wild. Their preferred prey are wild ungulates like ibex, blue sheep and argali, among other occasional small mammals like marmots, which live comfortably at high altitudes on the rocky mountain outcrops. As with any predator, snow leopards are naturally limited to the health and numbers of their prey. This is where the problem lies, as many of their natural prey are on the decline themselves, which forces the snow leopards to occasionally take advantage of livestock. When this happens, their reputation among the herders is put into question and they may be subjected to more persecution.

Why are their natural prey in decline? Well, they are subject to poaching themselves and have historically been overexploited. Kuban tells me that big numbers of domestic livestock are a big threat too, as wild ungulates are pushed out of their natural habitat to make space for pastures. Additionally, if these domestic animals encounter wild ungulates, they can transmit highly contagious diseases and parasites such as ovine rinderpest, MCC and sarcoptic mange. This can cause very high mortality in these wild animals, which are free-roaming and don't receive medical treatment.

If that wasn't enough, Kuban explained another threat facing the species: gold mines. 'In the last twenty years or so, our country has issued hundreds – even thousands – of licences for geological exploration. Many companies from around the globe received these licences and I see new videos every day of mining sites that are destroying the habitat. So, while these companies are helping our economy, they are travelling higher and higher into the mountain ecosystem. Not all the companies are working to the proper standards and massive destruction is taking place. They build roads in remote areas, making this landscape more accessible to poachers and herders.' Kyrgyzstan's largest mine is known as Kumtor and is predicted to produce between 160 and 200 tons of gold (worth $5 billion) in the next ten years. But as it expands, so do the potential dangers.

In addition to this, trophy hunting is popular across the country. It costs a shooter around $7,000 to kill an ibex and $31,000 for an argali, which both happen to be the snow leopard's favourite prey. 'I wouldn't say trophy hunting is destroying prey populations when properly managed, but the infrastructure used to accommodate the short shooting season does make it easier for poachers in remote areas. Sometimes there is a permit issue with trophy hunting too. Recently, rangers in the protected Sarychat Ertash Reserve found a foreign hunter shooting in the off-season designed to give populations a chance to recover. Although the evidence was strong, the investigation failed and there was no prosecution,' Kuban explains.

In a nutshell, these threats are all interlinked: the roads and infrastructure of gold mines and trophy hunting lodges give both herders and poachers access to the mountains. The herders' livestock degrade the habitat and outcompete the snow leopard's prey. The lack of prey causes the predator to hunt livestock, which leads to retaliatory killing and poaching. (And I haven't even touched on climate change, which overshadows all of this…)

Sometimes it is overwhelming trying to protect a rare species against the odds, but that feeling can change in an instant when you see the secretive animal you've dedicated your career to. 'We were setting up a camera trap and as we started to move back home to camp for the night, a ranger told me to look up. And there was a wild snow leopard watching us, sitting exactly like a domestic cat,' Kuban said, with a grin on his face as he recalled the memory. 'I got off my horse and started taking photos, trying to sneak a little closer. I walked behind the hill and around to where I knew the cat to be. It sat behind a rock and eventually stood up and walked off. It was so close, only about ten metres away!'

It just goes to show how amazing snow leopards' camouflage can be if the world's leading snow leopard trackers and scientists can't spot them right away! Surely that's got to be one of the best wildlife encounters anyone could ever wish for.

Kuban and his team spend a lot of their time in the mountains, living and working collaboratively with local communities as the severity of the conflicts fluctuates. Since there is still so much left to understand about snow leopard ecology, these baseline investigations are always a priority. Attempting to observe them continually would be too challenging, so the team deploy some technological help… the trusty old camera traps and GPS trackers. 'We put the camera traps out every year. Usually about forty cameras in 1,000 square kilometres, which helps us to estimate population size,' Kuban tells me. 'Like a human fingerprint, each

139

animal has a unique pattern on their fur so we can easily identify them, understand their territories, their reproduction and general population dynamics. We are restricted by the number of people that can go out and set up the cameras, but so far we cover one third of all snow leopard habitats in Kyrgyzstan.'

Data collected by the GPS collars worn by the cats are shared among the five countries that the Snow Leopard Trust works within; a couple have been used in Kyrgyzstan, but fifty have been deployed overall. These are fitted after the animal is safely anesthetised, and have provided some remarkable insights. Except for a female when she has cubs, snow leopards are solitary, each having a defined home range. They don't tend to defend these ranges aggressively, as males will purposefully stay away from one another, although their territories will overlap with nearby females'. And I use 'nearby' loosely, as home ranges can be up to 1,000 square kilometres in size! Male territories are usually larger, but variations can be seen between individual snow leopards, not just between sexes. The less prey available to them, the further their ranges will expand as they require more space to hunt in a less-densely populated area. If enough prey is available to them then their territory could be as small as 130 square kilometres – a stark contrast.

These movements might just seem like interesting facts, but every detail helps in their conservation. By understanding how snow leopards move and where they come into contact with humans and livestock, measures can be taken to protect everyone. A sister project in Mongolia studied nineteen snow leopards over five years, identifying over 250 kill sites and the species that were preyed upon. They found that wild ungulates were killed 73 per cent of the time in favour of livestock that were ten times more abundant in the area. When snow leopards did catch livestock, it typically happened at night in the corral or on a particularly rugged pasture where the herder was out of sight. Herders have since reduced grazing in rugged areas during the day and are welcoming support in the form of corrals, a type of paddock that protects the livestock overnight.

The situation as it stands in Kyrgyzstan is a positive one, as the population is stable and there is room for numbers to increase. Kuban rounds off beautifully: 'If you look at the global distribution of snow leopards on a map, you will see that Kyrgyzstan acts as a bridge between two large populations in Central Asia. Geographically, it is a very important area. Our mountains are a corridor. If snow leopards in Kyrgyzstan face a problem, it may fragment the species further. I hope we can save snow leopards; I believe we will. We can find a way for people to live in harmony with the mountain ecosystem and its predators. I hope the next generation will not repeat the mistakes of the elder generations.'

I sincerely hope to meet Kuban face to face one day, and if I ever get the opportunity to explore those mountains, I somewhat wish I won't come across a snow leopard. Not because I'm fearful or because they're not there or are low in numbers – I hope they will be thriving – but there's something comforting in the idea that they will be close by watching me trying to watch them. Maybe I'd get the feeling of being watched, or maybe I wouldn't notice at all and they would live up to their name of ghosts of the mountains.

Northern White Rhino

'There was always talk that he was the last of his kind, and I felt sorry for him. At that time I only ever saw him in passing, I didn't really know him. The personal connection happened when I came to work as one of his caretakers in 2014. I was scared at first because he was so massive and you really couldn't tell what he was thinking. But he was calm and really approachable. His demeanour made him unique and a perfect ambassador for his species.

With such a charismatic animal like him, I couldn't help but feel very sad about his fate. In my time developing that relationship, other than being his caretaker and the provider of carrots and bananas, I felt so deeply that his suffering was ultimately a consequence of our actions

as humans. He was the face of a species who has borne the weight of so much pain and destruction. I would wake up every day, watch him and talk to him to say that everything is going to be okay. It was emotional connecting the dots to what really awaited him and what he represented – which was always ultimately extinction.

I am so passionate about everything that I do, and I put so much effort into helping these animals, so when I realised that extinction was unfolding before my eyes… Well, I was not emotionally ready for that. I almost resigned. But I choose to turn this into an opportunity to create a buzz around species extinction and ask people to care for the planet, because we all depend on it.

Sudan may now be dead, but I am still trying to build more awareness for him today… perhaps even more so than when he was alive.'

The striking, powerful words of James Mwenda, one of a handful of caretakers who protected the last remaining northern white rhinos at Ol Pejeta Conservancy in central Kenya. Sudan was the last known male of his subspecies and he died on 19 March 2018 at the age of forty-five. Since his passing only two individuals remain, and as both are female – Najin and her daughter, Fatu – the species has become officially classified as functionally extinct, meaning that any hope of a natural recovery is lost for ever. Sudan's death made international headlines across mainstream media platforms and his story was even highlighted on David Attenborough's BBC documentary *Extinction: The Facts*. He captured the hearts of millions and his death was a huge wake-up call. I can vividly remember waking up to the devastating news. I just couldn't rationalise not only how we as a species had sat back and watched northern white rhinos slip through our fingers over decades but also how we were responsible for pushing them there in the first place. If I am entirely honest, I felt guilty and embarrassed. Especially when you consider that as megafauna, rhinos are among the most loved and adored animals on the planet; the ones whose pictures we use to decorate our children's bedrooms and our clothing, who've inspired music, art and poetry… but despite that long-standing connection and admiration, we let them disappear.

How could we have let that happen? And if we can't save rhinos, then what hope is there for everything else? What chances are there for the Socorro isopod or the El Rincon stream frog, or other lesser-known species that attract nowhere near the same awareness or global interest as rhinos? It's a thought that still crosses my mind often, and it can be overwhelming. However, I never imagined for one second that a few years down the line I would be chatting with some remarkable scientists who are pushing the boundaries of science to the extreme in order to potentially save a species already declared extinct. I promise, this is no *Jurassic Park* plot but is instead one of astounding human innovation and determination. (Although it is admittedly a bit sci-fi…)

I was six years old when I first saw a wild rhino. It was a male black rhino living in Lake Nakuru National Park, Kenya. It was late afternoon and we were driving along a bumpy dirt track away from our camp in search of a leopard, but as we turned the corner we were confronted with the giant backside of a rhinoceros protruding out of the bushes. It was unmissable. We sat, watched and took photographs as this male turned to watch us while munching on the surrounding vegetation. Rhinos are big anyway, but when you are young everything appears to be so much bigger, and in my eyes, he was HUGE. I couldn't take my eyes off him; I was fixated by the way his lips were moving, flexibly and with such precision. Black rhinos have a prehensile top lip that points downwards in a 'V' shape that evolved to allow them to grasp and manipulate their food. This lip essentially acts like a finger, selecting the twigs and leaves that they'd prefer to eat. After what felt like only minutes, but was in reality a couple of hours, the sun began to set and we headed home. To this day, I can still see that rhino's face as he tucked into his evening meal.

There are five species of extant rhinos:
1. Javan rhino: critically endangered; only seventy-two individuals remain.
2. Sumatran rhino: critically endangered; fewer than 100 individuals left.
3. Greater one-horned rhino: vulnerable; between 3,300 and 3,600 alive.
4. Black rhino: critically endangered; fewer than 5,600 remain.
5. And finally, white rhino: (near threatened; fewer than 18,000 left.

White rhinos are split into two subspecies, the southern white, which is doing incredibly well in comparison to its other close relatives, and the northern white rhinos, of which only Najin and Fatu remain. These bleak and frankly uncomfortable statistics haven't always been so low – in fact, far from it. Prior to the evolution of humans, rhinos were once among the most successful mammalian groups to have ever existed. They emerged during the Eocene when the temperature was much warmer than it is today. Very little ice was present and this environment promoted the evolution of many large mammals, such as tapirs, zebras and modern-day horses.

Growing bigger was an adaptive strategy for species to cope with the large expanse of open habitats. Studies suggest that rhinos, which belong to a group of animals named perissodactyls (meaning odd-toed ungulate), originally appeared approximately 55 million years ago in what is now India, before it attached to the rest of Asia. The early rhinos looked nothing like the ones alive today – amynodonts had no horns, broad torsos, forward facing eyes and more closely resembled modern pigs with longer legs. The metamynodons – a genus of the amynodontidae family – spent a lot of time in the water and looked similar to hippos. Later, during the Oligocene period, between 34 and 23 million years ago, the species *Paraceratherium* evolved. This animal likely holds the title of the 'largest land mammal' to have ever existed, and with its long legs and long neck it would have been totally unrecognisable as a rhino of the kind we all know and love today. We can't be sure of its exact size due to an incomplete fossil record, but it probably stood at about 5 metres tall and weighed up to 20,000 kilograms. It was an absolutely phenomenal beast, in every sense of the word. It lived in social herds and, despite its size, young and weak individuals were predated by gigantic crocodiles. What a time it would have been to be alive – when true giants wandered the Earth!

It will come as no surprise to read that all rhino species alive today are under immense pressure. Their iconic horns have caught the greedy eyes of human beings for the last 2,000 years. Humanity's obsession with obtaining power and status extends not only to the ownership of various animals, but also to the acquisition of various parts of their bodies. With any species that develops an impressive, imperishable feature, it's often the case that people will attempt to take it for themselves. In the case of the rhino, its horn has been the

inevitable target of poaching. Rhinos' faces have been mutilated
– cut, sawn and hacked at – in the attempt to remove their horns,
inflicting immeasurable pain and often death. We have all seen the
heartbreaking images of rhino mothers in agony, left for dead in pools
of their own blood and flesh, their faces torn apart, as petrified young
calves nestle in, trying to wake them. These images are unforgettable
and emotive, but there is power in showing the truth; it can unite
people, increase awareness and ultimately instigate action.

The international trade of rhino horn has been illegal under CITES
since 1977, but in some countries domestic trade continues. Rhino
horn is made from keratin, the protein in our fingernails and hair.
Despite this now being common knowledge, a horn is still one of
the most valuable appendages on the exotic black market alongside
tiger penis, elephant ivory and pangolin scales. A 'top-quality' horn
can reach a price of £40,500 per kilogram, meaning that, gram for
gram, rhino horn is worth more than diamonds, gold and cocaine. The
demand primarily comes from Asia, specifically Vietnam and China, the
two biggest destinations for black-market wildlife products in general.
In 2019, a haul of 125 kilograms of rhino horn was seized at Hanoi
Airport in Vietnam, estimated to be worth £6 million.

The horns are ground up into a fine powder and used in traditional
medicines that are centred around the misplaced belief that when
consumed, everything from aggressive cancers to gout to hangovers
will be magically cured. And it's supposedly meant to help men wake
up their own 'horns', if you know what I mean… But none of this has
any scientific backing. It has no medicinal value whatsoever. Zero –
zilch – none – not a bit. And if that wasn't bad enough, rhino horn is
also used as a sign of status among some members of wealthy society,
who decorate their homes with horns detailed with elaborate carvings.
It's a very damaging and deep-rooted mentality that is fuelled by

corruption and criminal activity, and it is seriously threatening the rhino's entire existence. The demand for their horns has increased massively since the 1970s and a huge peak was observed between 2008 and 2015. In South Africa, where most wild rhinos live, 5,048 were poached during that seven-year period. Currently, on average one rhino in South Africa is killed for its horn every twenty-two hours – a catastrophic statistic, especially when you take into account the population levels listed above. One bit of good news to come out of 2020 was that rhino poaching fell by 33 per cent, likely due to coronavirus restrictions, although since pandemic restrictions have lifted the number of poaching cases has been on the rise. In the first six months of 2022, 259 rhinos were poached in South Africa alone.

The northern white rhino was once abundant and could be found widely across the north-east of Africa. But by the 1960s there were only 2,360 known individuals remaining, and this number kept sinking… and fast. By 1984, there were only fifteen northern white rhinos left. Poaching and the civil wars in the Democratic Republic of the Congo (DRC) and Sudan caused an already small population to collapse even further. These fifteen rhinos survived in Garamba National Park in the DRC. An international rescue action was put in place to help them recover, and slowly the numbers grew to about thirty animals. But when the next wave of illegal poaching began in 2003, many were lost. An aerial survey carried out by the park in July 2004 with the aim of counting the number of northern white rhinos found evidence of only seventeen to twenty-two animals. With grave concern for the future of this subspecies, a proposal was given to the DRC government to translocate five rhinos to a secure, temporary home. Initially the proposal was well received but, after a protest by a group of politicians, it was declined, perhaps due to ignorance, or because of the profits involved in the rhino horn trade. All conservation support for Garamba National Park was suspended and the rhinos were left to fend for themselves. No live rhinos have been seen there since 2006, and no signs of their presence (dung or tracks) have been spotted since 2007. As far as anyone could tell, northern white rhinos were extinct in their last wild stronghold.

At this time, six northern whites were living in captivity in the Czech Republic at Dvůr Králové Zoo. In an attempt to stimulate breeding, which had been unsuccessful at the zoo, in 2009 four of the six rhinos were translocated to Ol Pejeta Conservancy in Kenya, where anti-poaching units and caretakers would provide them with round-the-clock care and protection. Everyone crossed everything and hoped that being in their native rich-grassland habitat might – perhaps – help in their recovery. The fate of the subspecies rested heavily on the females Najin and her daughter Fatu, and the males Sudan and Suni. To keep them happy and healthy, they lived in a 700-acre enclosure, were fed a balanced diet and were protected by armed guards 24/7. There was a lot of excitement in 2012 when Suni was seen mating with Najin, but sadly she did not fall pregnant. It must have been so excruciating to wait and to learn that there was no baby rhino on the way. Just two years later, in October 2014, Suni died of natural causes, leaving Sudan to hold the title of the 'last remaining male'. What a burden to bear. And with every day that passed, they got older and their chances got smaller. The results of a veterinary check-up in 2015 nearly obliterated any fragments of hope that remained; both Najin and Fatu were deemed unable to carry a pregnancy to full term, and Sudan's sperm count was low. Artificially assisted reproduction was the only possible solution – sperm and egg samples were collected from each rhino and frozen, and the samples joined a number of others belonging to other northern whites who had passed long before.

Then, in 2018, the difficult decision was taken to euthanise Sudan after his joints and muscles started to disintegrate.

I got in contact with Ol Pejeta Conservancy and caretaker James Mwenda because I wanted to better understand the rhinos as individuals, but also what it must have been like to witness their struggle. This is a subspecies that was dealt bad card after bad card, and, even just looking into their background, I found myself feeling hopeless. It was so refreshing speaking to James, because while he understandably holds great sadness, I was touched by his powerful, emotive and inspiring words.

James grew up in a small village in Kenya where human/wildlife conflict was rife. He has vivid childhood memories of his family working tirelessly growing crops on the farm, only for the elephants to descend from Mount Kenya National Park under cover of night to eat and destroy their food and livelihoods. James used to spend nights in the cold trying to scare them back into the forest by banging metal and making as much noise as possible.

James recalls, 'Sometimes the Wildlife Service would come with their guns, firing into the air, and the elephants would be scared back. If someone from my village knew how to do that, that would really help handle the problem. Deep inside me I always had a feeling that elephants were animals that never knew what they were doing, it wasn't their fault. At that stage, I realised that maybe if I carried a gun and became a ranger then I would know what to do when the elephants came into the community. My experience of going days without food because of elephants ignited my passion for conservation, and I started thinking that I wanted to be part of the remedy to help my community and the wildlife safely.'

As someone who has never repeatedly gone hungry because of these conflicts, I find it hard to know what I'd do in that situation.

I'd love to say that I would be as forward-thinking and resilient as James clearly was… but it's very hard to put yourself in those shoes. Luckily his village was fenced off in 2014 and both the community and the elephants are now much safer.

James finished high school and went to train as a ranger at Ol Pejeta; he wanted to study conservation, but wasn't able to attend an expensive college or university. I asked him what it was like to train as a ranger. I was curious because it's something that I myself have dreamed of doing since I was very young. The idea of being in the African bush all day surrounded by such a wealth of biodiversity, and getting visitors to connect with it too, sounds like such a dream, but it certainly doesn't sound easy. James replied, 'You don't necessarily need any strict curriculum or papers to be a ranger, you just need to be brave. It's one of the biggest requirements. It requires a lot of commitment because you are literally on the frontlines. We must know tactics for survival out in the bush and also be able to interpret animal behaviour – from knowing how to track and read footprints, etc, to knowing when it is best to run away. You have to be physically very fit but also emotionally strong and able to rely on your senses. Every animal – lion, rhino, buffalo, etc – is different so you need to know how to approach and run away from each of them as individual species. Apart from the wild animals, there is definitely a risk of being killed by poachers too. Some people aren't brave enough – on their first day they might get chased by a lion and go home. It goes way beyond a job, we do this because of a passion to protect our animals. That's why I do it and I salute other rangers for the commitment they have made for the well-being of our planet.'

After Sudan died, James and his team's focus was on Najin and Fatu. He smiles slightly as he relays their personalities to me:

'They have unique characters just like every other being. Fatu, the youngest, is a bit unpredictable just like any teenage girl. She's excited about life and wants to experience everything, she can be quite pushy to get what she wants. Her favourite activities are wallowing in the mud and sharpening her horn on the trees – she's girly, into her appearance I suppose. And Najin is very calm; she is similar to Sudan in that respect. She loves food and can eat and eat to the point her stomach is so full that she will struggle to sleep.'

A day in the life of a northern white rhino caretaker varies but typically begins early, at 6 a.m., when the team wake up to clear their enclosure, followed by conservation talks to guests throughout the day. James endearingly refers to the two rhinos as his 'girlfriends', and shares the responsibility of caretaking with ten others and a team of approximately fourteen anti-poaching units.

These rhinos are an emblem of their persecution; they represent the greed, corruption and short-sightedness of mankind and the sad reality that many other species will inevitably end up facing the same fate. As humans, we often act only once it's too late. We are a reactive and not a proactive species. That is a fundamental mindset we have to change. But for these northern white rhinos, there is now an incey-wincey-teeny-weeny glimmer of hope: an international consortium of scientists put their heads together and, in 2019, the news hit that northern white rhino embryos had been successfully artificially created! A seriously jaw-dropping moment.

Professor Cesare Galli is an IVF specialist for the pioneering Avantea Laboratory in Cremona, Italy. I spoke with him about the process and what it might mean for the future of the species – if there even is a future. Cesare said, 'Our labs' expertise is in breeding large animals, especially livestock, and we were approached in 2014 to help with rhino conservation. Our objective was to help the northern whites, but due to their limited availability (only two females remaining) we had to perfect the techniques on other subspecies.' Cesare and his team worked closely with southern white rhinos and Sumatran rhinos so that when it came to creating northern white embryos they would be ready. He continued, 'It took us about five years to develop the technique, and our first success was when we created a hybrid embryo using a southern white egg and northern white sperm in 2018. As a result, we knew then that the male sperm quality was good enough and that our techniques would work. We were confident enough that we could approach the Kenyan authorities to get approval for harvesting eggs from Najin and Fatu.' After the long process of securing approval, the team flew out to Ol Pejeta in August 2019 to meet with a number of other experts. Since artificial insemination and natural pregnancy was not a viable option for Najin and Fatu, veterinary expert, Dr Thomas Hildebrandt, from the Leibniz Institute for Zoo and Wildlife Research (IZW) in Berlin, travelled to Kenya to perform a procedure to collect their immature eggs, or oocytes. Rhino anatomy makes egg collection quite challenging as the ovaries are at least 1.5 metres inside their bodies and intestinal loops can block the route. Cutting the skin was also not an option as rhino skin is approximately 5 centimetres thick and is slow to heal, meaning any infections could be fatal. So Dr Hildebrandt instead designed a bespoke tube with a delicate needle that entered through the anus and went into the ovary follicle, where the eggs are stored. Using ultrasound as a guide, eggs could then be collected and rushed to Italy with Cesare, where the frozen sperm of Sudan and other deceased male rhinos (Suni, et al.) awaited.

Subsequent to their trip in 2019, the scientists have made two more visits to Kenya for egg collection, although Covid regulations during 2020 seriously restricted progress. They managed to

successfully harvest a number of immature eggs from daughter
Fatu, but sadly nothing from mum Najin. Rhinos have a life
expectancy of anywhere between thirty and forty years and, while
Fatu is only twenty-one years old (born in 2000), her mum Najin
is thirty-two (born in 1989) and, devastatingly, vets have recently
located a large tumour in her abdomen. With this diagnosis and
her increasing age, Najin isn't a candidate for egg collection and
her health is expected to decline some time in the near future.
They don't know how long she has left. So, all the weight falls upon
Fatu – and what a weight it is. I know I am anthropomorphising
massively, and as a scientist myself I always try to steer away from
doing so, but when the fate of an entire subspecies rests solely on
one female, it's hard not to. I suppose, though, when we make these
emotional connections and sympathise with what an individual
animal may or may not be thinking and/or feeling, it can be a big
driver for conservation engagement and awareness. So, in this case,
I'll allow myself to feel sad for the responsibility Fatu carries.

The procedure to create an embryo is very similar to the IVF
treatment available for humans struggling to conceive. Cesare tells
me, 'The immature eggs are allowed to mature in incubators with a
temperature of thirty-seven degrees for one or two days, and then
they are fertilised with thawed male sperm. The sperm quality is
poor with not a lot of motility, so we inject the sperm using a micro-
manipulator into the egg. It's a technique called intra-cytoplasmic
sperm injection (ICSI). We leave it to develop for ten days until it
reaches a stage called blastocyst, which is when it can be classified
as a viable embryo. They are then frozen in liquid nitrogen. They can
be frozen indefinitely but we hope to put the embryos in a surrogate
southern white rhino female soon.' Currently, somewhere in a freezer
in Cremona, there are five northern white embryos – just a small

group of cells frozen in time – the product of modern science and a
lot of remarkable people. Who knows what their fate will be?

The idea of implanting embryos of one species into another – as
long as they're closely related – is a technique that could really help
species on the very brink. In preparation for the embryonic transfer,
in November 2020 a southern white rhino bull was transferred to Ol
Pejeta Conservancy from Lewa Wildlife Conservancy. Now, you may
think that a male would be redundant in this process, but he has
a very important role to play. He has fathered many young rhinos
– he's good at what he does. Having already done a great job in
passing on his genes and increasing the southern white population,
he was transferred to Ol Pejeta where he was sterilised, in a small
non-surgical procedure. This might seem like an odd thing to do
but, when he mixes with the southern white females, his behaviour
can tell scientists about the reproductive cycles of potential
surrogate mothers. He can't impregnate them himself, of course,
but his excitement and curiosity are really reliable indicators of
their fertility. Once the scientists are aware that one of the southern
white females is in season and ready to become pregnant, they will
artificially inseminate her with a northern white embryo.

It would be such a huge achievement on many levels, but there
are also big concerns. As with any species whose population has
crashed so severely, the lack of genetic diversity causing inbreeding is
a major issue, and especially in this case when Fatu is the only female
providing eggs. I voiced this concern to Cesare, because as much as
I personally dream of a world filled with northern white rhinos, you
do have to ask yourself whether or not it is ethical to bring them back
if they are only going to suffer. My mind was blown by what he said
in response – this is when it gets seriously sci-fi. He replied, 'Genetic
variability in this case is too low, which is why rhino IVF is just one

part of the solution. We will always need the technology to make embryos from natural eggs and sperm, but we are also working with a project called BioRescue to create artificial gametes (eggs and sperm) using stem cell technology.' In other words, scientists are developing methods to artificially grow eggs and sperm cells in Petri dishes using fibroblasts (connective tissue cells) that are cryopreserved in liquid nitrogen. This is highly controversial and contains a lot of complexities.

In 2018, researchers in Japan actually managed to grow a very immature human egg. It was far too underdeveloped to be fertilised and more studies are needed to make sure it's safe for human reproduction, but essentially it proved that in the future we may be able to mass-produce human eggs and sperm in a lab setting. Babies could, in theory, be created from the blood, hair and skin cells of women who cannot conceive. Or those who are too old or too young, or even those who have died. Imagine that: creating offspring from the cells of your late great-grandmother or favourite deceased superstar. It is fascinating and almost unbelievable that we have the capability to do this… but it is a little Frankenstein-y, isn't it? If successful, then it's not such a far stretch to think that in the future people may be able to design their babies, choosing their offspring's appearance and personality traits, which would raise huge ethical and societal problems. Similar studies in this area are also taking place in Berlin. But human considerations aside, for the northern white rhinos this development couldn't have come at a better time. Currently the cells of at least eleven genetically distinct rhinos in labs across the world could be used to create eggs that will increase the genetic diversity and strengthen the population. It's a long way off yet but Cesare hopes that in the next twenty to thirty years, there will be a viable population of northern white rhinos roaming the plains of Africa once more. From a human perspective the way they plan to get there is a little scary, but as a tool for conservation it might just save these rhinos. And maybe even many other species currently caught in an inbreeding bottleneck.

When Sudan died in 2018, Ol Pejeta Conservancy held a small funeral in his memory. Caretaker James Mwenda gave a powerful and poignant eulogy, and I felt it was right to let his words finish this story. It is James and his team who are really on the frontline, after all. His message to Sudan is beautiful, and we can all learn a lot from it. Standing at Sudan's headstone and surrounded by other grieving caretakers, James read aloud:

'Goodbye Sudan, I don't need to say here that I loved you. You know it well from all the talks and the moments we had together, being with you for the last few years completely changed me, and as you taught me daily I continued to teach and inspire my fellow humans to be conscious and sensitive of our environment. I promised to be your voice, I'm not sure whether I duly and diligently fulfilled that, but I did my best… If I was powerful in the face of the conservation world then nineteenth April would be "Sudan the legend day". A day when parents would take their kids out and teach them how and why we need to embrace our environment. A day where a picture of you, Sudan, could be presented in the classroom and the kids would grow conscious of extinction and what your existence meant…

On the other side of life, greet Lola, Saut, Nasima, Nabire and the rest of the rhinos. Tell them that some humans still uphold the madness that rhino horn is a cure but there are others that still are fighting for your future. I will try my best to honour all that we talked about and live for what you have taught me.'

Southern Hemisphere

Pygmy Sloth

There's a lot to be said about living life in the fast lane. It's energetic, full of excitement with an edge of danger. Imagine how it must feel to be a peregrine falcon diving through the air at 200 mph. Or to leap out of the ocean like a dolphin, just for the fun of it. Do these animals find it thrilling, or just part of everyday life? Who knows, but I'd imagine that within those species there are individuals who like to live more energetically than others. Just how some adrenaline-fuelled humans seek activities like sky-diving or heli-skiing while others choose a more comfortable existence with their feet planted firmly on the ground. Personally, I love to challenge myself and am usually the first in line for anything adventurous, but I wouldn't be without my chill days, lounging on the sofa catching up on my favourite TV series. (I am also partial to the occasional lie-in – something very few wildlife enthusiasts will ever admit to!) In our fast-paced world we often forget to value the essence of slowing things down, but it's a virtue not lost on some animals…

It is well known that sloths are the slowest mammals on Earth. They were first described by French naturalist Georges Buffon in 1749, in his encyclopaedia of life sciences, as 'the lowest form of existence… an imperfect sketch of nature'; he claimed that 'one more defect would have made their lives impossible.' Safe to say sloths probably weren't among his favourite animals! Little did he know how wrong he was. Today, sloths are still labelled as lazy and stupid by those who don't understand them. Some say they're drugged by the leaves they eat, while other think they'd be 'so dumb' as to mistake their own arms for tree branches. These are all misconceptions about an animal that, in reality, is cleverly designed for survival and perseverance. After all, who was it who won the race? Was it the hare? Or was it the tortoise?

There are seven species of sloth alive today, divided into two genera: the *Bradypus* (three-toed) and the *Choloepus* (two-fingered). The Hoffmann's sloth and Linnaeus's sloth belong to the *Choloepus* genus and the others – the brown-throated, pale-throated, pygmy northern maned and southern maned sloths – sit together within the *Bradypus*. When I first started writing, it was thought that only six species existed worldwide but new genetic analysis in September 2022 identified that maned sloths had speciated and were completely distinct. All species have three fingers on their hind feet but on their forefeet their digits differ, as suggested above. When most people talk about sloths, they simply group the two genera together. They look and behave similarly and live in relatively close proximity to one another in Central and South America – so, why not? But when looking a little closer at their genes, scientists found they were actually a prime example of convergent evolution, sharing a common ancestor thirty million years ago. As a result, they aren't closely related at all – their strategy is just so good, they evolved separately twice. There are some subtle differences though: the two-fingered species are larger and tend to move that little bit faster, but the three-fingered species are much better swimmers.

But the question remains, why so slow?

Sloths are folivorous, meaning that they feed almost exclusively on leaves. It's a low-calorie, low-energy diet but, unlike other mammals that feed on similar foliage, sloths have exceptionally slow digestion. Its precise rate is often debated but estimates suggest it takes somewhere between eleven and thirty days for food to pass through their large, four-chambered stomachs before being excreted out the other end. Typically, a healthy sloth's stomach is always full, accounting for 30–40 per cent of its entire body weight. Many folivorous organisms, like koalas and howler monkeys, simply make up for their low-calorie diet by constantly consuming more and more leaf matter, but a sloth's ingestion is dictated by their slow digestion, meaning that on a daily basis, they don't actually eat very much at all, so have limited energy available. Their digestion rate and metabolic rate (i.e. the number of calories burnt for normal bodily function) are some of the lowest in the mammalian world and, as a result, they need to conserve as much energy as possible. Luckily for them, they have a few ingenious ways of doing so:

1) Sloths are poikilotherms. As heat is energetically costly to produce and maintain, sloths have bypassed this by thermoregulating themselves using behavioural methods like basking in the sun to keep warm. Their core temperature fluctuates a lot throughout the day: by up to 10 °C.

2) They sleep for 80 per cent of the day.

3) They are approximately three times stronger than the average human when it comes to gripping strength. This is especially incredible when you consider that they only have 30 per cent of the muscle mass expected for a species their size. While they might look dense and muscular, they have reduced their muscle tissue extensively to preserve energy. They are actually rather skinny under all their dense, long hair (which they use to stay warm by trapping in heat from the sun).

4) One of the most iconic sloth adaptations is their long, curved claws, which they use to hang upside down on in the tree canopy. They grow continuously, get filed down naturally over time and are formed of protruding distal phalange bones coming out of the arm. These claws help them sleep, eat and give birth while suspended, limiting energy expenditure. They're so strong that sloths can even die in that position, upside down, and still remain suspended in the trees.

5) Two-fingered sloths have more ribs than any other mammal. Humans have twenty-four ribs, elephants have twenty, but sloths have forty-six! These ribs help support their otherwise vulnerable stomach while they're hanging upside down and they are particularly flexible, meaning that if they fall, their ribs rarely break. Sloths have been known to survive 30-metre falls. I'll admit this isn't so much an energy conservation tactic but it's such an amazing fact that I knew I had to sneak it in somewhere!

Ultimately, these adaptations have led to a unique animal successfully filling a very specific, beautifully bizarre evolutionary niche. And they've been doing it for a long time; sloths and their ancestors have been hanging in the trees for nearly 64 million years. To survive, they rely on camouflage to stay hidden from predators, as running or jumping is out of the question, and scarcely move, staying still to go undetected by species further up the food chain, like jaguars or harpy eagles, that are visually scanning the environment to find something to snack on. But they have another defence mechanism: their *fur*, which is not only very dense, consisting of two layers to aid thermoregulation, but also contains a whole ecosystem of organisms within the hair. Sloths are solitary animals by nature, but when you take a look at what lives *on* them in the micro-cracks of their fur, you'll find a whole ecosystem of moths, beetles, parasites, arthropods, fungi and algae, some of which can be found nowhere else on Earth other than on the back of a sloth. It's a symbiotic, mutually beneficial relationship; these organisms have a safe place to live while the sloths are not only visually camouflaged – thanks to the photosynthetic algae tingeing their fur green – but it also helps them remain inconspicuous in the olfactory sense, as it means they smell just like the jungle they live in. (How remarkable is that?! Really shakes up the phrase 'you can run, but you can't hide'!)

There are some who might label sloths as lazy, but I firmly believe that they are in need of a new reputation – one that symbolises their stealth, patience and subtle genius. Among the scientists trying to help save these elusive mammals, there's a lot of love for their unusual abilities, even if they are notoriously hard to find. Dr Becky Cliffe is one of the world's leading experts on sloth biology. Originally from the UK, Becky completed her PhD at Swansea University helping to lead the longest recorded sloth ecology project, and has raised nearly $1 million for the 'Save Our Sloths' campaign. In 2016, she founded a non-profit organisation called the Sloth Conservation Foundation in Costa Rica, which aims to save wild sloths through community initiatives that promote the peaceful coexistence of sloths and humans.

There are only two sloth species, out of six, that are considered threatened by the IUCN. One of those species is the pygmy sloth, which is listed as critically endangered; the last population count in 2012 found there were only seventy-nine individuals left in the wild, making them one of the rarest mammals on Earth. They are endemic to a small island, only 4.3 square kilometres, off the coast of Panama, known as the Isla Escudo de Veraguas. The population has been isolated for 9,000 years, since the island was cut off from the mainland due to rising sea levels, and they have since diverged into the small sloths we know today, approximately 40 per cent smaller than other mainland species. They are these beautiful, striking creatures that live among the mangroves and just as I was gearing up to ask Becky about their terrifying plight, she offered me an insight.

'The IUCN Red List looks at the imminent threat of global extinction for a particular species, it essentially assesses the likelihood a species could disappear tomorrow,' Becky begins. 'So, because the pygmy sloth is one of the most critically endangered mammals on the planet, everyone panics. But if you take a step back from that and look at what their situation is, they're actually relatively stable. They live on such a small island and while there's only very few individuals, there's probably only ever been a very low density of numbers. I've been to the island many times, and the government is great at protecting the pygmy sloth for the habitat and for ecotourism. It's actually illegal to visit the island without permission and guidance from a ranger. They're critically endangered because of their small population, and if something happens, like a massive hurricane or a new virus, they could get wiped out overnight. But that's always been the case – they've always been in that precarious situation. So if you want funding for scientific research or for conservation, it's easier to succeed when focusing on the pygmy sloth. It's great that people want to help save these animals but I believe the money could be better focused on the mainland species where numbers are being decimated and it's going completely undocumented.'

It's common knowledge that wherever there is a uniform scoring system, which the IUCN classifications primarily are, there will always be some outliers that don't quite fit within the set boundaries. It's a great system that works for most species but in this case, it's probably not working in the best interests of other sloth species. Pygmy sloth numbers are undeniably low, and their conservation is very important, but we cannot overlook other species just because they have a lesser listing – or no listing at all.

'There are four types of sloths that are listed as "least concern" that live on the mainland in South America,' says Becky. 'And of those, there's not a single population count. There's no population monitoring. Nobody knows the distribution of the species. Nobody has any idea what is going on. You are dealing with animals so difficult to count to any degree of accuracy. I'm stuck between a rock and a hard place; I am watching species literally slipping silently towards extinction and nobody knows about it, so it's hard to find enough support.

It's like their most successful survival method, which is to go unseen in the forest, is working against them. They're so secretive that they're evading the science that's needed to get them protected.'

It's odd that a species or a group of animals, like sloths, that are world renowned and generally adored can be on the brink of extinction. It would be an understatement to say that people love sloths; it was only yesterday that someone told me that if they could be reincarnated they'd like to return as a sloth. I think it's their quirky characteristics, and the markings on their faces that give them their smiling, cheeky appearance, that we adore so much. Perhaps if people were aware of what was happening, they would be more motivated to save them.

Scientists might not know precise numbers, but the threats are glaringly obvious. 'They are creatures of habit. Everything about their biology and ecology is geared towards surviving in a very stable and predictable environment,' Becky says. 'And obviously, when humanity comes in and we start doing what we do best, aka changing things, sloths are the first ones to struggle. Unless trees are physically connected at the top, they can't move. They have to come to the ground, where they get attacked by dogs or run over by cars, or climb across power cables, where they get electrocuted. Deforestation for agriculture means that a lot of the populations are becoming genetically isolated, and studies are finding pesticide residue embedded in their claws, saliva and fur.'

The one thing that is clear is that threats are coming from all directions, but the main cause of the trouble is deforestation, followed by electrocution on power lines. Three thousand electrocuted wildlife casualties are brought into rehabilitation centres in Costa Rica every year; over half of those are sloths, and there's only a 25 per cent survival rate.

Dr Adriano Garcia Chiarello is a scientist working with maned sloths in Brazil. He has studied the impact of forest fragmentation on mammals since the start of his academic career and has been working with this species, listed as vulnerable, since 1995. 'When I first began,' Adriano says, 'there was only some preliminary work about their distribution, so I started studying their ecology and behaviour – we confirmed that their diet consisted of 99 per cent leaves, which was to be expected, but we also realised that each individual will only occupy very small spaces in the forest, somewhere between one and two hectares. Some individuals are diurnal, some are nocturnal and others are cathemeral, i.e. active in irregular patterns day and night. These were all things we uncovered relatively recently.'

Sadly, these sloths are restricted to 10 per cent of their former range and live in three genetically isolated populations along the coast of Brazil. Genetic research by Adriano revealed that these three populations likely separated a long time ago as a result of geographical features. But the threat of further isolation continues, as the expansion of major cities along the coast puts additional pressures on the forest. 'A lot of the habitat that the maned sloths occupy happens to be close to the major cities – like Salvador or Rio de Janeiro,' he continues. 'Human expansion is causing people to clear the forest for infrastructure, cattle pastures, coffee plantations, charcoal production and logging. When you clear the forest, you don't only lose big areas but the forest boundaries get exposed and are subject to the edge effect.' The edge effect is a term used to describe the changes in the microclimate that can occur when part of a habitat is destroyed. The new boundary gets exposed to new levels of light, wind, humidity and/or temperature that could make the border and beyond unsuitable for species that are used to living in the depths of the forest. So, while the people participating in deforestation might think they are leaving enough habitat behind, the sustainable healthy land is restricted to a far greater degree than they realise.

The maned sloth is the most studied species, although there is still so much to learn about them. For every isolated population around the world, for every species, there need to be specific solutions. Adriano is embarking on a project using thermal drones to locate sloths in the treetops, and Becky is training dogs to sniff out their poo! Both these methods will help these two scientists better understand how numbers are faring, but it's the community conversation that really makes me smile. I talk a lot in the UK about getting wildlife corridors in place throughout our gardens so that hedgehogs, amphibians and other creatures can have better access to mates and resources. You can imagine my delight, then, when Becky told me of the Sloth Friendly Network she established In Costa Rica! 'We are trying to get everyone to love sloths, so we go into villages to help reforest borders and corridors. We help build wildlife bridges for the sloths to cross on and also talk about the damaging impact "sloth selfies" can cause. It's important to talk about that as some people will capture sloths for the tourist selfie industry. But, it's been so well-received by the community, it's a win-win! Sloths are a great model for coexistence. If we can get it right with them, then it means we'll be able to coexist with everything else too.'

It would be fantastic to see the right support and funding appear before sloths disappear further. It goes to show how important the IUCN status is: yes, we must fight like hell to protect those that are critically endangered (that's what this book is all about), but we must not overlook the ones that are 'data deficient' either.

White-Headed Vulture

My fascination with vultures began in 2001, aged six, on a family holiday to Kenya. This was the same trip where I encountered my first rhino and so many more remarkable species. However, the purpose of the trip was not actually to see wildlife but to attend a wedding of a family friend who lived in one of the local towns. It was a gorgeous traditional wedding and she'd made me a beautiful bridesmaid's dress. When I returned home, my other family members asked what had been my favourite part of the trip. They expected me to say it was the day I got to be a bridesmaid in a beautiful dress… but that came a (close) second because nothing could compare to watching vultures tucking in to a rotting old giraffe.

Before the wedding on one early-morning game drive, we had come across a giraffe that had recently died and was lying stretched out on the plains. It was out in the open, which meant that we could drive up close and inspect it in detail. Unfortunately for my mother, I was adamant that we had to revisit its quickly decomposing body every day until we left. This was okay until its stomach started to expand with natural gases, which eventually led to it bursting, leaving the most indescribable, vile smell hanging in the air. We weren't present when it happened but nevertheless it was gag-provokingly disgusting, and I can still smell and taste it now. It was probably at this point that my mum would have been desperate for me to forget about the dead manky giraffe, but I knew that smell only meant one thing – scavenging animals were on their way to feast. And there was no way I was missing out on that. I forced my family and our guide to sit in the stench of this giraffe for hours so I could watch as black-backed jackals, hyenas and, of course, vultures all swooped in to feed. They each took their turn and within days the carcass was stripped bare. It was the best week ever, and the smell was a small price to pay, even if no one wanted to sit next to us at the wedding or on the plane journey home.

American author and environmental activist Edward Abbey, who died in 1989, once said, 'if my decomposing carcass helps nourish the roots of a juniper tree or the wings of a vulture – that is immortality enough for me. And as much as anyone deserves.'

He was a controversial, eccentric man; he hated being referred to as a nature writer, for why would anyone truly interested in the outdoors wish to stay in and read when they could step outside to experience nature for themselves? Abbey was certainly divisive and had some questionable outlooks, but he was perhaps among the first to look upon the vulture with admiration, which is something I can relate to. I have always gravitated towards the animals most people think are 'gross', 'ugly', 'weird' or somewhat 'disturbing'. There is something about a misunderstood underdog that intrigues me; perhaps they appeal to my empathetic side, or maybe it's the challenge of changing people's preconceived perceptions, which is no small ambition. But I always recognised that if successful, you would have the power to change the world – or at least change the world for that given species.

Nothing can compare to observing behaviour in the wild, but to see vultures in the UK there was always one place I could visit: the Hawk Conservancy Trust, based in Andover, Hampshire. It was founded by Reg Smith, who originally bought the land in 1952 to run as a farm; but, after developing a passion for birds of prey and conservation education, he opened the trust with his wife, Hilary, in 1980. Our two families have always been close, and I have learned so much from visiting the centre over the years. Meeting Marmite the barn owl, watching bald eagles fly above my head and seeing secretary birds up close are some of my favourite childhood memories. Today it's home to over 130 birds of prey and, while people can go and visit, the work of the trust is focused on the research and protection of wild species.

Around the globe there are twenty-three extant species of vulture; they can be found on all continents except for Antarctica and Australasia. Originally all vultures were grouped together in the same genus and were believed to have evolved once from a diurnal bird of prey, something we shall forgive based on the striking superficial similarities between the species, but biologists looking past the aesthetics and behaviour quickly realised that they needed to be split into two groups based on their distinct genetics: old world vultures inhabit Europe, Africa and Asia whereas new world vultures can be found in North and South America. The two groups are an example of convergent evolution, which happens when two very distantly related organisms evolve similar traits. Essentially, their role is so important or features so successful that they evolved twice in different areas.

Old world and new world vultures do share a number of characteristics that scream 'I'm a vulture': a bulky body, long, broad wings for lift, sharp eyesight for high-altitude soaring, scavenging behaviour, long intestines, powerful stomach acid for digesting rotting meat and a bald or semi-bald head for thermoregulation and cleanliness. But there are some subtle differences apart from their genetics: for example, new world vultures don't have a syrinx (avian vocal organ) and they engage in urohidrosis, a habit of defecating on their unfeathered bare legs to prevent overheating – a trait they share with storks. A sexy image if ever there was one, but hey, it's functional and who are we to judge!

Every organism has an important role to play in our world's complex, interconnected ecosystem and vultures are a significant cog in this delicate eco-machine. They are predominantly scavenging birds that feed on dead carcasses, otherwise known as carrion. Their eyes are densely packed with cone receptors, giving them acute vision, sensitive to detail and movement. They are experts at spotting a meal from great heights, in some cases up to 11.5 kilometres. Some species, like the turkey vulture, forage by sense of smell (which is unusual in avian species), being able to detect the odour of rotting flesh in the air in tiny concentrations, as small as a few parts per billion, before flying in a circular motion to home in on the scent's origins. It's a myth that vultures can literally 'smell death', but you wouldn't be wrong in saying they can certainly detect the chemical compounds produced by decaying meat. Each species has its own way of finding food; new research even suggests that some, like the hooded vulture, use sound too. A combination of all these scavenger senses means it's highly unlikely that an animal can die and decompose without them knowing about it!

There are billions of wild and livestock animals around the world and vultures play a huge role as 'nature's cleaners', consuming carrion that would otherwise decay and foster disease. In addition, decomposing bodies produce methane and carbon dioxide, and new research shows that vultures prevent tens of millions of metric tonnes of greenhouse gases from entering the atmosphere by scavenging. We mustn't underestimate how crucial this service is to the ecosystem; it benefits our economy, climate and even human health. Once vultures have found a meal, they will gather and consume a carcass in a matter of hours – or even minutes, depending on its size – making the most of every part from flesh to bone. They are the dominant scavenger, with a tolerance that no other animal can match, able to safely consume meat so rotten and decayed that it would poison other species if eaten. And if that isn't remarkable enough, evidence suggests that their diets help to prevent and suppress zoonotic disease outbreaks, like rabies. Vultures are key workers, acting as remarkable barriers, but how do they survive it themselves? Well, the pH of a human stomach is between 1.5 and 3.5, but a vulture's stomach acid can range from 0 to 1; that's more acidic than battery acid, which has a pH of 0.8! It is so corrosive that some species' stomach acid can even dissolve metals.

Ironically, it's their impressive scavenging methods that are leading vultures into trouble. Out of the twenty-three species, fourteen are listed globally as threatened with extinction. In the early 1990s, they were making headlines as conservationists were confronted with free-falling statistics that predicted these birds were well on their way to becoming the world's most threatened avian group. This was the beginning of the Asian vulture crisis, where vultures, who had once bred in their millions throughout India and Pakistan, declined dramatically: by 99 per cent in just fifteen years. It came as a shock – how could one of the world's most successful and adaptive birds be declining so rapidly? The causes were initially unknown; many assumed it was the fault of a new virus. In 2004, J. Lindsay Oaks from the Peregrine Fund connected the dots when he discovered quantities of the anti-inflammatory drug diclofenac had led to kidney failure. At that time, diclofenac was an inexpensive drug being administered to cattle in order to reduce the likelihood of fever and illness, which sadly led to its incidental poisoning of vultures when they ate them. It wasn't until the vultures had disappeared that people started to realise just how important they were at cleaning the landscape and, potentially, and reducing disease transmission. Nepal, Pakistan and Bangladesh were quick to outlaw diclofenac for livestock use, although in spite of this it is still available for human consumption, and ornithologists today are still concerned about the quantities that remain in the food chain. But it's slowly looking up.

Across the Arabian Sea, another issue reared its head: the African vulture crisis. Home as Africa is to eleven out of the sixteen old world vulture species, they have always been a familiar sight across the continent, from the heart of city centres to the wide-open plains. But in the last fifty years, there has been a 97 per cent population decline, with four species now listed as critically endangered. The rates mirror that of the Asian crisis, which is frankly all too familiar.

To get a handle on what these African vultures are up against, I got in contact with the head of conservation and research at Hawk Conservancy Trust and lecturer at the University of Reading, Campbell Murn. When Campbell first started working at the Trust there were a number of vultures there, but it was one species that captured his attention. 'There was a very, very old white-headed vulture there when I arrived,' he tells me. 'She was flightless and the story went that she was rescued from the bill of a marabou stork as a chick. She was given a home at the conservancy and shared an open-topped aviary with a rescued lappet-faced vulture who was a sad relic of the old days of the zoo industry, when people used to think that the way to display big birds was to pinion them.' Pinioning is a terrible surgical procedure to remove the pinion joint in a bird's wing, historically done without anaesthetic at just a few days old, to prevent the growth of primary feathers, which stops them from ever taking flight. It's essentially like someone cutting your toes off to prevent you from walking.

Watching the Asian vulture crisis unfold, with species rapidly on their way to extinction, it became obvious that hardly anyone really knew very much about vultures. Campbell ended up doing his Master's degree on the distribution and behaviour of white-backed vultures in relation to different types of land use. 'Vultures are flavour of the month now but twenty years ago there were very few people working with them,' he says. 'My master's was based in Kimberley in the middle of South Africa; there is a mixture of land use but it is principally either cattle, game or sheep farms. The overall result showed that the vultures strongly preferred land that had a reliable management with stable ownership. They like stability in the landscape.

'It was difficult to get precise population numbers, but there were five main breeding areas around Kimberley,' he goes on. 'They're very dynamic. And so between the first set of aerial surveys and the most recent, one of the colonies disappeared completely and another one grew by almost the same amount. It's tempting to make the conclusion that the birds had picked up sticks from one and then settled in another one, but it's probably far more complicated than that. The number of threats facing those birds is increasing as there's a lot of disturbance from mining – Kimberley was the original mining town where diamonds were first found in huge numbers in South Africa.

'You've got two types of white-backed vulture nests,' Campbell explains, 'they favour tall trees either in the savannahs or along the riverbanks. However, alongside the rivers is where you get a lot of land use change from diamond mining and agriculture, where the old camel thorn trees used for nesting are chopped down. Luckily, in that area there weren't other threats like there were elsewhere.'

Later in his research, Campbell turned his attention to the species that he first got to know at the Trust: the critically endangered white-headed vulture. They have a beautiful dark plumage, a naked baby-pink face and neck, a fluffy white head and a blue and coral-orange bill, and are unique in their behaviour. Vultures are primarily scavengers, but white-headed vultures have been observed actively hunting and killing their own prey, leaving no evidence behind. Campbell was lucky to see this for himself, after weeks watching the birds: a male and a female swooped down like a pair of goshawks with wings bent to catch a mongoose, before devouring it in seconds, leaving no trace! 'Nature rewards the patient,' he says with a smile.

Population estimates of vultures are notoriously hard to judge, but a consensus six years ago suggested there may be as few as 5,000 wild white-headed vultures left, having experienced a decline of about 96 per cent in forty-five years, or three generations. 'I would say white-headed vultures are unique because they are almost completely reliant upon protected areas in Africa,' Campbell goes on. 'I am not aware of any nests outside a protected area for this species… they might head out to forage but they favour areas that are not subject to human developments like cities or agricultural crops. I spent a long time trying to understand why, but what was alarming was that we identified about four hundred protected areas where white-headed vultures could potentially nest successfully, but there were only five areas where there were more than forty nests. This tells us that there are only five places in all of Africa that can be considered as having a secure population of these birds. Most white-headed vultures live in small numbers in tiny, protected areas with one or two nests, which makes them prone to local extinctions. It's alarming because one poisoning event could wipe out huge numbers and be devastating,' he concludes.

The poisoning of vultures, whether intentional or unintentional, is a problem growing in magnitude and is responsible for 61 per cent of reported deaths. You may automatically assume that poisoning events happen because of a disdain for these scavenging birds; it's an assumption I jumped to when I first learned of the issue years ago. But the vast majority of farmers and landowners in South Africa support vultures; they have a cultural and/or ecological appreciation for the role they play. Admittedly, there are some who find them to be a nuisance, particularly when a new cattle water trough is installed only to be christened by vultures bathing in the fresh water after a messy, often bloody and definitely smelly meal. But the main cause of vulture poisoning is connected to another dark wildlife atrocity. As excellent carcass locators, vultures circle at great heights in the sky to locate food. Consequently, they are visible indicators of a dead animal: a type of exposure poachers could do without.

Vultures were originally poisoned incidentally when carcasses, coated in toxic agricultural pesticides, were laid out to reduce the numbers of other animals that posed a threat – like hyenas or lions, or to control the local feral dog populations. Poisoning is a non-selective method that inevitably always goes beyond the initial target. But as the demand for elephant ivory and rhino horn amplified over the years, poachers armed with pesticides started going after the birds. Poachers enter reserves to kill game, buffalo or zebra, and lace their bodies with poison to remove vultures from the area before returning a few days later to kill an elephant or rhino. This is called sentinel poisoning. In June 2019, 537 vultures belonging to five species were found dead at one single poisoning event linked to elephant poaching in Botswana. It just goes to show the impact one incident can have.

Of course there are other reasons for persecution of vultures, but it varies depending on the region. Overall, 29 per cent of deaths are linked to African belief-based use, which purports that ingesting parts of the vulture can enhance gambling success and child intelligence, among other things; 9 per cent are linked to electrocution from power lines; and just 1 per cent of incidents are related to food.

Campbell was part of a study in 2018 that predicted the long-term survival of white-backed vultures, based on a statistical modelling programme called VORTEX. The outcomes were worrying at best. Worst-case scenario: without intervention, at the current rate of poisoning, the species was 100 per cent likely to go extinct in the next fifty-five to sixty-two years. But with a little bit of help, mortality at each carcass poisoning attack could be reduced by 70 per cent, allowing the population to keep going for at least another 100 years, giving them a fighting chance to bounce back.

'Aside from working on vulture ecology, I focus a lot on minimising the damage that poisoning events can cause,' Campbell tells me. Having played such a huge part in vulture science, if there is anyone who can implement a solution, it's him! 'You can't easily stop poisoning from happening in the first place,' he goes on. 'It's a bit like trying to stop poaching – some of the best and brightest minds in the business have tried to stop elephant and rhino poaching and so on, but it continues. So I know that poisoning is going to keep happening. Typically, rangers tend to patrol in pairs. Imagine they're going through the bush when they suddenly come to a clearing and there's a wildlife poisoning scene. It is utterly horrific, it's like a wildlife bomb has gone off: there is the poisoned carcass, half-dead tawny eagles, dead vultures, lions and a hyena staggering around. All these animals, everything from the insects all the way up to the largest mammals, get affected. It's devastating. And if you don't know what you're doing or you don't have the kit to deal with it, then more animals come and get poisoned. The poison doesn't stop working after the first animals have died.'

Campbell helped develop poison response training to train groups of field personnel, rangers or law enforcement officers in exactly what to do in a poisoning situation: how to neutralise and decontaminate the scene, how to take forensic samples and how to catalogue the disaster. 'It's a whole *CSI*-type situation,' he says.

'The kits they get provided with contain all the stuff needed for decontamination and safety, so when the inevitable happens the poisoning source gets shut down, which prevents the situation from getting worse. Instead of four or five hundred vultures being killed at one elephant poaching event, rangers have the field skills needed to significantly reduce the number of birds killed.'

While I am all for preventative conservation to stop wildlife crime before it happens, in some cases it is idealistic; and we need to be realistic when it comes to saving the species on the brink of extinction, because they frankly don't have time to waste. By reducing the reach of poisoning and slowing down the decline, we can buy valuable time that can be used to find alternative solutions and, hopefully, change perceptions about traditional medicines.

What will the future hold for white-headed vultures and the other African species?

Well, only time will tell, but Campbell is positive, even if he is a little hesitant. He thinks for a moment before responding: 'Can we repopulate a safe protected area with white-headed vultures? Probably, yes. Can we make vulture safe zones across Africa? Well, that's a difficult nut to crack. But you know what, thinking of the Asian vulture crisis twenty years ago, we really thought extinction was imminent. For all intents and purposes, they were going to go extinct and nobody knew what the hell was going on as they were dying faster than anybody could count them. And then, in my opinion, Lindsay Oaks made the greatest contribution to conservation in the last hundred years when he found the link between diclofenac and vulture renal failure. For the last fifteen years that population curve was low and flat – we knew we could still lose them – but in the last two or three years, we've seen the curve blip upwards. And now I am fundamentally optimistic about

Asia and the vultures there. African vultures face a lot of challenges, but if we look at Africa in the same way we looked at the situation in Asia, it's similar. Twenty years ago, we were head in hand saying, good grief, what are we going to do? And then it slowly turned around. I can only be hopeful.'

Obviously Campbell's work is far from over, but the increase in Asian vulture populations is proof that conservation efforts can work if action is taken quickly. Whenever I visit Africa, my gaze will always float towards the sky in the hopes of seeing white-headed vultures circling above, moving as one large spiral. These misunderstood birds should be admired and respected; they navigate a strange space between life and death and, in doing so, provide a sense of balance in the natural world. They might not be conventionally beautiful or cute but, to me, they are perfect.

Kakapo

I t's the dead of night, and you are walking down a
mountain trying to keep up the pace because time is of
the essence. There's no anthropogenic noise whatsoever –
all you can hear is the rain falling on the leaves around you
and the squelching of your boots as they hit the surface of
a giant puddle. It's difficult terrain, but as long as you don't
fall over you don't care, because in your hands is one of the
most precious things on the planet. A small box containing
a couple of kakapo eggs. With only 208 individuals alive
today, every egg is critical. You're concentrating on the 1.5-
hour trek ahead of you so that you can safely deliver these
fragile eggs to base camp where they can be checked over,
and you're critically aware that they need to be under the
incubator soon. Each egg is important, but these are extra
special as they came from a female who hasn't produced
viable eggs in thirty-five years. So, no pressure.

Walking down this mountain, you're totally reliant on
the torch to help you find your footing and navigate a way
down. But all of a sudden, the torch fails. It's okay; you have
prepared for this – you carefully reach into your backpack for
the back-up torch. But that won't switch on either. What do
you do?

That is exactly the situation Dr Andrew Digby of the Kakapo Recovery Group found himself in: on the side of a mountain, a fair distance away from camp, with no light, grasping on to eggs that could potentially secure the next generation of kakapo and help to save an entire species. Luckily, he was able to radio a nearby team member, who came to the rescue with a functioning torch!

Islands are relied upon by 600 million people, equating to one-tenth of the world's population. So from a human standpoint they are incredibly valuable; but for me, it's the non-human life that is most exciting. They are hotspots for biodiversity because over time in isolation, species diverge from one another, creating new endemic species that are perfectly adapted to the specific conditions and resources available on that particular island. Despite only contributing to approximately 5 per cent of the global land mass, islands hold 20 per cent of all vascular plant species and 15 per cent of all mammals, amphibians and birds. The species living on remote islands have an increased level of endemism on both the genetic and ecosystem levels. They are unique. Hence why many scientists – like Charles Darwin and Peter and Rosemary Grant, who investigated natural selection and evolution of finches in the Galapagos – were fascinated by these patches of land.

Evolution and species divergence happens incredibly quickly in these environments. Studies suggest that mammals evolve three times quicker than in mainland ecosystems, which is mind-blowing! But extinction rates are higher too. Isolation can leave populations vulnerable, especially when human-aliens from outside the boundaries of the island invade, bringing with them disease and non-native species. It changes everything: the scales tip and the ecosystem becomes unbalanced. In fact, of the 724 declared animal extinctions in the last 400 years, roughly half were island species. And sadly, many more charismatic unique island-living species are following the same trajectory...

Strigops habroptilus, also known as the kakapo, is a nocturnal parrot endemic to New Zealand. It is the heaviest parrot in the world, weighing up to 4 kilograms, and is therefore a ground-dwelling species. They are so distinctive in appearance that you question how such a bird could really be real. Do you remember at school those competitions where you had to design and draw a new species? Well, it is almost like the kakapo has jumped straight out of someone's imagination, onto the drawing paper and then somehow into existence. With facial discs that resemble the face of an owl, whisker-like facial feathers used to help feel in the dark, a bill almost too large for its body and a mottled moss-green plumage; it is a secretive bird full of charisma and character. They are a nocturnal and solitary species that are sensitive to environmental changes, and are lek breeders; males gather on high ground, each creating a series of bowls (or scrapings) that are connected by tracts within the scrub and trees. They attempt to impress the females by settling in their bowls and inflating their thoracic air sacs enabling them to emit a low-frequency booming sound throughout the night every 1–2 seconds. If successful, a female will approach and select her partner. Females only produce between one and four eggs once every two to four years; this is largely dependent on the abundance of fruit that is produced by the rimu tree. This is an evergreen coniferous species that is native to the lowland and montane forests of New

Zealand and, on a two to four-year cycle, produces lots of small red berries. These are believed to be the kakapo's most valuable food source as the berries contain high concentrations of calcium and vitamin D, which are important minerals needed for egg production. The birds are not solely reliant upon them; their vegetarian diet also includes seeds, bulbs, roots, leaves, buds, flowers and even bark, depending on the season. Their nests are shallow depressions on the ground created inside natural cavities or under dense vegetation. I have never seen a kakapo myself – in fact very few people have. It would be a dream come true for me one day to see them in their wild habitat.

New Zealand is composed of over 600 islands with two larger primary islands in close proximity – the North and the South Island. Collectively as a country, it has been geologically isolated for 85 million years and has given rise to the evolution of many fabulously unusual animals and plants that are found nowhere else on Earth. But to tell you the story of the kakapo and how the fate of the species has ended up in the hands (quite literally) of a small group of conservationists, we have to go back in time to the arrival of humankind. Indigenous Polynesian people arrived on mainland New Zealand on canoes known as waka some time between 1320 and 1350. Up until this point no other mammal species, with the exception of bats, had colonised the country – it was simply too far away across the ocean for mammals to disperse to. When the Māori arrived they were isolated from other civilisations for centuries and had a unique culture centred around mythology, performing arts and craft. Living off the land, the Māori would often hunt kakapo; as a flightless and relatively bulky bird, they would have been an easy catch and would provide a substantial meal for the entire family. As well as their meat being eaten, their skins and feathers were used to create soft capes and cloaks for the daughters and wives of leading chiefs within the community. However, it wasn't this hunting that directly caused the major decline of the kakapo. On the original voyages bringing in these Polynesian settlers, humans were not alone. Other alien invaders were on their way too.

When the first human settlers arrived they were accompanied by their dogs, but also stowed away was the Polynesian rat, also known as the Pacific or little rat. Little did the Māori know that the first domino had fallen in a succession of catastrophic blows for native wildlife… It was here that things began to change. The dappled green plumage of the kakapo blends perfectly into their preferred habitat of tussock land, scrublands and forests of beeches, tawa and rata trees. In fact, as a completely flightless bird, its camouflage and its instinct to freeze rather than flee when threatened was a very successful survival strategy for millions of years. It worked so well that the kakapo was once the most common bird in New Zealand, and was widespread throughout the islands.

Evidence of their historical distribution can be found in the caves where old bones remain and in the middens (archaeological food sites) of old civilisations. However, camouflage was no longer a successful defence when up against the highly sensitive noses of dogs and rats. And kakapos' instinct to freeze certainly didn't help; they were essentially 'sitting ducks'. Dogs could easily sniff them out and notify the human hunters of the birds' presence, and the rats would locate their nests and prey upon their eggs and chicks. These introductions didn't solely impact the kakapo, but also many of New Zealand's other endemic species like the land crabs and the iconic kiwi bird.

By the time European settlers arrived in the early 1800s the kakapo had already declined from much of its natural range and was now confined to the central parts of the North Island and the forested areas in the South Island. And, sadly, the Europeans brought with them some additional pressures that would eventually push the kakapo to the very brink of extinction… cats, stoats, ferrets, weasels, brown rats and black rats. It was, and still is, a bleak picture. All these species were far better climbers than the Polynesian rats brought by the Māori and therefore many species nesting off the ground in bushes and trees were now in serious trouble too. An estimated 26 million chicks and eggs are preyed upon every year by these invasive predators, and as a result a quarter of New Zealand's endemic bird species have been driven to extinction. The huia, the laughing owl, the bush wren, New Zealand little bittern, South Island snipe and North Island snipe, New Zealand owlet-nightjar and Eyles's harrier – to name just a few – are specialised species that evolved over millions of years, only to be eradicated by the careless nature of human beings. They now only exist in books, dusty museum displays and the rare old photograph.

The kakapo was once on that list too, or at least we believed it to be. Conservation efforts for this species date all the way back to 1894, when pioneer conservationist Richard Henry began trying to relocate the birds from the mainland, where predation was wreaking havoc, to the predator-free island of Resolution in Fiordland. Despite his efforts, that translocated population vanished a few years later. By the mid-1900s they were officially a 'lost species', with the only whispers of their whereabouts coming in from a handful of people who had ventured into the remote heart of the islands. The New Zealand Wildlife Service was determined to find these remaining individuals, so between 1949 and 1973 they set out on sixty expeditions across New Zealand. In all that time, they only found six individuals. That's one every ten expeditions. They were all male and, devastatingly, all but one died within a few months of being taken into captivity. They were officially thought extinct.

You'd have thought at that point the government and the scientists would have given up hope, but I am so happy that they didn't because eventually two small populations were found in the extremely rugged, mountainous areas of Fiordland and Stewart Island. Amazingly, eighteen kakapo were located in Fiordland and ninety-two on Stewart Island. There were many more males than females but as soon as the presence of a female was confirmed on Stewart Island, researchers saw their first glimmer of hope and the journey to bring them back from the edge of extinction could begin. To escape the stoats in Fiordland and the cats on Stewart Island, their only hope was to be translocated to predator-free islands like Codfish, Anchor and Little Barrier, which is where they can be found today.

To understand exactly how the conservation of such an elusive and unique species works, I spoke to Dr Andrew Digby – the same man who found himself clutching a couple of eggs on a mountainside without a torch. Originally from the UK, Andrew studied a PhD in astronomy at the University of Edinburgh before moving to America in 2003 to conduct a postdoc with NASA, looking for new planets around other star systems. It was all part of a big push at the time to find life on other planets.

While a lot of his time was spent questioning the universe and staring up into the stars, Andrew also volunteered his time to local wildlife charities to aid his other passion – biology.

'I came to New Zealand in 2006, and there was very little astronomy,' he tells me. 'There were like five people employed within the field here and I was told someone had to die or retire before I got a job. So I ended up working in meteorological forecasting for a while and then got involved in conservation volunteer work. That's when I thought seriously about a full-time job out of conservation, and ended up getting a PhD in conservation biology.' He also mentioned that he found a striking connection between astrophysics and nature: in both cases, you're trying to solve unanswered mysteries.

Before working with the kakapo, Andrew had been spending his time trying to understand more about the kiwi. Kiwis are another funky species of ground-dwelling bird endemic to the islands of New Zealand – a well-known fact is that they have the largest egg on the planet relative to their body size. Seriously, the egg is about 20 per cent of their body weight and would be the equivalent of a human giving birth to a three-year-old child (ouch!). Using automatic microphones and recorders, Andrew was trying to understand their vocalisations. They exhibit sexual dimorphism – the females are much larger than the males – so you might expect them to have different call frequencies based on their size differences. But this wasn't the case at all. Andrew's research led him to coin the term 'vocal cooperation', as it turned out that the birds had actually evolved to shift the frequencies of their calls to match one another. So, when you hear what sounds like a single kiwi vocalising, you may actually be listening to a male and female calling in synchronicity. This discovery was extremely helpful when it came to monitoring the kiwi because researchers could analyse the bioacoustics more effectively and know how many were present without needing to physically see the birds, which are very well camouflaged on the forest floor.

When a job with the Kakapo Recovery Group came about, Andrew applied, although he was originally sceptical of getting the position as he knew very little about the birds. But his analytical skills in science were exactly what the group were looking for to help save the species.

As of right now in 2022, there are only 252 individual kakapo left on the planet.

'This is actually quite a big increase from just a few years ago around the mid-90s when the population was at fifty-one individuals,' Andrew says. 'And even in the early 2000s when there were just eighty-six or so. But when you can name all of your individuals and know each one within an entire species, that's a bad sign that they're in big trouble.'

I asked Andrew if he remembered the first time he saw a kakapo, and he replied, 'It was in the wild on a place called Anchor Island and it was just amazing. The first thing I thought was, "Look how big they are," which is many people's first reaction. You might have seen pictures, but you don't actually realise until you see one, and it sits on your lap, just how massive they actually are. Their camouflage is incredible too. I've been in a situation where I knew I was within two metres of a kakapo because I could smell it, but I just couldn't see it. It ended up being just over a metre away but was totally hidden. They're birds whose characters are larger than life.' Andrew smiles as he recalls these stories. I think I'd have been smiling too if I'd been lucky enough to get so close that I could smell a kakapo!

'The first priority when those eighteen individuals were found in the 70s was to translocate them somewhere safe,' he goes on. 'Once that was done, things ticked over very slowly because no one really understood their biology. We know a lot more now, but it's still a learning process. Currently we monitor every single nest, artificially incubate the eggs, provide supplementary feeding to ensure birds are in optimal breeding condition and even hand-rear the chicks that don't look like they are going to make it. We have also been trialling artificial insemination for a long time; it has been quite challenging but we are getting there with it now and it has the potential to make quite a difference.' He goes on to say that one of the main issues they face in trying to increase kakapo numbers is that they have a major infertility problem and are susceptible to disease. As mentioned earlier, the females only breed every two to four years; and research shows that a huge 61 per cent of eggs fail to hatch.

To better understand why the kakapo were struggling to breed, the Kakapo Recovery team, alongside the Genetic Rescue Foundation at Duke University and Pacific Biosciences, in 2015 decided to sequence the genome of all living birds – which at the time was 125 individuals. This was the first and only project to have ever sequenced the genomes of an entire population. Doing this allows researchers to genetically manage which kakapo breeds with which by moving certain individuals between islands to meet new, more genetically distinct mates. Of course, when you have a population whose numbers have plummeted as low as 110, if not lower, inbreeding will almost definitely occur. But by understanding the genomes, Andrew and his team were able to judge the degree of relatedness of each individual, and increase the viability of artificial insemination. The other positives were that each individual could be aged using DNA methylation, and sperm quality, vitamin deficiencies and disease resistance could be assessed.

One of the big challenges around kakapo infertility was trying to identify where the problem is: is it with the males, the females or a combination of the two? To get a clear picture of the bird's movements, each kakapo wears its own small smart transmitter. Not smart in that they look exceptionally dapper with it on, but because it's a very high-tech piece of kit. It essentially works like a Wi-Fi network, uploading the activities of all the birds – everything from who has mated with who, how long it lasted and even quality of the mating (would love to know how it works that last one out!) – onto a system that can be remotely accessed by the scientists wherever they are in the world. In addition to this, each nest site has infrared sensors and cameras to remotely determine how attentive the females are to their eggs and chicks. But this type of intensive surveillance cannot go on for ever. Andrew and his team have helped raise the kakapo population by 70 per cent in the last five years, which is wonderful – but the species needs to stand on its own two feet. The overall aim is that one day these individuals will be thriving in the wild without the need for transmitters and continual monitoring.

To say that they have tried and tested many different methods would be an understatement. For successful artificial insemination you of course need a reproductive female, but also some good-quality sperm. But how do you go about getting that sperm? Well, they've certainly had some creative ideas! A kakapo helmet was designed for people to wear on their heads, a bit like a rugby cap; the idea was that the person wearing the hat sat low with their head close to the ground so that the male kakapo could climb onto their shoulders and attempt to mate with the contraption on their head; if successful, the helmet collected the sperm. (It's a real thing, I promise – google it!) Surprisingly, it's not such a far-fetched idea; kakapos have actually been documented trying to mate with humans before. In fact, when British zoologist (and friend of mine) Mark Carwardine was filming a BBC documentary in 2009, a male named Sirocco attempted just that: he climbed onto Mark's shoulders and was quite insistent on having his way with him! The clip is still available on YouTube if you fancy a giggle.

The helmet wasn't the only invention though. A remote-control car, fondly named Chloe, dressed up to resemble a female kakapo, was also used to try to entice the male. But sadly, neither the helmet nor the remote control worked. There was no success at all. I have to say though, if it meant saving a species, who wouldn't have volunteered to wear the kakapo ejaculation helmet? I know I would have. In hindsight, perhaps they should just have asked Mark Carwardine to pop back to New Zealand and wear the helmet!

It actually took a few years before the team were able to successfully artificially inseminate a kakapo, and even then it has only worked three times, despite efforts being made every breeding season: once in 2009, again in 2019 with three females and most recently in 2022. This was a huge first for the conservation community because artificial insemination had never before been attempted with a wild bird species. In 2019, experts were brought in from around the world and a team of parrot insemination specialists from Germany came to provide their very niche expertise. But, Andrew said, 'These are people who really know parrots, but even they were really surprised with how different the kakapo was. They don't follow the parrot "norms" at all; even something as seemingly straightforward as locating the female oviduct to inseminate the semen was hard at first. We ended up putting the sperm in the wrong place for quite a few inseminations! But ultimately there are three important steps. Firstly, collecting the sperm from the male. We're able to do that quite successfully now by holding the male and using a special massage technique to stimulate ejaculation. Second step is how to transfer the sperm quickly to the female. In captivity, birds would be next door to one another, but on these islands where the kakapo live, a female might be on the opposite side to the male. Last time we actually used drones to get the sample there more quickly. And finally, you have to inseminate the female. Kakapo females only breed every two to four years, so when they do come into season it's a big effort. It's a real slow gain, but we think we've got the process working for next time it comes around.'

The most critical period of time after successful insemination is once the eggs are laid. As you might imagine, it's both an exciting and a nerve-wracking experience for the team, who have no clue what to expect. Venturing out into kakapo habitat to see if their efforts have paid off, the team set up a base camp on the islands. Every day they trek to the nests where, if all is well, the female is incubating. Keeping a reasonable distance, they set up a small tent close by and wait for nightfall, when the female leaves the nest for short periods of time to find food. It's the perfect opportunity for Andrew and his colleagues to get a sneak peek and check the health of the eggs. 'You candle the eggs to see if they are fertile or not. It's one of the most bitter-sweet moments of the programme because if you have three eggs and all are fertile then that's a significant proportion of the population, especially if the parent birds are genetically important,' he relays. Genetic importance refers to the birds that have a stronger, more distinct genome as opposed to those with a high degree of inbreeding; and candling is when you shine a bright light towards the egg in a dark place to see through the shell and determine whether or not an embryo is developing. 'But more often than not, the eggs are infertile,' Andrew goes on. 'You'll be holding these eggs knowing that the female has gone to so much effort. She might not have bred for three years, or, in some cases, even up to thirty years.'

The percentage of eggs that fail to hatch, as we've noted, is 61 per cent, which is very high compared to other avian species. So why is that?

Despite the best efforts of the Kakapo Recovery Group and the New Zealand government, no one really understood why so many eggs were not hatching, so they enlisted the help of Dr Nicola Hemmings in the UK; she specialises in variation in bird reproduction, with a focus on infertility and embryo development.

Nicola has a keen eye for detail, and she applied very specific techniques to piece together the mystery behind the kakapo hatching rate. After a lot of patience, persistence and paperwork she secured the funding, and 128 failed eggs made their way around the world to her lab at the University of Sheffield. Firstly though, to appreciate the intricacies of her work, it's important to have an understanding of avian egg formation. Ovulation begins with just the yolk, which then moves into the reproductive tract, where sperm are being held ready for fertilisation. Triggered by hormones, the sperm move up the tract to penetrate the yolk's surface. About fifteen minutes after the yolk is released from the ovary into the tract, glycoproteins are produced, which essentially stick to the yolk's surface and act like a glue, preventing any sperm from nestling their way in. All the sperm that are present at the time of fertilisation are quite literally stuck on to the outside of the yolk – although hopefully one has made its way inside! Finally, the albumin (or egg white) is produced, followed by the shell and then any pigments. If all is well, once the egg is laid it will begin to develop as the incubation period begins.

Nicola vividly remembers the day that the kakapo eggs arrived for her research. 'Ever since I started working on hatching failure in birds, this was always the species I wanted to work with because it has one of the highest levels of hatching failure,' she tells me. 'I just couldn't believe that I had those eggs in my lab. They arrived and I just had to examine as many as possible straight away. It takes a while, only about four or five can be done in one day. But the first time I looked at the slide under the microscope, I just felt like I wanted to cry with excitement because I could finally see what was going on.'

Nicola and her colleagues analysed each kakapo egg meticulously. 'When an egg doesn't develop, we can open it up and look at the layer surrounding the yolk under the microscope, and we can actually still see all the sperm that were there at the time of fertilisation. They don't disintegrate, they're essentially held in suspended animation. I use a fluorescent dye that binds to the DNA, so all the sperm heads light up clearly and you can also see if and where sperm made it into the ovum by looking for tiny holes in the layer. If that all looks good, then the next step is to locate the germinal disc, which is where embryo development begins. Under the microscope, you can see if there are any cells present in that disc. By doing this with the eggs we can work out whether sperm made it to the egg, whether the egg was fertilised and whether the embryo started to develop at all.'

Listening to Nicola, I was just astounded by the depth of the study and how detailed the analysis was. But it wasn't good news. 'The majority of eggs failed because of early embryo mortality and not infertility,' she continued. 'About 80 per cent had sperm around the yolk and had cells in the germinal disc, suggesting the first stages of embryonic development had occurred. The other 20 per cent were infertile, which is still a high percentage when compared to other bird species, but it wasn't as high as we were expecting. We don't know for sure why there is such a high rate of early embryo death but my overwhelming hunch is that it's probably a consequence of inbreeding depression. The kakapo population went down to such a tiny size and when you get down to those really small numbers of individuals, the genetic diversity of the population becomes very low. Even though numbers have increased, there is still low genetic variability. I know from studying other species that inbreeding depression heavily affects the earliest stages of development because at that point there is a lot of gene expression occurring, which can have big survivability consequences.'

The Kakapo Recovery Group have really considered and exercised every method possible to try to save this species from the brink of extinction. There is no other initiative quite like it. I suppose it makes it that much more frustrating if it fails because it shows that while you can do everything imaginable to try to save a species, ultimately causes out of our control – like severe inbreeding – can determine the success. Sometimes, we do just have to let things go. That's the sad reality that many species face. But it's still not time to give up hope for the kakapo yet – far from it.

Previously I wrote about how every single kakapo had its genome sequenced, which has proven to be very useful because it gives such a detailed genetic portrait of each individual. For example, in 2019 a male kakapo named Gulliver fathered offspring for the first time, a total of three chicks! A huge success. Gulliver himself was one of the few offspring of a male that was originally found in Fiordland back in the 1970s. The birds that came from

Fiordland had a greater level of genetic diversity than the other population, on Stewart Island. Looking specifically at Gulliver's genome, there are genes present there that no other kakapo has. This makes him (and potentially his three offspring) a kakapo of very high genetic importance. This unique gene is responsible for disease resistance, which could be of great value as kakapo are very vulnerable. The aspergillosis fungus outbreak that occurred in 2019 on Codfish Island, for instance, killed nine kakapo out of twelve receiving treatment. This is a disease that can affect many species of animals, including humans, so experts from all over the world are pitching in to help understand what happened. Investigations are currently under way, but a couple of theories are that there was an unusually high concentration of the fungal spores present in the environment, or simply that the kakapo had low immunity. Gulliver lives on Codfish Island, and survived the aspergillosis outbreak. While his genetic make-up could be entirely irrelevant, there's a chance that it afforded him extra protection. His genes could go on to increase the immunity of future generations and also promote greater genetic diversity. And that sounds pretty exciting. It's knowledge and hope that we wouldn't have had without having the entire population genome sequenced, so perhaps this could be a way forward in conserving other organisms that are looking down the barrel of extinction too.

This book has taken nearly two years to write, and when I began the kakapo population was hovering at only 197 individuals. I have been excitedly – and tentatively – observing the progress that has been made over this time as the population grew. The breeding season of 2022 was the second most successful on record since the 1970s. The rimu tree reached the peak of its four-year cycle and had a 'mast year', meaning a bumper year for fruits and crops. Think of your local woodland at home; have you noticed in particular years that there are a lot more acorns on the ground than in others? Well, it's exactly the same thing. Many different trees adopt this strategy whereby the plants produce more fruits than any animal could possibly consume, thus securing the next generation of trees, or so it is theorised. A ranger who visited Ulva, a small island close to Stewart Island, counted the number of berries and estimated that there were between 4,000 and 5,000 per square metre! As a result of all that extra vitamin D, a total of forty-nine chicks were raised at the nest and six were hand-reared. The hand-rearing is a last resort and only occurs when – for whatever reason – the parents are unable to care for it, or it looks as though the chick won't survive. As of 8 August 2022, the population stands at 252.

This huge victory was followed by a stark reminder that we cannot take our eyes off the ball just yet. In 2020, a proportion of kakapo were translocated to Chalky Island and they successfully hatched three chicks in 2022, a first for the breeding site. The island had been predator-free – stoats were eradicated in 1999 – but a field trip in August 2022 found footprints. Stoats are good swimmers, capable of swimming up to 1-1.5 kilometres away from shore. The animals themselves were later spotted in various locations across the island causing alarm. The Department of Conservation is running an immediate incursion response, which includes a stoat detection dog team and trapping.

The government in New Zealand is taking a very firm approach to restoring all the islands of the nation by attempting to totally eradicate rats, possums and stoats by 2050. Called the Predator Free 2050 initiative, it's a very ambitious project to take on, especially considering that the largest area ever cleared of invasive predators is Australia's Macquarie Island, which is 50 square miles. New

Zealand on the other hand is 2,000 times that size. There is some scepticism around the ethics of it too, but there is no doubt that if effective it would protect future generations of the native wildlife that we risk losing for ever. The kakapo could be reintroduced to much of its original range, which it desperately needs; it can't be forever restricted to three islands, as the population needs room to expand. But until that point, when it's safe for the kakapo to return, the Kakapo Recovery Group will continue with their mission to better understand and protect this unique and fascinating species. When asked if he is hopeful, Dr Andrew Digby said, 'I am quite a pessimistic person by nature, but I am very optimistic for kakapo. I think given the current trajectory, they will survive.'

Black-and-White Ruffed Lemur

The term 'biodiversity hotspot' is thrown around a lot these days to describe landscapes and as a result it's been somewhat diluted. I could argue that I have a hotspot in my garden or inside my local woodland that I know will be more 'busy' with life than elsewhere within those borders, but it's all relative, based on location and knowledge. Over time we've forgotten part of its original definition, as these places aren't defined solely by their biological beauty. The first mention of a biodiversity hotspot was made in 1988 by Norman Myers, one of the first environmentalists and campaigners to really start sticking his neck out for climate change and the extinction crisis. It took a while for people to catch on to 'biodiversity hotspot' as a concept, but once they did it quickly became very popular. According to Myers, 'A biodiversity hotspot is an area with unusual concentrations of species, many of which are endemic. It is marked by serious threats to its biodiversity by humans.' Officially, the area must meet two strict criteria: it must 1) have at least 1,500 endemic species of vascular plants, and 2) have lost over 70 per cent of its original habitat. A hotspot is a place that is not only characteristically irreplaceable but has been (and continues to be) the victim of great anthropogenic destruction. It's a place to be celebrated based on its strengths but also protected due to its vulnerability. It's a place with more to lose.

In 1989, one year after Norman's paper 'Threatened Biotas: "Hot Spots" in Tropical Forests' was published, Conservation International adopted the idea to help them identify biodiversity-rich habitats around the world that need extra attention and preservation, essentially helping to direct funds to the critical areas that need it most. In the years since there have been numerous reviews to ensure no hotspot was missed from the list. And I think you might be surprised about how few there actually are. To date, there are only thirty-six recognised biodiversity hotspots. The latest addition was in 2016, when the North American Coastal Plain was added to the group due to its significance; it houses many rare and endemic species, like the broadspotted molly fish and the Florida bonneted bat.

The reason the biodiversity hotspot concept even exists is because biodiversity isn't evenly distributed around the world. Life on Earth is patchy and, while lots of organisms do thrive in the most challenging, inhospitable of places, those locations are not suitable for most. The United Nations' 'A–Z of Biodiversity' details how biodiversity hotspots represent only 2.3

per cent of the Earth's land surface but – brace yourselves – hold approximately 50 per cent of all endemic plant species, 42 per cent of endemic terrestrial vertebrates, 55 per cent of primates, 22 per cent of carnivores and about 80 per cent of all threatened amphibians. These places are vibrant, holding such an immense abundance of life, but – ironically – because of this they are more threatened with extinction than anywhere else and, collectively, have already shrunk by a staggering 86 per cent from their original habitat size.

Madagascar, the world's second largest island nation, is one such hotspot. Eighty per cent of its flora and fauna is endemic, making it one of the world's most unique biological bubbles. Its environment is unparalleled. Located just 250 miles off the coast of Mozambique in south-east Africa, it is geographically isolated and has been for millions of years. The island was formed due to two major tectonic rifting events. Approximately 160 million years ago, a land mass broke off from the supercontinent, Gondwana, and rifted 1,000 kilometres southward, leaving behind what we now call Africa. The second separation event followed 88 million years ago when that land mass further divided, forming India, the Seychelles and Madagascar. India and the Seychelles gravitated slowly northward, but Madagascar stayed relatively close to the African continent. As you'll know from reading about the kakapo previously, it's the geographical isolation of islands that gives rise to the evolution of endemism. Madagascar is 592,000 square kilometres in size – a little bit larger than France – with forest, savannah, river, wetland, mangrove and reef habitats.

Ornithologists travel there to check off rare roller and fly-catcher birds, botanists come for the endangered baobab trees and

orchids, and herpetologists gravitate towards the chameleons or
the Madagascan tree boas. All fascinating species in their own right,
but I'd hazard a guess that there is one group of endemic animals
that everyone travelling to Madagascar has on their bucket list.
Whether you have an interest in natural history or you're just into
animated movies, you'd have to make a trip to the forests to catch a
glimpse of the lemurs.

I have a lot of love for these special primates. I spent my teenage
years at the Wildheart Animal Sanctuary in the UK, working
alongside various species; I helped hand-rear a red-ruff lemur
called Andro, and dedicated my university dissertation to the
study of social hierarchies within the ring-tailed lemur troop.
I grew very close to them all, although I suppose that's to be
expected when you spend over 250 hours meticulously watching
and recording their intricate behaviours. They're full of character
and energy, with strong social bonds to one another that make
them so much fun to watch. There are currently 111 species, with
new ones still being discovered, but their evolutionary history is
a bit of a puzzle. Madagascar was isolated long before the rise of
placental mammals, so their ancestors must have colonised the
country after it split from Africa. Looking at the DNA they share
with their closest relatives on the mainland, the bush babies and
lorises, suggests that the lemur lineage split off from a common
ancestor approximately 60–65 million years ago. It's thought
that the first 'lemurs' would have floated on rafts of vegetation
across the Mozambique Channel to Madagascar before rapidly
diversifying on the island. But, until recently, fossil specimens
found in Kenya and Egypt contradicted this by indicating that
lemurs evolved much later, only twenty million years ago. There

have been a number of hypotheses and theories to suggest what might have happened, but sometimes it's just the case that the right bones haven't been dug up yet! It wasn't until palaeontologists at the University of Oxford found a fossil that dated back 35 million years that scientists agreed it was likely that lemurs colonised much earlier.

Lemurs come in all sizes, from the smallest 30g Madame Berthe's mouse lemur to the largest 9kg indri. They share some characteristics with mainland primates but are easily distinguished by their unique adaptations. As with any social animal, communication is important, and lemurs particularly utilise scent. They have glands on their wrists, chests and genitals that secrete smelly chemical compounds that they rub onto objects in the environment, or sometimes themselves. This helps establish dominance within their groups, mark territorial boundaries between troops and even communicate readiness during the breeding season. Interestingly, new research has found that the chemicals are slightly different in each gland and change throughout the seasons. During breeding, the scent is supposedly more fruity and floral and the behaviour is referred to as 'stink-flirting'. Their sensitive snouts are elongated, they have wet noses and forward-leaning incisors on their lower jaw, known as a toothcomb, that they use for grooming; allogrooming (grooming each other) is essential in lemur societies as it helps to maintain relationships within a troop that can contain (depending on the species) up to thirty individuals. Lemurs also have better night vision than most other primates (indicating their ancestor might have been nocturnal). Another cool fact that distinguishes them from most other primates is that the females are in charge.

Based on the IUCN update in 2020, 98 per cent of lemurs are endangered and 31 per cent within that are critical. These statistics are frightening regardless, but even more so when you consider that the animals are confined to one isolated island. Some reports say that within twenty-five years, if things continue the way they are, they could all disappear.

Black-and-white ruffed lemurs are one of those critically endangered species. They've declined by 80 per cent in the last twenty-seven years. I'm twenty-seven years old as I write this, so that's happened within my lifetime! It really hits home. I've never been to Madagascar but I was lucky to work in the UK with two females called Liberty and Lalaina. As soon as I entered their enclosure, they immediately came over to sit on my shoulders, hoping that I might have a few blueberries tucked away in my pockets. Their long fluffy black tails would drape down my back as they balanced themselves effortlessly. They always made me smile with their laid-back attitudes and inquisitive faces.

Overall though, this chapter isn't about any one particular species. It's about the collective threats they all face and the people doing what they can to find a solution.

Dr Erik Patel is the research and conservation director for the Lemur Conservation Foundation in south-west Florida. It was founded in 1996 by Penelope Bodry-Sanders and their overarching focus remains the same: to protect lemurs and their habitats. They have a 130-acre captive breeding centre in the USA that is currently home to all kinds of these endangered and critically endangered primates, from the famous ring-tails to the charismatic red-ruffs and even the lesser-known collared brown lemurs. The centre currently has fifty resident individuals and was created as a safety net for wild populations, to preserve their genetics and safeguard their future. Having these animals in captivity also gives valuable new insights into their secretive lives that can help guide conservation decisions back in Madagascar. As ambassadors for their wild counterparts, they have a role as educators, inspiring people to become more aware and potentially engage the next generation of budding primatologists.

Erik began his career working with well-known American primatologist Dr Patricia Wright at her research centre in Ranomafana National Park when it was just a couple of huts in the forest. Patricia specialises in the social and family dynamics of lemurs and even rediscovered a species thought to be extinct: the greater bamboo lemur, one of the rarest primates on the planet. Due to her dedication and the contribution of other scientists, the huts are now long gone and in their place is a $5 million research facility. Erik's main species of focus is a lemur called the silky sifaka. It's an arboreal species, spending most of its time high up in the treetops, with fluffy bright-white fur and a black face – most of the time. It's one of the largest-bodied lemurs and, for some unknown reason, they lose their facial pigment with age. As they grow older, the black disappears and their skin turns pink. And yes, you guessed it, they're critically endangered too, with only 2,000 remaining individuals.

'Patricia was one of the people who initially suggested that I take a look at the silky sifaka in the far north of Madagascar in Marojejy National Park,' Erik explains. 'The lemurs live in the steep mountains at high elevations but the park had been closed to research for a long time. Patricia got permission to visit and was able to put a radio collar on a female. She wanted me to follow up on that. So,

I received some grant money from Cornell University where I was studying, and that was it. To help me I brought along two very smart research assistants, and we had a horrible time. We spent a lot of money and for two months couldn't find any of these lemurs. It got to the point where we almost left. Tensions were rising and we were running out of food, but as the end of the trip was near, I thought it would help to hire some local people who really knew the area… And we finally found them. Lemurs habituate more quickly than other primates, so the group got used to us quite quickly. I realised how rare and unique these animals are, and so I ended up staying.'

Marojejy National Park, one of 4,000 national parks across the globe, is a 214-square-mile pocket of wilderness. Joining the Great Barrier Reef, the Taj Mahal and the Pyramids of Giza, Marojejy National Park became a UNESCO world heritage site in 2007 due to its 'rugged and untamed' jungle. 'We're very lucky, the national parks in the north-east are some of the earliest established national parks,' Erik says. 'And that makes a big difference. Marojejy was first recognised in 1948 for its biodiversity by a French botanist, Jean-Henri Humbert, who wrote a book called *A Marvel of Nature*. He was one of the most influential scientists in Madagascar during that time and he set up the first protected area network. He made it a very strict nature reserve. You could say it was heavy-handed in a lot of ways but nevertheless, because it was established so early we're experiencing far less disturbance than many of the more newly established parks in Madagascar.'

The leading cause of lemur suffering is habitat destruction. Madagascar is a spectacular biodiversity hotspot, but that biodiversity is being increasingly squeezed and restricted into small patches of fragmented forest; 80 per cent of the nation's natural habitats have already been removed, and an estimated 200,000 hectares are thought to be cut down every year for deforestation. 'Slash and burn agriculture for rice – or "swidden agriculture", as it is also referred to – is the primary threat leading to deforestation in lemur habitats,' Erik explains. 'It's important to remember that most of the people engaged in this are desperately poor and have very few other options.' Madagascar is one of the world's financially poorest countries. The World Bank estimated in 2019 that 75 per cent of its human population of 29 million live on less than $2 a day, which is far below the international poverty line. Half of Malagasy children suffer from malnutrition at some stage in their lives and at this poverty rate, half of all children between the ages of five and seventeen are forced into harmful labour industries to survive. 'Most people don't inherit flat land that's well irrigated, so they're forced to try and farm these steep hillsides,' he continues. 'If you burn the rainforest, the ash will come down and will temporarily fertilise the soil for a few seasons, but very quickly if you re-farm it, the land will become completely dead. And that's what's happened all around the central highlands near the capital. The rivers there have dried up and there's just nothing there any more. People can't live there and they say it looks like the surface of Mars or the moon,' Erik tells me, with a slightly more sombre tone than before.

'Another reason why Marojejy is more protected is because the standard of living is slightly higher in the north-east thanks to vanilla. Most of the world's vanilla comes from this region of Madagascar, so there is less pressure to slash and burn, but the newest problem we have inside the park is vanilla plantations.

It's not like palm oil where you have to cut down all the forest to a clearance, as vanilla can grow in the shade. But it's causing corruption, as the people farming it are bribing rangers. We know we need to act on it but we aren't sure yet what to do.

'Selective logging continues to be a major source of disturbance too,' he continues. 'In the past, we had rosewood logging, which was a total disaster. Madagascar had some of the best rosewood in the world and the trouble was all of it was found only inside protected areas. The demand in China was unbelievable; they found one bed frame made out of Malagasy rosewood selling for $1 million. That's how expensive it was! So we were dealing with that for a long time, between 2009 and 2013. We made four or five big international films about it, some of which won awards, and that helped. But demand also slowed as the numbers of large rosewoods worth logging has dropped massively, sadly.'

Now, this is where it gets morally complicated – and, if I'm honest, a little bit uncomfortable. I live in the western world, where we, as individuals, consume more resources than the planet has to offer. At the rate it's going, by 2050 we will need three Earths to satisfy our demand on resources. We expect next-day deliveries, eat food that has been shipped around the world, wear fast fashion and have multiple cars parked on our driveways. Our families might be generally smaller than in developing nations but, through consumption, our impact is far greater. I don't plan on having any children but regardless, my carbon footprint (although I do my best to limit it) is probably double that of the average Malagasy family. I felt that this was important to flag as in this next section, Erik discusses the link between deforestation and communities, as well as family planning.

Overpopulation is often blamed for our environmental struggles. And while it is true that with more people comes a greater pressure on our planet's natural resources, we must always remember to factor in the disproportionate rate of consumption and unequal human rights. 'The relationship between poverty and unsustainable swidden agriculture is complicated,' he begins. 'On one level, there is a relationship between extreme poverty and deforestation, but if you talk to the people that really study this, you will consistently find that it's the population size of the villages, but not the socioeconomic status per se, that is associated with deforestation rates.' Twenty per cent of the world's population lives inside a biodiversity hotspot, and population growth within those areas is 40 per cent higher than in other areas due to their remote nature and lack of healthcare and education services. Having noticed this, some conservation organisations, notably Blue Ventures, who work to protect Madagascar's oceans, are trying to do something to help. They've partnered with MSI Reproductive Choices (formerly Marie Stopes International), an organisation championing every woman's right to reproductive choice, and are supplying contraception to rural villages. By providing women with the option to choose as and when they want to have a baby, as well as providing educational and employment opportunities, you are supporting gender equality, the economy and, by default, the environment.

My final question for Erik: what does the future look like for lemurs?

'The Lemur Action Plan is a national strategy that many of us at the IUCN Primate Specialist group worked on in 2016. We came up with a strategy that had three main objectives in order to save lemurs in the wild. The first is ecotourism. It generates a lot of money for local people living around protected areas and, fundamentally, if we can valorise the forests, we can find ways for local people to earn money by protecting lemurs. That's key. It's a safe place to visit, it's a very friendly culture and the wildlife is very special to see.

'The second part of the plan is to build and maintain long-term research centres. Not only will these help us understand what's going on in specific areas but they also help generate more income and awareness. They're great at involving and teaching lots of Malagasy and foreign students too.

'The third and final goal is to support community managed forestry and local guide associations. There are a number of forests in Madagascar that have been given to local communities to manage. They call them community-managed forests. Some of them work really well and others not so much. We're learning that outside training and support is wanted and needed, so we are trying to provide that as well as supporting guide associations. For example, Marojejy has a very strong guide association with ten or twelve local individuals who live near the park entrance. They're the main guides for visiting researchers and tourists so they're in the forest all the time, you know, live there. They know what's happening in the forest. They can find the lemurs before I can and should be in leadership roles!

'If we were to lose lemurs, it would be a tremendous loss for the world because you cannot recreate these things,' he goes on.

While there's still lemurs in the trees of Madagascar, there's still a lot worth fighting for. Maybe soon I can make my dream a reality and help with stage one of the action plan…

Erik, I'm coming to visit!

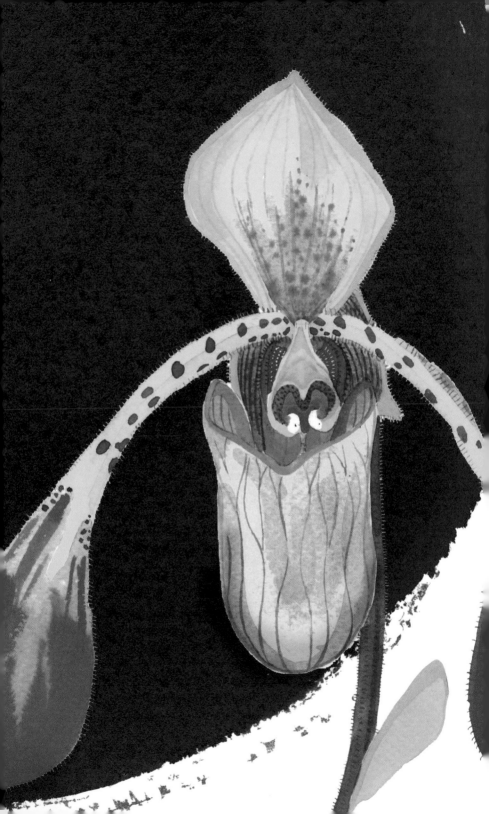

Lady's Slipper Orchid

In the year 2021, much of the world found itself in a lockdown. The coronavirus pandemic rapidly travelled from country to country and we were told by scientists and governments to 'stay home' to 'save lives'. We spent what felt like for ever in our houses, making the most of the one hour of exercise we were allowed outside for each day. In the UK and around the world, some of the most popular hobbies were baking, reading, Zoom quizzes, gardening, home workouts, painting, mindfulness, TikTok, vlogging, running and hairdressing. A few people got creative and started a trend, like building miniature benches for squirrels, creating pancake art or learning the art of calligraphy. Another fad that gripped the nation was: house plants. We became obsessed. But what impact does that have on our environment?

I went around my flat and counted a total of fifteen plants: a fern, two peace lilies, two orchids, a few cacti and succulents. If I am honest, I'm not a brilliant botanist, and I certainly don't have the greenest of fingers, but I have always enjoyed decorating my home with beautiful plants, bringing the outside inside. During the lockdowns, purchasing and taking care of plants became hugely popular, but it's been a growing trend for the last twenty years. And there is lots of science that explains why. Indoor plants keep you happier and healthier as they can reduce fatigue, lower stress and improve focus and productivity, which can subsequently boost recovery from illness. So it's understandable that the demand exploded exponentially in lockdown, as we searched for ways to ease our stress during the pandemic. Yet sudden growth in demand often leads to unforeseen negative consequences. Fuelled by social media sites like YouTube, Instagram and TikTok, 'plant collectors' or 'plant hunters' have sprung up around the globe, supplying rare and endemic plants straight from the forest floor to your doorstep.

It's important to note that, of course, not all plants come from the wild. The sale of ornamental plants can be divided into two main categories: 1) the mass-market trade of potted species that tend to be easy-to-grow hybrids and 2) plants supplied by specialist growers and sellers. The latter typically have large collections, ready to ship when demand surges. Most common house plants will have been grown from seeds or produced through tissue culture propagation close to home – wherever that may be for you. However, the ever-growing drive for ownership of unique and rare species is resulting in the extinction of wild plants; so much so that people are now referring to this time as a 'plantdemic'. The illegal plant trade has been around for a long time but it's never discussed to the same detail as animal poaching, despite having similar impacts, causing ecosystem imbalance and collapse. For example, succulents have massively grown in popularity as they are relatively low-maintenance to look after and give a rustic feel to your home decor. They're recommended as the plant you'd struggle to kill as they don't need watering as frequently as others. The dudleya, commonly known as 'liveforevers', is a species of rare, small rosette succulent endemic to southern California and is being poached in its hundreds of thousands; this is making it incredibly rare and having a drastic impact on the local environment. Some of the plants that have been uprooted are over 100 years old! This species is one that lives in dry habitats on top of rocks and cliffs where many other plants are unable to grow, and helps prevent erosion. These succulents are highly sought after and can be sold for over $50 in the USA and other countries. State and federal wildlife agents estimate that the quantity of poached dudleya overall has contributed tens of millions of dollars to the illegal poaching trade. It is very rare to prosecute plant collectors, as the areas they operate in are vast and governing bodies have a lack of funding that prohibits them from monitoring the situation effectively. But unusually, in 2019 there was a successful prosecution. Three men were found with over 3,700 succulents after they had travelled the length of the Californian coast – they were sentenced to ten years in prison.

On average, a person spends 144 minutes scrolling through their apps each day. My phone and profiles are a huge part of what I do as a science communicator, so I often see the best of what social media has to offer. But it can be a dark place too, when the algorithms promote animal exploitation, exotic pets, violence, bullying, poaching and so much more. These internet outlets mask, and consistently promote, the black markets while consumers remain none the wiser. On Instagram, the hashtag #houseplants has 9.2 million followers, and #planttiktok has over 5.3 billion views. Almost inconceivable, and that represents just a fraction of the people who seek out or happen upon video content of house plants. A lot will simply be about plant appreciation or the top tips for looking after them, but you'd be shocked if you dug a little deeper. It's a minefield if you haven't done enough research or don't know what you're really looking at. Influencers promoting their favourite plant groups are (in some cases perhaps unknowingly) driving the demand and giving plant poachers their target species to obtain from the wild. Some of the most sought-after are aroids, carnivorous plants, orchids, cacti, hoyas and many more. In comparison to forms of poaching involving dangerous animals, plant poaching has arguably fewer risks, and requires less training. It can be very lucrative, too, as long as you don't get caught. Rare and endemic species are now paying the price for our greed as plants once present in the wild are being plucked from the ground and, in some cases, plucked into local extinction.

Pungky Nanda Pratama is a conservationist and environmental educator from Indonesia. He has a passion for all plants, but is especially dedicated to saving orchids. 'Orchids are one of the most fascinating plants on Earth and so smart too, sometimes I don't know how they do it! They don't have eyes and yet they are able to visually mimic pollinators so that they can spread their pollen. Some orchids even mimic the scents of pollinators to draw them in! It's crazy! I love all wildlife but plants give me oxygen every day and orchids just make me happy.' Pungky beams as he describes his love of flora. Globally, there are between 25,000 and 30,000 described orchid species, with many still believed to be undiscovered. This represents approximately 10 per cent of all flowering plant species and they're widely renowned as the most diverse group too. And DNA analysis has previously indicated that they are also one of the more ancient groups, with evidence suggesting some species have been present for over ninety million years! They can be located on every continent with the exception of Antarctica, although many are native to tropical regions, with the number of species increasing with proximity to the equator. However, despite their wide range of success in evolutionary history, 1,000 of the described orchid species are currently listed by the IUCN as threatened with extinction today, and many of these exist in Sumatra, Indonesia, which is internationally regarded as an orchid hotspot.

As a general rule, you can identify an orchid by their floral arrangement, which typically consists of six parts: three green sepals (aka modified leaves that surround the developing flower inside) and three petals. There are orchid species that are subterranean, meaning that they grow and flower underground or at the soil surface, and some are lithophytes that have the ability to grow on rocks, but the majority, approximately 70 per cent of all species, are epiphytes that grow on a host plant species. In this way, they are similar to a parasite, except unlike parasites they do not derive nutrients from their host and instead absorb water and minerals from the air, rainfall, organic matter or from symbiotic relationships with fungi. With each species being highly specialised to the local environment in which they evolved, there is great concern that the endangered orchid species may be lost if their natural ranges aren't protected. So, that's where Pungky steps in...

Pungky's work is based in Kerinci Seblat National Park, which was also one of the last known refuges of the Sumatran tiger. It's a huge area, covering 5,400 square miles, that stretches from the centre to the south of the island, and is the second largest of its kind in the whole of South East Asia. This forest is under immense pressure from deforestation for palm oil, rubber, acacia and other plantation crops. In fact, a study by the University of Maryland using satellite data revealed an alarming decline in tree cover between August and December 2020, most likely due to illegal clearing for smallholder agriculture. Of course, this deforestation has a huge impact on the plant diversity under the forest canopy and it's a subject that is widely spoken about. I wanted to know what, from Pungky's perspective working on the ground in this region, he felt was the biggest threat to orchids and other plant groups. Was it deforestation or poaching? He replied, 'It's probably fifty-fifty. The plants are being taken now by poachers from the wild before they even become threatened by deforestation. It's a very stressful situation – animals can at least run but plants cannot. We are trying to save species from unprotected areas, which are more at risk, but the hunters are much faster than we are as there is such a strong demand for orchids and other rare plants across Europe and in the USA. Once a plant is collected here in Indonesia, the hunter will sell it to a buyer for about 1,000 rupiah, which is 5p. It might then be flown through one of the big cities, like the capital Jakarta, and would then sell at its destination for 50,000 rupiah (approximately £3) depending on the species. It is driven through the black markets by the mafia.' This might not seem like a lot, but in Indonesia every single penny goes a long way – especially when you can collect a lot of plants on one trip. Once in the hands of the sellers abroad, the price sky-rockets.

The most expensive recorded house plant ever sold was an incredibly rare white variegated *Rhaphidophora tetrasperma*, sold in June 2021 to a buyer in New Zealand for AU$25,100 (around £14,000) on an auction site. The plant was on 1,600 people's watchlists and had 248 bids. It sold a long way from home; the species naturally grows in southern Thailand and Malaysia. I have no clue where this individual plant originated but it just goes to show the money that can be made.

The most common types of ornamental orchid that can be purchased are moth orchids, which have a long flowering period and grow in wide colour varieties, but others including oncidium orchids, vanda orchids, dendrobium orchids and paphiopedilum orchids are widely available also. Despite being notoriously hard to look after, requiring precise microclimates that replicate the conditions of their tropical homes, they seem to be the pinnacle of any household plant collection. 'People can easily find free information about how to look after all these different species, and most can afford equipment like humidifiers or misters to tend to them. This adds to the demand,' Pungky explains. 'Currently there is no balance or sustainable approach to harvesting so it's about educating local communities and raising awareness to save these plants. One species, the *Paphiopedilum bungebelangi*, was found for the first time in 2018 and we noticed after only one month it was up for sale online. It was driven to extinction by poaching – we believe – somewhere between three to six months after it was first described.' Imagine being the first person to see a 'new-to-science' orchid, and for your incredible discovery to have led to almost immediate extinction driven by the desire of people in western countries to own it. I'd be devastated. In fact, when I heard this story I *was* devastated. All orchids have very long life cycles, so it is possible that one or two individuals could reappear in the wilds of Sumatra somewhere, but scientists believe that is a very small chance. I just hope that, if it does happen, it's kept as one of the nation's best-kept secrets. A necessary shame.

Pungky's favourite orchid, the *Paphiopedilum lunatum*, is a species belonging to the lady slipper orchid genus. It is an exquisite flower, with moss-green petals that have dusty pink tips and mottled leaves, that grows on the forest floor. At the bottom of the flower head is a pronounced labellum, a modified petal, that is common among orchid and canna species; its purpose is to provide a landing platform and to attract pollinating insects. They massively vary between species but in lady slipper species, the labellum is characteristically shaped like a pouch. When it comes to the legality of smuggling, Pungky tells me, 'All orchids of the *Paphiopedilum* genus are listed in Appendix I in CITES, so the trade is forbidden internationally, yet the black market can spread out everywhere. The biggest collectors of slipper orchids are mostly from outside Indonesia. There is a lot of demand in European countries, like the UK, and in the United States. Plant poachers harvest the wild orchids and send them mainly through Thailand and, in some cases, Singapore, to reach other parts of the world. These routes are a gate for illegal trade which makes it easy for the hunters to transport the plants around the world, so we are all very worried.' Despite the protection given by CITES towards these orchids, in 2015 it was noted that 97 per cent of listed species were recorded as threatened largely due to deliberate poaching. Noticing this devastating trend, in 2017 Pungky established the Flora Rescue Project in collaboration with the Natural Resources Conservation Agency of South Sumatra, with the aim of transplanting endangered species from damaged land or unprotected areas across southern Sumatra. He collects them, propagates them in a greenhouse and finally releases them back into the wild within Isau Isau Wildlife Reserve, in higher numbers than he found them, safeguarding these rare species against localised extinctions.

To date, Pungky has rescued over forty different species of plants, including some of the rarest orchids endemic to the region. 'I can spend hours out in the plantations and forests looking for orchids. Some are easier than others to save depending on where they grow. Species that grow at the tops of trees or on the side of a cliff can be challenging, but it's worth it. I can remember in just one day, I walked for ten hours and found twenty-three species of orchids that I brought back to the greenhouse,' he recalls. 'We have a new greenhouse built in 2021, which is 150 square metres, and that could potentially fit up to 10,000 plants inside. Our first greenhouse was only 32 square metres and it's overloaded right now, so I am very grateful for the funding for the new building provided by a local company and the Natural Resources Conservation Agency of South Sumatra. We will start flora expeditions soon into the most unprotected areas and bring back the species into the new greenhouse, where they can be checked over and habituated for one year before they are propagated with tissue cultures. Our mission currently is to save as many species as possible and then next year we will be focused on propagation.'

This is a process that's widespread in the horticultural world, and you may well have propagated yourself for a school project. It simply means to take a plant cutting, or tissue culture, from a parent plant to grow new individual plants. While this is a pilot project, relatively small-scale and new, Pungky has returned over 200 plant specimens successfully to safe zones within the forest.

His success so far has led to more funding and opportunities to grow the project further.

Another of his initiatives is the Sumatra Camera Trap Project, which involves setting wildlife camera traps in areas that might confirm the presence of endangered mammals within the national parks. The hope is to capture on record the likes of flagship animals, such as the Sumatran tiger, sun bear or clouded leopard. The cameras are set in areas where there is evidence of activity (footprints, poo or scratch marks) and then left for fifteen days before being collected to see what, or who, has strolled by. With this evidence comes more data, more awareness and more chance of safeguarding the forest for those wonderful creatures as well as the lesser-known and lesser-protected flora and fauna. Pungky has managed to capture a clouded leopard but is still holding out hope for a Sumatran tiger!

The whole concept of plant poaching for ornamental collections is something we all have a hand in. It's not that we shouldn't be buying and displaying plants in our homes but that we need greater education on the origin of these species, and to understand the impacts our purchasing can have, so that we can make informed choices as consumers. I mentioned earlier that I have a number of plants in my flat, and when interviewing Pungky they were on display behind me. I showed them to him, curious to find out more, and was devastated to hear that one of the species I own, a rubber plant, originated from Sumatra. The species is common as a house plant and the individual I own certainly wasn't picked from the wild, as they are easily propagated locally, but nonetheless I felt very guilty. Going forward, I'll be much more critical about which species I am buying and who I am buying them from.

As consumers we have a lot of 'power in our pounds' and should be spending wisely to reduce the demand of all animal and plant products that cause detriment to our fragile ecosystems. Individual action is critical. Simply put, if the demand for rarities stops then so does the trade. But there are some things you can do to be aware of when identifying which plants have been wild-collected. Firstly, look out for buzzwords, such as: 'native variety', 'new species' and, more directly stated, 'wild-caught' or 'wild orchid.' Another method is to check or request an image of the plant before purchasing; you may be able to identify damage or broken roots caused when it was taken from the wild. Finally, research the scientific name of the species you're buying. If it's newly described then it may be possible to locate its origin. For example, after artificial propagation it can take some orchids up to twenty-two months to grow to the point where they meet with CITES regulations for sale. If it's a new species and is under that time, it could be that the plant was wild-harvested. For as long as we love plants, I am sure we will share our homes with them, and yet very few everyday consumers will be aware of this issue. This is why education is key and legal labelling should be more honest and obvious.

Pungky occasionally works undercover with some of the plant hunters, and he mentioned that many individuals involved will purposefully drive rare species closer to the brink of extinction in order to raise the price of their collections. People will pay more if an orchid is one of only a handful of remaining plants. Studies show that at least 347 species of orchid found in South East Asia can be found on the black market, including 106 of the tropical slipper orchids. It's truly a dire situation when a species is worth more extinct than alive in the wild. But there is a group of companies that could change everything for the species caught up in wildlife trades around the globe, and help in the fight against anthropogenic-induced extinctions. I am of course referring to the social media outlets that provide platforms for illegal traders and facilitate communications pathways from them directly to millions of unwitting customers worldwide.

Social media platforms are quickly overtaking the traditional e-commerce sites, like eBay, when it comes to black-market products, regardless of their prohibiting terms and conditions. It is difficult to statistically track how this has changed over recent years, but the shift is pretty clear as it's within plain sight on our news feeds and 'for you' pages. Research is currently taking place at the Royal Botanic Gardens in Kew, UK, to develop an algorithm that scans internet sites for more information on the sale of endangered plants. This will hopefully go a long way towards safeguarding future populations, but we also need social media companies to take more responsibility for what's shared on their platforms. They should, after all, be held accountable. This not a matter of free speech or infringing on privacy, but a matter of halting illegal markets, educating their users, protecting species and ultimately protecting ourselves. In March of 2018, the Coalition to End Wildlife Trafficking Online was formed by the World Wildlife Fund (WWF), TRAFFIC and the International Fund for Animal Welfare (IFAW), with the aim of reducing sales of animals and their parts. The number of companies signed up to the coalition doubled in 2021 from twenty-one to forty-seven, and includes organisations like Google, Facebook, Instagram and, most recently, TikTok, who promote the hashtag #offlineandinthewild. To date, collectively these tech institutions have reported blocking over 11.6 million transactions involving endangered species. Credit where credit is due – this is great, really great, and certainly moving in the right direction. But...

These reports are about animal exploitation. I mean, the coalition does say 'wildlife' in the name, but why is there no alternative for flora? Why are they always forgotten and bypassed. It's devastating that these rare and endemic floral species aren't afforded the same attention and protection as fauna. Plants get massively overlooked, and the impact of their declines will be inexplicably underestimated. The research from Kew Gardens can't come soon enough to encourage (and politely, peacefully demand) that social media platforms take plant poaching more seriously than they have done before. It's thanks to the incredible work of Pungky and his team at the Flora Rescue Project that I have been made aware. I'll be sharing his story as widely as possible, and I hope you will too.

And next time I buy a house plant – and I will – I'll be more careful about where and what I am buying.

African Wild Dogs

African wild dogs are a species like no other. Often overlooked, these apex predators demonstrate some of the most remarkably complex social behaviours expressed anywhere within the animal kingdom. They are intelligent, vocally expressive, and beautiful beyond compare. With elegant long legs, Mickey Mouse ears and intense hazel eyes, each individual wild dog has its own unique coat, made up of striking brown, beige, black and white markings. The patterns are as exclusive and varied as our fingerprints. When people come to Africa for the first time, they expect to see a dramatic blood-orange sunset draped across a flat savannah horizon highlighting silhouettes of distant grazing elephants and gazelles. The hope of seeing lions, leopards or cheetahs on the hunt is always top of the bucket list too. I totally understand why – these species are the celebrities of the bush. But, it's often what you don't expect that has the most impact and meaning... and for many people, that's an encounter with a pack of wild dogs.

The species has many different colloquial names – African wild dogs, painted dogs, hunting dogs – but genetically speaking they are not closely related to dogs at all, other than the fact that both species belong to the vast Canidae family. They were first described scientifically in 1820 by Dutch zoologist Coenraad Jacob Temminck, when he assigned them the Latin name Hyaena picta in reference to their lanky appearance; he actually believed that they belonged to the hyena family, but that wasn't the right fit for them either. Wild dogs are in fact the largest canids in Africa. Domestic dogs, jackals, coyotes and wolves belong to the Canis genus, whereas wild dogs split from that lineage about 3.9 million years ago and are the only living members of the Lycaon genus. They are out on an evolutionary branch of their own!

I was volunteering in Namibia when I was a teenager, at a place called AfriCat located just a couple of hours north of the country's capital, Windhoek. There was a small pack consisting of five wild dogs (four females and one male) that roamed the reserve, but, sadly, before I arrived, they had to be taken into a semi-captive enclosure for emergency veterinary care and rehabilitation. Wild dogs are expert hunters with an 80 per cent success rate. Lions, by contrast, only make a kill about 25 per cent of the time, and leopards around 38 per cent, all depending on conditions. As individuals I wouldn't say they were particularly impressive hunters, but working as a pack they are formidable. (Although, it might surprise you to learn there is a group of predators that leave wild dogs in the dust when it comes to predatory efficiency... Believe it or not, those predators are dragonflies, which are successful a staggering 95 per cent of the time! Best not tell the dogs that though.) One of the first things I did at the reserve was visit the wild dog pack. They were being supplemented with food while in the enclosure and I was invited to watch them tuck into their meal – an impala if I remember correctly. It was a very sad situation because the male, named Rex, had been recently kicked by an adult giraffe, presumably while the pack were trying to hunt its newborn calf. A giraffe's kick can be deadly, yielding 2,000 psi (pounds of force per square inch), and it had shattered the bones in Rex's leg. He was lucky to survive, but the leg had to be amputated. For any solitary predator, this would be a death sentence because they simply couldn't hunt to survive, but, luckily for three-legged Rex, he had the support of the group, who always ensured that he never went hungry. When he was well enough, they were re-released into the reserve, where the pack supported him – probably in more ways than we know – for the rest of his life. It was really touching to see first-hand how strong their relationships were despite great trauma and individual cost.

Pack size averages between seven and fifteen individuals, but can reach up to forty members in regions where the environment allows. That might seem like a lot but, prior to their decline, numbers of over 100 wild dogs had once been recorded within the same pack! Now that would be remarkable to have seen but it's actually quite a striking example of shifting baseline syndrome (how we accept the current damaged environmental standards as normal, believing that they've always been that way). Within their packs, they have a complex social hierarchy where the dominant male and female pair have a lifelong bond, typically producing all of the offspring. Litters range from four to twelve pups, and it's a team effort to raise them all. The subordinate adults will help feed the youngsters by regurgitating partially digested meat and will always help protect them from any potential dangers.

It's a very strong family unit that will always provide for one another in their old age or when injured, like poor Rex. An amazing piece of research was released in 2017 that revealed new insights into pack dynamics. If a member of the pack wishes to leave a resting site and move on to hunt, for example, it will sneeze. And if the notion is reciprocated by more individuals, then they will also sneeze – essentially voting on what they'd like to do next. If the original sneeze comes from one of the dominant wild dogs then the pack is more likely to move off, although if ten or more subordinates engage in the behaviour then the dominants will follow suit. It's a specific vocalisation that they use in decision-making as a group. As a species, they have an outstanding vocal repertoire of yelps, whines, barks, groans and squeals that they use to communicate. Decoding the sneeze is just the tip of a very big iceberg; there's still a lot to be transcribed! Their beautiful appearance is enough to make you fall in love with them, but when you also see their interactions and hear their vocalisations, you can't help but be mesmerised. The fact that we don't understand the significance of their social intelligence – and perhaps never will – makes them that much more alluring.

Sociality is a spectrum, from the solitary species that only intentionally come together out of the necessity to breed (like polar bears, blue whales or platypuses) to the eusocial organisms, living life at the highest level of sociality. These species live in cooperative colonies of overlapping generations, where there is an obvious division of labour – non-breeding individuals will work to support the reproductive success and offspring of one singular queen. It's mainly observed in social insect species, like within some bee or termite societies, although the naked mole rat has evolved the same structure, too, the only mammal to have done so. Lots of species have evolved to reap the many benefits of social living – predatory defence, mating opportunities, cooperative foraging efforts, etc. But within the Carnivora order, roughly 85 per cent are considered solitary and only 15 per cent social.

In the case of the wild dogs, it's always been historically accepted that this life strategy evolved due to the immense benefits gained from cooperative hunting. Attacking in groups means they can target bigger prey species, chase over shorter distances and increase their chances of success – if they're lucky, they might even catch more than one. One study looking into the diet of wild dogs found that 90 per cent of the prey was composed of wildebeest, impala and warthog. Smaller packs with fewer than ten adults would typically target the smaller prey species, whereas the larger packs were found to go for wildebeests that weigh a colossal 250 kilograms! This argument has been disputed by a few, but there is still a lot of evidence to support it and I think it makes sense. I am sure there are other important factors that encouraged the evolution of their social society, but hunting has got to play a role.

The species has officially been listed as endangered by the IUCN since 1990, and now there are only 700 packs remaining in the wild across sub-Saharan Africa. The IUCN makes these official counts based on the number of mature, sexually reproductive adults. But in the case of the wild dog, only two individuals per pack will make the cut. The species were once found living across thirty-nine countries on the continent but, today, can only be found in thirteen. The loss of any apex predator has catastrophic impacts for the ecology of a habitat.

They occupy the highest position on the food web, so, when they disappear, there is always a risk of a top-down trophic cascade. With the removal of predators, prey species become unregulated and the whole system gets put under unprecedented pressure. The numbers of prey can boom and their behaviour will change as a result. For example, wolves and bears being absent from the UK has resulted in way too many deer, which has had devastating impacts on the environment; without the threat of predation, the deer stay in one place, feasting on all the vegetation and preventing new growth in woodlands. The concept of the 'ecology of fear' is what keeps prey on the move and allows for regeneration. Predators don't get enough credit for the way they shape the entire ecosystem but they are so fundamental to its overall health and function.

While wild dogs have been facing some serious decline in recent years, there are a lot of people getting stuck in trying to pull them back from the brink. Professor Rosie Woodroffe is renowned for her fascinating research specialising in animal behaviour, epidemiology and human/wildlife coexistence. I had been following her on Twitter for some time even before the concept of this book was drafted, intrigued by her refreshing and consistent approach to science communication. Plus, she fills my news feed with adorable photos of wild dogs that would be enough to brighten anyone's day! I asked how she got into biology, and she responded, 'I would spend a lot of time hiking up and down mountains with one of my closest friends, Tim Scoones, and we would be yakking to each other about how we were going to save the world when we were older. There was no question that conservation was what we needed to do. He got into film-making (and became very successful) and I got into the science of animal behaviour. I ended up doing my PhD studying badgers in the UK and then started a project studying the sociality of banded mongoose in Uganda.'

Rosie confessed that despite never having actually seen one, she had always wanted to work with wild dogs. It wasn't until her former supervisor reached out with an opportunity that she could delve in. 'He called me up out of the blue and said that four years prior he had agreed to write a conservation action plan for wild dogs but never got around to it. The donor who supplied the funding was asking where it was so he gave me his notes and asked whether I would spend six weeks writing it up. I had no clue what I was doing or what standard it needed to be completed at, so it took me a year and a half to do it!' she says with a laugh. 'I'd made recommendations that we desperately needed to understand how or if people and wild dogs could live together peacefully. Wild dogs are such a wide-ranging species, living in territories ranging between 150 and 4,000 square kilometres. Most reserves simply aren't big enough for wild dogs. They don't mind ranging into areas where prey densities are lower, so they don't stop when they reach the reserve borders. Many packs that spend time in reserves also range onto unprotected land next door, where they meet livestock that look like food and domestic dogs carrying diseases, as well as roads with high-speed traffic. These causes of death can drive a population to extinction, even if it mostly occupies protected lands. For a reserve to keep wild dogs safely inside, it would need to be either the size of a small country, or surrounded with a predator-proof fence which would break connectivity for wild dogs and other species. So instead, we started to look at whether we could help wild dogs and people to coexist.'

It's been twenty-five years since the action plan was published by Rosie and her colleagues in 1997, and since then she has initiated field projects that are active all across Africa. 'They are really badly affected by habitat fragmentation because they range so widely,' she says. 'So the average range for a pack in East Africa, for example, is about 600 square kilometres. I remember giving a talk in New York once and trying to explain that the size of Manhattan Island would be just about big enough for one dog, without the rest of the pack. It's quite difficult to grasp just how large an area they need. As the wild land becomes more fragmented, there is less chance that any pack will not be in contact with people in the adjoining lands. They venture into hostile land where there are communities and surrounding agricultural fields that have a number of goats and sheep. If there is no wild prey for them, then they might attempt to kill the livestock. But as a species which hunts during the day, there is a reduced likelihood of an attack because generally herders are with their livestock constantly.'

Habitat fragmentation is one of the world's biggest environmental catastrophes. Without joining up international efforts from governments, NGOs and local communities, I fear we will lose a lot more habitats before the situation gets any better. I can only hope that we will still be around to see it when it does. But there is another threat causing havoc throughout their range. When Rosie first started working in Kenya, there was huge controversy as wild dogs had suddenly become extinct in the Serengeti. Prior to that, a reintroduced population in Etosha National Park had all died suddenly. In both cases, post-mortems were carried out as soon as possible and the packs were found to be positive for rabies. As you may well know, rabies is a viral disease that causes the progressive inflammation of the brain and nervous system. It is a brutal illness that can be easily transmitted up through the food chain and to other pack members. It was clear to Rosie from the outset that disease would be a significant threat; but, to what degree, she was yet to learn.

'The populations I was working with in Kenya lived alongside people and livestock so I assumed that the big threat was going to be human/wildlife conflict. We were really careful for that reason and we collared a couple of dogs from each pack so we could keep track of their movements. As soon as any individual had died, we would go straight in and do a post-mortem. I quickly realised that conflict wasn't the issue. Disease was the big killer, and we lost a lot of packs in the early stages,' she told me.

It was recognised early on that rabies was being transmitted to the wild dogs from domesticated dogs. The team took blood samples from all kinds of wild carnivores (jackals, hyenas, lions, etc) but found that the virus was only persisting in man's best friend. There is a lot of prior research about how best to control rabies in dogs, so to some extent that was good news! The World Health Organization has a project called Zero by 30, which aims to eradicate rabies in domestic dogs by 2030. It's an ambitious task but, if successful, it is one that could have great benefits for all kinds of species worldwide. 'We vaccinate the local domestic dogs and even have the ability to give the vaccinations directly to wild dogs if we need to,' Rosie tells me. 'It's safe and it works. It's a complicated decision because we don't like to intervene if we can avoid it, but we know we've got the solution. Touch wood, but we haven't had a rabies-related death in years.' In Rosie's study area, and beyond, the population started to recover quickly. By 2008, the number of packs had increased from zero to twenty! A massive success and a credit to the team's work.

Things were going so well – as well as being a success it was a huge relief, I'd imagine. But in 2017 there was a devastating outbreak of canine distemper. With the exception of one animal, all of the packs Rosie worked with died. 'It was horrible to see that happening. We previously thought distemper wasn't an issue as previous blood samples from the wild dogs showed that many of them had natural antibodies against it. We saw no signs of ill health, nothing. There had been outbreaks historically elsewhere in two single wild packs and once in captivity, but we didn't expect this massive epidemic to hit when it did, where we nearly lost everybody. It doesn't persist in domestic dogs, like rabies, but is transmitted through airborne exposure and is highly contagious. Even if it did persist in domestic dog populations, it would be difficult to achieve the vaccine coverage needed as there are no human health benefits from controlling canine distemper virus. With rabies, everyone wants to support the search for a cure because that intervention saves both wildlife and people,' she says, looking more sombre than before. Canine distemper is closely related to measles and impacts the respiratory, gastrointestinal and nervous systems.

It might surprise you to know that wild dogs are considered to be more at risk than lions, elephants and even rhinos. They really are on the brink, so a solution was desperately needed. 'We knew we needed to find a vaccine. And I think we have done just that! I have just completed some trials of a new vaccine on wild dogs in captivity and it's been very successful. We are confident enough now to try out in the wild,' Rosie tells me with a grin. This is a major breakthrough for wild dogs as a species, and for Rosie, who grew concerned about such events over twenty-five years ago!

Only time will tell what the outcome will be, but the vaccine should give wild dogs a shield from one of their most prolific threats. Once a virus hits it has the capability of wiping out the entire population all at once. It's been a sprint to find a solution, but working on coexistence and the improvement of their habitat will be a marathon. It's just about the only marathon that I'm prepared to run!

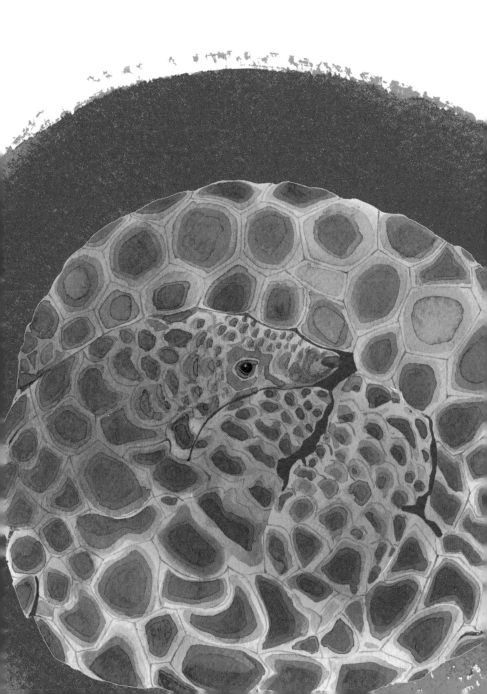

Temminck's Ground Pangolin

B ack in 2012, I had been at AfriCat in Namibia for a couple of days when something extraordinary happened. It was beyond any encounter that I could have wished for and if it wasn't for the photos, I would probably have convinced myself it was a dream.

We returned after a busy day in the bush, hungry and in need of a good night's sleep, but as we were finishing our evening meal, a call came through over the radio. Everybody looked at each other, wide-eyed in disbelief. We all froze for a split second before grabbing our cameras and sprinting out to the vehicles as fast as we could. It was pitch black and the nocturnal sounds of the African plains were in full swing. I knew it was going to be good based on the fact that even the most experienced of guides and staff looked flustered by the announcement... did we hear it right? Were they sure? Could it really be... a pangolin?

We were moving fast. Not because the pangolin was going anywhere – it was being monitored by one of the reserve's security guards, who had happened upon it – but because everyone was bursting with trepidation. After making our way across the reserve, we finally arrived at the fence line where the sighting had taken place. Our headlights lit up the road ahead as we inched forward with caution. Getting closer and closer.

I will never forget the curled-up ball of scales that appeared as we edged around the corner. Under the cover of night and to any untrained eye, like my own, it could have easily been mistaken for a basketball-sized boulder. But there it was – a Temminck's ground pangolin – and it was more beautiful than I could have ever imagined. It had travelled too close to one of the reserve's parameters, so we were invited to help redirect this bizarre-looking mammal back into the park. Every so often, its soft pointy nose and beady little eye would appear inquisitively from under the protective tail that was wrapped around its entire body.

Once it had moved, we stepped back and watched it unravel itself slowly, first revealing its head as it checked for safety, before rolling over and scuttling off on its hind legs into the bush like some kind of living artichoke on legs, or friendly miniature crocodile.

Pangolins have gained more publicity in the last ten years but still very few people are aware of their existence. So, how do you go about saving an animal that many people haven't even heard of? The pangolin is in a realm of its own. There is no other creature to compare it to, with its prehistoric appearance and utterly unique behaviour – they are the epitome of weird and wonderful, so secretive and under-studied that they are almost mystical.

Yet they are believed to be the most trafficked animal in the world, a badge no species wants to claim. There are eight species worldwide: four live in Asia and four in Africa. They are the only known mammal that is entirely covered in scales, which is partly why they were previously thought to be related to the Xenarthra suborder, consisting of anteaters, armadillos and sloths. But, unexpectedly, science shows they are more closely related to the Carnivora order, home to big cats, bears and dogs. Due to their rarity and secretive nature, very little research has been conducted, but they are known for resting in burrows or hollow trees (depending on the species) during the day and emerging at night to feed upon nitrogen-rich ants and termites. They have sticky tongues that when extended can reach up to 40 centimetres long – sometimes longer than their own bodies – and are internally attached at the pelvis! And with curved claws on the end of their specialised front legs, they are the perfect insect predator, excavating termite and ant mounds in very little time at all. They eat different ant and termite species in specific seasons, making them very difficult to keep in captivity away from their natural habitat that provides the range of food required. No one knows how many are left in the wild, but scientists agree that numbers are steeply declining. It's for this reason I never thought I'd be lucky enough to see one, let alone get to film them and lend a helping hand.

I was seventeen years old when I embarked on my first international volunteer programme. I wanted to get as much practical experience as possible in the zoological industry and it was my dream to one day work in the bush with native African wildlife. The idea of learning how to track leopards and hyenas using only my senses, watching the dramatic red and orange sunsets and camping out under the stars, seemed idyllic. It still does, in all honesty. I wanted that *Born Free* lifestyle, but obviously with some modern-day ethics. It was all I could think about when I imagined my future – that maybe one day I'd get the opportunity to live and study somewhere deep in the wild. Africa always felt like a home away from home in many respects; there is nowhere that I feel freer or more content. So when I got the opportunity in 2012 to volunteer at AfriCat, a reserve in Namibia, to work in their big cat conservation programme, I was elated. It took me about five minutes from stepping off the plane in Windhoek to realise that Namibia was going to be a very special place for me. There are so many different breathtaking habitats, from the sand dunes and ocean to the woodland savannahs and floodplains; there is the Etosha National Park in the north and the Orange River in the south; the people, the wildlife, and landscape – it's incredible. I knew I had found my favourite place on Earth.

After my first incredibly lucky encounter with the pangolin I spent two more months volunteering at AfriCat and had some amazing close encounters with lions, giraffes, porcupines, honey badgers and so much more, but no more sightings or evidence of the elusive pangolin. It's an understatement to say they are challenging to find. I left my internship having learned so much, but I was very aware that this was likely to be the only time in my life I would see a pangolin (this turned out – luckily – not to be the case, but more on this later). You see, one of the most unusual features of the pangolin is their scales, which are made from keratin, the same fibre as our hair and fingernails. These scales have a crossed lamellar arrangement in a hierarchical structure that makes them incredibly strong, with a tensile strength of between 60 and 100M Pa. Now perhaps that figure doesn't sound particularly impressive, but when I say that they are sturdy enough to protect the pangolin from the bite of a leopard, which has the second most powerful biting force of any big cat in comparison to body size, then you can appreciate just how strong they really are. They are almost invincible. But their smartest defence strategy is also their downfall. Pangolins do not run, bite or scratch when under attack and, while their scales might provide safety from jaws and claws, they do not deter the threat of the human hand. When intimidated, pangolins roll up in a ball to hide their soft underbellies, making themselves easy targets to be picked up, tossed in bags and shipped off to become just another statistic in the illegal wildlife trade.

As economic globalisation continues to increase, we are seeing a simultaneous increase in the illegal wildlife trade. It's hard to evaluate exactly what this industry is worth because poachers and suppliers rarely submit spreadsheets of their expenditures, but the annual value of the trade could be as high as $20 billion, making it one of the most profitable industries in the world and one of the greatest threats to biodiversity. The trade in pangolins is thought to account for 20 per cent of the global illegal wildlife trade. That's potentially $4 billion annually. They have been persecuted for centuries, the first evidence of pangolin persecution dates back to 1820, when King George III was presented with a coat made from the scales of the Indian pangolin. As of January 2017, all eight species became protected by CITES, which meant that all international trade became prohibited, and in addition over 180 governments signed a treaty to stamp out poaching and help protect them from extinction. Yet pangolins are still being lost at an alarming rate due to the demand for their scales and meat in traditional medicines. They are boiled, sometimes when still alive, before their scales are ripped from their bodies. They can be either dried, roasted or cooked in oil (or historically boys' urine) and then sold to supposedly help with skin diseases, deafness, nervousness, women possessed by the devil, crying children… The list goes on but the fact remains that pangolin scales have zero medicinal value whatsoever – you may as well bite your fingernails.

In a study looking at where the majority of demand comes from, China and Vietnam were the main countries. In fact, in Vietnam until 2015 a prescription for pangolin scales was covered under some health insurance plans. Pangolins used to be commonplace in the wilderness of southern China, but their population has dropped by approximately 90 per cent since the 1960s. They have a low birth and survival rate, so their potential recovery is extremely slow. But currently there's little hope of recovery because if they're not being taken for their scales, it's their blood, meat and young, which are delicacies. It's impossible to tell how many pangolins are taken from the wild each year, but there were 128 tonnes of them seized in 2019 alone, which shows that the problem is still rife. And that's only the quantity that was traced, so you can only imagine the number that slipped through the net. It must be in the tens of thousands of individuals, if not more.

Back in 2019 I was working for Lush Cosmetics in the UK, in their wildlife film unit. Other than making bath bombs, the company often spearheads campaigns focusing on human rights, climate action and the biodiversity crisis. While there, I got to work closely with my wildlife film-making mentor Ruth Peacey to develop an idea for the BBC. Now, I can't say what that idea is because I hope that one day it'll happen, but what I can divulge is that we decided to film the pilot in Namibia, at AfriCat, where I had volunteered years before. I was confident that there would be a bonanza of wildlife to film and some incredible stories – and I wasn't wrong. We had two key species we wanted to feature: 1) the brown hyena and 2) the Temminck's ground pangolin.

In the time that I had been away, AfriCat had employed a number of scientists to live on-site monitoring wildlife movements and tracking the rare and endangered species. That's when I first met Kelsey Prediger, a student from Michigan, USA, who had moved to Namibia to complete her Master's thesis. Her job was to shine light on the patterns and basic ecology of the pangolins living there, everything from their breeding cycle to their diets. She guaranteed me a pangolin sighting – something I was sceptical about because I was well aware of how rare they were; and I know you should never make promises when it comes to wildlife because the moment you do, the animal in question will invariably never show up. I should have had more faith because that week I saw *four* pangolins. It wasn't that numbers on the reserve had necessarily increased, but, with Kelsey's research, she was able to familiarise herself with their territories and movements like no one had before. We were able to film Kelsey tagging them using specialised GPS tags, but my favourite experience was trekking into the bush under the cover of night, watching and following a female pangolin as she went about her nightly duties of eating termites and prowling around the undergrowth like a miniature T rex. Watching her behave naturally in an environment she was clearly thriving in, totally unaware of our presence, was a sight I'll never forget.

When I caught up with Kelsey to find out exactly what she's hoping to discover about this endangered species now, she said, 'When I started it was the first in-depth research project in Namibia. There had been one pilot study previously, but not much else.

I thought about what I could learn from wild individuals that might one day help pangolins getting released back into the wild after being seized by the authorities in the wildlife trade. My thesis focused on home range size, habitat preference, burrow preference and prey selectivity. We started to realise that they are very territorial, much like a leopard, and the pangolin will defend their territories against members of the same sex. And so we found males would have a large territory that would overlap with several females. This is so important to know when it comes to releasing pangolins because you want to avoid conflict and maximise success. We're still just scratching the surface because there is so much to learn.'

It's always shocking to see the images that have hit the headlines over the years of bags piled up at airports and in dodgy sheds when you know a living pangolin is lying tied up within them. But it's quite comforting to know that for the lucky few that get found, there is hope of them going back into the wild. 'Another aspect was looking at the prey selectivity because other studies have found that they are very picky,' Kelsey continued. 'By understanding what they choose to eat at what time, we will be able to choose a better release site with their preferred species of ants and termites. But also, their preferences vary massively regionally, so we're hoping to be able to get a better idea of the origin of trafficking based on their diets. I also found pangolins in this region of Namibia prefer burrows originally created by aardvarks, which makes sense as they're deep and act as a thermal refuge, maintaining a temperature between twenty and thirty degrees. We know so little, so every bit of information is crucial.'

Collecting data on any species in the wild is difficult; it has come on in leaps and bounds in the last fifty years or so, but harsh environments and often unreliable technology still make things tricky. One common method is to use tracking devices, which means scientists don't have to be following animals 24/7. There are lots of different types of tags and depending on the study subject they often need to be adapted so that they can't be pulled, rubbed or shaken off, or cause any behavioural change or damage to the animal. Pangolins are no different! As they are a species that spends a lot of time underground, we can't use batteries powered by solar energy, which is the usual method in bird tags and for other mammals, and we're also unable to place them around the neck or ankle as they could potentially slide off or prevent the animals from digging effectively.

'We've got a 20 to 50 per cent fail rate with our tags but it is improving; we now use a GPS local download and a GPS satellite transmitter that looks like a cattle tag that we place into one of their scales on their mid-back,' Kelsey told me. 'We carefully create a hole and loop the tag through. Before the GPS tags I was having to track them on foot every night but now I've got more flexibility because the data is transmitted by satellite to my laptop.' This will be especially helpful to Kelsey now because over 2020 and 2021 she expanded her sights, and has set up an NGO focused on creating pangolin awareness and conservation, called the Pangolin Conservation and Research Foundation (PCFR). 'Going forward, I'm tagging pangolins in new regions of Namibia, collecting data on all the usual behaviours but also researching what happens after rescued individuals have been released back to the wild. In July 2020, alongside the Namibian Pangolin Working Group chaired by the Ministry of Environment, Forestry and Tourism, we released our first trafficked pangolin,' she excitedly revealed. 'She gained 1.5 kilos and in December 2020 I visited her to find she had a male in pursuit, which suggests she has settled into the area. It's the first documented release that we can consider a success. It'll be a true success if or when she starts reproducing but so far, it looks very promising.'

The female in question had been seized by Namibian police and the Blue Rhino Task Team after a tip off from the public and had spent a few days in rehabilitation to make sure she was strong enough to return home. Luckily they knew of the area she came from, where trafficking is at its highest, so the PCFR and other organisations were there to release her in the best location possible. A very lucky pangolin, but hopefully more will be following in her footsteps thanks to pioneering scientists like Kelsey pushing for tighter regulations and more public awareness.

As brilliant as rehabilitation is for ex-trafficked individuals, there needs to be a big push to end the demand in the use of pangolin in traditional medicines because those individuals should never have been trafficked in the first place. A greater education on the importance of these species is needed because they are vital for the health of the ecosystem. One pangolin can consume over seventy million insects every year, acting as a natural population control, and they also aerate the soil when they use their claws to dig for food, spreading nutrients around their environment. Asian species of pangolin have experienced more drastic declines but, as those numbers become increasingly low, there is more pressure on the African species to satisfy the demand for traditional medicines. At the risk of sounding controversial, the word 'tradition' always seems to cause trouble. I personally love tradition… like a vegetarian roast dinner on a Sunday with the grandparents, celebrating Christmas and going trick-or-treating at Halloween with my younger brother… but I have also stopped participating in traditions once I have learned about the damage they cause. If we are unable to grow and change our minds – change our traditions – for the benefit of one another and the planet, then we are in deep, deep trouble.

256

There is zero medicinal value in pangolin scales. It's as simple as that. And even if there were, consuming pangolins to the extent of wiping them off the face of the Earth just because it's 'tradition' is not an excuse. Let's make new traditions, ones that are healthy and can withstand the test of time so that future generations can partake in them and perhaps one day see a pangolin too.

Times are changing for the better. In 2020 China announced that they were removing the species from the official list of traditional medicines and were raising the pangolin's protection status to the highest possible level, which is also held by the much-loved giant panda. Authorities have promised to crack down on the trade and protect areas of viable habitat that are left in the country. Big promises, but we also need big action. Still, it is positive because when people see the government moving towards conservation, it gets us to think and reconsider. Younger generations are driving this change; they're less likely to use wildlife products and more empowered to speak up for the environment as the pressure grows to be eco-conscious. The solution is simple – if there's no demand then there'll be no trade.

Pangolins hold a special place in my heart, so I'd like to ask you to do something to help: go and tell a friend all about pangolins. Not necessarily the doom and gloom bits, but describe to them this prehistoric-looking mammal covered in scales with a tongue as long as your arm. Show them a photo of their adorable, quizzical faces and wow them with facts of their ecology. I guarantee you'll be so surprised by how many people are totally unaware that they even exist. But now that you do know, please use your voice for pangolins, because then we might just be in with a chance of saving them. It would be devastating to see them vanish completely. There is no other organism like them, after all.

Northern Royal Albatross

Weary eyes, sore muscles and missing luggage were what awaited us when we finally touched down in Ushuaia, Argentina, after two long-haul flights and a swift overnight stop in Buenos Aires. I was only ten at the time and this was the furthest away from home I'd ever been.

Located in the Tierra del Fuego province, Ushuaia is considered the globe's southernmost city and holds the title 'end of the world'. It's not exactly what you'd expect, with tourist stops, brightly coloured houses and a welcoming atmosphere – it's home to a population of 75,000 people. Its title struck me as odd because, for me, the journey had only just begun. I was going beyond the 'end of the world' (which should really be renamed 'end of civilisation') to the land of piercing blue icebergs, ancient glaciers, elephant seals and clumsy, flightless seabirds. I was on my first voyage to Antarctica, and what an adventure it would turn out to be!

Naturally, penguins were at the top of my list to see, but I was unsure of what else we could reasonably expect to encounter on the frozen continent. We had plans to retrace Ernest Shackleton's footsteps, take Zodiac cruises around the epic icebergs, watch fur and elephant seals hauled out on the beaches, and, if we were lucky, maybe even see hunting orca or humpback whales. But, it was all an unknown. We boarded the Russian research icebreaker ship, the *Vavilov*, and set sail. To reach the Antarctic peninsula you have to cross the notorious Drake Passage, which takes two days and is one of the most treacherous journeys any ship can make. They say there are two versions of the Drake Passage: if you're lucky enough to pass during smooth conditions, you'll have experienced 'Drake Lake' but at its worst it is called the 'Drake Shake'; 55-mph winds whip up unpredictable storms, raising 12-metre waves that crash down against and aboard your vessel. Many wrecks lie victim at the bottom of the infamous passage, with many lives lost. I have experienced both the 'lake' and the 'shake', which is not for the faint of heart (or stomach). Midway through this journey with no land in sight, I stepped out from the shelter of my cabin to see what was happening on the deck. The wind whipped my face as soon as I opened the door and I had to use all my weight to push against it, slowly moving forward to the railing. It was choppy but no way near the 'Shake' state. With one hand gripping the cold, white railing and the other holding a pair of binoculars up to my eyes, I tried to focus my gaze. Hundreds of seemingly fragile birds were gliding elegantly across the waves. Their effortless movements were a stark contrast to the peaks and troughs of the menacing dark-blue water. I could barely stand upright in the wind; how on Earth could they be flying with such ease?

There were black-bellied storm petrels, blue petrels, southern giant petrels, south polar skua, southern fulmars and even the occasional pair of beautiful storm petrels. It was mesmerising to watch them dance between the sprays of spume, spat out by colliding waves, flying on the updraught of air created by the ship as it ploughed on through the deep. Each species was stunning in its own way: their plumage, movement, and their proximity to me and my camera. But one bird stood out above the rest. It appeared to be defying the laws of physics with its flight, occasionally swinging left into an upswell of wind to give me a side-profile glimpse of the piercing jet-black eyes in its bright-white head. A wandering albatross. Despite the clear day with little cloud cover, this magnificent bird appeared out of nowhere, soaring effortlessly right front of me. Wandering albatrosses have the longest wingspan in the world, measuring up to 11 feet (twice the height of me). It's hard to appreciate their scale in flight, but on land it is a different story.

Bird Island is situated just off the north-west tip of South Georgia, separated from the mainland only by a 500-metre channel. It's home to 50,000 penguins, 65,000 fur seals and a very special population of breeding wandering albatrosses. When we visited, ships following strict protocols were allowed to bring passengers onto the island, so we jumped at the chance. Little did we know that we would be among the last group of non-scientists allowed to visit the island due to concerns for human safety and wildlife protection. It was another clear day with bright-blue skies, and the water was calm – the perfect conditions for landing ashore.

We arrived on the beach and were immediately surrounded by wildlife – probably more than I had ever seen before in such close proximity. Carefully weaving our way through hundreds of fiercely territorial fur seals, we made our way towards the grassy tussock parts of the island where the albatross nest. At a respectful distance, I sat with my camera and started taking photos of a sleepy adult. At first it was peaceful (except for the penguins on the beach below), but that changed the moment the second adult returned back from foraging at sea. The pair immediately began displaying to one another, performing their courtship dance right in front of my eyes. They both spread their giant wings, while head-bowing, sky-pointing and vocalising in the form of a rattle and sky call. It was such a tender moment to witness between such epic birds.

According to BirdLife, a global partnership of NGOs, there are twenty-two albatross species soaring our planet's skies, with most residing in the windy regions of the southern hemisphere. They're the oldest known wild birds, with individuals often reaching over the ripe old age of fifty. One record-breaker, a female Laysan albatross fondly known as Wisdom, was tagged as an adult in 1956 and is now estimated to be at least seventy years old and was still successfully hatching chicks in 2021! Giant, long-lived creatures that they are, you'd presume that many people would have the chance to see one; but sadly few ever do, and there's a couple of reasons for that.

Firstly, albatrosses are known for spending the majority of their lives far out at sea. Once fledged from their natal grounds, young birds can spend up to six years flying over the open ocean without ever coming into contact with the land – 2,190 days spent out at sea! – before they become sexually mature enough to breed. They can fly 805 kilometres a day, reaching speeds of over 50 mph, while rarely beating their wings and maintaining a heart rate similar to their basal rate when resting on the ground. The famous 1873 novel *Around the World in Eighty Days* would be nothing for an albatross, a mere joke in fact – an insult even, as it would only take them forty-six days to circle the Earth if they so wished.

Albatrosses do this by flying 'smarter, not harder'. Just as planes use the power of their engines to take off, these birds use vast amounts of energy beating their long wings to take off and gain altitude. Though impressive, they are not the most graceful when taking to the air (or when landing) as their physiology is designed for gliding. Once in the air, they are able to use the wind to their advantage. Dynamic soaring is one method they utilise frequently. From high altitudes, they descend towards the ocean surface gaining kinetic energy, or speed, pulling up just before they hit the waves, where the wind levels are much lower; this allows them to travel further towards their desired direction. Slope-soaring is another technique; when the coastal winds collide with cliffs or mountain ridges it creates an upswell of air that the albatrosses then ride upon. By using both flying techniques, albatrosses can fly for hours without hardly ever beating their wings. If you've ever held your arm out horizontally, you'll know how quickly a painful aching sensation creeps into your tensed muscles that are holding the weight of your limb. So, how do these birds glide with their wings outstretched without discomfort? Well, evolution has devised a solution in the form of a specialised shoulder-lock tendon; the wings essentially click into the soaring position. This takes pressure off the muscles in the wings and requires less energy, subsequently keeping their heart rate low. Energy is valuable for any species, but for a bird navigating such an unpredictable environment where in a lifetime they could travel over 8.5 million kilometres, conserving energy is paramount for their survival.

Aside from their far-flung sea-dwelling lifestyles, the second reason why most people will never catch a glimpse of an albatross is that fifteen of the twenty-two species face extinction. That's 68 per cent of their entire group teetering on the brink. Seabirds are brilliant indicator species and are reliant on the health of our oceans, so when the whole taxonomic groups start to tumble, you must look beyond individual populations and ask why. Since the 1950s, seabird numbers have fallen by 70 per cent. That statistic is not only sad but is also an indication that something much bigger is going on. The northern royal albatross in New Zealand is one such species whose population is feeling the pinch. Sharyn Broni works for the Department of Conservation as a wildlife ranger at Pukekura/Taiaroa Head and has been monitoring these special birds during their breeding season ever since 1997. Hardly anyone will ever get to know the characters, quirks and intricate behaviours of the albatross, but she is one of the lucky few.

'I grew up in Dunedin, on the South Island of New Zealand, which is pretty much the only city in the world with albatross nesting nearby,' Sharyn begins. 'They're a long-lived species so you get to work with individuals for a long time. There are birds that I work with today that were there when I started twenty-five years ago. It's amazing to think about!'

Before jumping into the issues and the measures being taken to pull the species away from extinction, I wanted to know how the birds are faring today, so I asked the baseline question, 'What are the numbers you're working with?' Sharyn replied, 'From a world perspective, they are declining quickly. They're listed by the IUCN as endangered but are nationally classified as threatened.

When I started there were about 20,000 individuals and now that number is probably closer to 17,000. While they are endemic to New Zealand, there are only four breeding sites; numbers at three of the sites are in decline but at Pukekura/Taiaroa Head where I am based, the population is growing slowly – but the colony is small and accounts for less than 1 per cent of the entire population. The other three breeding sites are home to the other 99 per cent, all located on the Chatham Islands, 800 kilometres east of New Zealand, and are extremely isolated and hard to study, though over the last few years there's been aerial surveys from aeroplanes to assess them. We are lucky to be able to work so closely with the ones at Taiaroa Head but understanding the problems they face out at sea is important too.'

The threats to albatrosses are vast. One of the biggest things pushing them to the brink of extinction is pelagic longline fishing, a commercial fishing technique that uses a main floating line with suspended baited hooks hanging down in the water column at various intervals to catch target species like tuna, swordfish and other billfish. Each line can be over 80 miles long, supporting thousands of deadly hooks. It has been a popular fishing method since the 1980s and, according to Callum Roberts, author of the 2013 book *Ocean of Life*, there is now enough longline set in the oceans to wrap around our planet a staggering 500 times.

Overfishing is a giant problem and one we need to tackle – preferably yesterday. The issue with these longlines is obviously their abundance and distribution, but also their non-selective nature. Fishers pull up their lines to find by-catch of all sorts: dead endangered sharks, turtles, dolphins and whales, all caught or tangled up in their nets. And it can be equally fatal for seabirds, which dive down attempting to take the bait as the lines are being set.

The life-history strategy of all albatrosses makes their populations more vulnerable. They take years to reach sexual maturity, live a long time, are monogamous and only produce one chick every other year. The turnover between generations is slow, which means that the survival of adult individuals, as opposed to generations, is the most important thing to secure the future of the species. There's little room for mistakes, yet a hundred thousand get caught on longlines each year. Albatrosses are sexually monogamous and return to the same nest site to breed with their partner every year, but during the non-breeding months the sexes segregate out at sea. For example, male wandering albatrosses – which on average have longer bills, larger wingspans and heavier masses than the females – typically forage and spend their time further south, in the Subantarctic. In contrast, the smaller females favour regions slightly further north, in the subtropical regions. It's a way to reduce competition for resources but as a result there's a stark contrast between the sexes; more longlines are set in subtropical regions so, as a consequence, there is greater loss of females.

Collaboration between BirdLife and the RSPB has led to a project called Albatross Task Force, which tries to teach fishers how to safely remove any albatross that gets caught on the line. It's clearly working; since they started in the South African trawl fishery in 2006 they've reduced albatross by-catch by 99 per cent, a brilliant accomplishment. Training is desperately needed all over the world. In 2015 images surfaced of a northern royal albatross flying over the waves with a mutilated beak. There have been a number of these cases in the south-west Atlantic, where fishers simply cut off the upper or lower mandible of the bill to release it from the hook, not necessarily realising the damage that will cause. I asked Sharyn about the impacts of longline fishing on this species and she said, 'Fishing is a major cause for the loss of most endangered albatross species, but comparatively very little is understood about how northern royals spend their time in the ocean. We think that they spend less time interacting with fishing boats than others but that could be changing.'

Breeding adults return to the colony from late August, hopefully to be reunited with their partner after months at sea. Studies show that males in particular are very loyal to their natal grounds and choose to breed within 40 metres on average from where they hatched themselves! 'They put so much energy into choosing a mate that it makes sense that they're loyal to their partner and nest location, but they sneakily mate with other individuals when their partner is not around. It's something called extra pair copulation,' Sharyn tells me. Nests are built on flat mounds of grassy vegetation and mud on the ground near the coastline. Once the eggs are laid, between October and December, the pair will share incubation duties for an average of seventy-eight days before the chick begins to hatch, some time between January and early February. The majority of avian species stay at the nest for a matter of weeks before fledging into the world (but then again, most birds don't have the life expectancy or strategy of an albatross); a northern royal chick will stay at the nest site for roughly 240 days, or thirty-four weeks. They are reliant upon their parents returning with partially digested food until they are ready to take to the air themselves.

Just like any monogamous species, break-ups or divorces do happen, but for albatrosses the rate is low – or at least it was. New data from the Royal Society in 2021 detailed how the divorce rate of the black-browed albatross, a species found breeding in the Falklands, has increased between 1 and 3 per cent each season, to 8 per cent. These birds struggle to maintain long-term relationships, and successfully fledge chicks, because they are under increasing stressors caused by the warming waters of climate change. There's less fish in the ocean, meaning individuals have to forage for longer periods and travel further out to sea; they can disappear for weeks at a time. All these impacts trigger more stress hormones, as the birds try to survive and adapt in the changing environment. Although this study hasn't been replicated on all species, it's a window into the future for these birds unless we all take responsibility and do our bit to stop climate change in its tracks.

Sharyn's main role during the breeding season is to provide some critical extra support to the northern royal birds on Taiaroa Head, helping them to successfully fledge their chicks. The best way I can describe it is that it's essentially like an 'albatross adoption service'… and in the face of the harrowing challenges faced by the species, it's proving to be a successful, heartwarming conservation strategy.

Sharyn describes their method: 'All the birds have stainless steel bands around their legs with a unique number and then two or three colour bands' on the second leg to help us identify them. The unique number and colour of bands is unique to an individual. We record the birds every time we see them and these records go back to 1938, so we have nearly ninety years of data on them. Until the first few eggs are laid in the season we are just adding to that data, especially if there's pairs of first-time breeders, but once the egg is laid we start looking at how long the birds spend incubating. After about ten days we carefully check if the egg is fertile. Fertility rates are generally high but sometimes eggs can be infertile and we also see embryo deaths. We candle them by shining a light through the egg to see the blood vessels (hopefully) radiating from the yolk. One adult should always be on duty at the nest while the other goes on a foraging trip, but if that takes longer than thirteen days then the egg becomes at risk, as the incubating adult might be forced to leave to find food for itself. The egg could be deserted, so we move it into an incubator and put a ceramic dummy egg in its place to hold the adults at the nest for as long as possible. If they end up deserting, it doesn't matter as the real egg is safe.'

On the occasions where they do come across an infertile egg, they will remove it and leave a dummy in its place as well. The adults will continue to incubate, unaware of the replacement. You might be thinking, what's the point? Forcing the birds to continue using their precious energy reserves to keep an egg-shaped piece of ceramic warm might seem unusual, but the adult pair could be very valuable foster parents to an abandoned chick later in the season.

'The first four or so weeks of the chick's life is called the guard stage, where the parents are with the chick all the time. But they will be completely happy to feed and raise somebody else's chick during that time as long as it's in their nest. After four weeks, they will avoid taking on a chick,' Sharyn said. I was quite surprised to learn how easily the foster parents would take on a chick that was three or four weeks old. A few days old, sure, that would be understandable, but nearly a month? It's a pretty remarkable demonstration of instinct.

Fly strike is a common and severe problem at the colony. It occurs when flies lay their eggs onto the skin of an animal, in this case the newly hatched albatross chicks, before they emerge as maggots consuming the skin of their host. The summers are hot and the vegetation type supports huge numbers of these flies, which can kill the young birds easily in the first two weeks of their lives. As a precautionary measure, Sharyn and the team remove the eggs as they begin to hatch, placing them into artificial egg incubators. The chicks are sprayed with a liquid called Avian Insect Liquidator to protect them from the fly strike, and are put back into the nest as soon as possible. It might seem like an intensive measure, but every individual counts in the battle against extinction.

To carry out the work, Sharyn spends a lot of time observing these magnificent animals in intricate detail. She knows many of them well and looks forward to their return. Naturally, some are more tolerant than others of human interaction. I asked if there were any individuals that really stood out to her over the years, and she replied, 'There's a female called White Orange who is very calm. In fact, if you are working near the nest she will try to preen your hair. She's very gentle.' Imagine, getting your hair cleaned by an albatross!

Over the coming years the main aim of the conservation project is to maximise the number of chicks that are fledged every year. The numbers of successfully fledged chicks have increased from 80–100 birds twenty-five years ago to now over 250. Sharyn concludes, 'In the Chatham Islands where 99 per cent of the population breed, we are still only just understanding the problem causing the population decline. We need to know more about the impact of fishing mortalities and climate change on the northern royals. Things are changing all the time, so we have to adapt too. The oceans have warmed up and we have had more heatwaves in the last few years, which is sending certain species further south to seek out colder regions or causing them to disappear altogether. Albatrosses learn the best fishing spots around New Zealand, but that's changing as the fish move and decrease in numbers with the warming waters. They're an apex species at the top of the food chain, they bring nutrients into the land where they nest, they engage people with seabirds and the health of the ocean – they're so important to the global ecosystem.'

Epilogue: Humans

Multiple adaptations have driven the evolution of Homo sapiens. From the development of bipedalism (standing on two feet) to the enlargement of our complex brains, our opposable thumbs, our ability to use tools and to understand and communicate with detailed language. It's amazing to think that our world, our physical bodies and way of life, is essentially just a snapshot of this moment in time in our planet's history. We are still evolving and, in 1,000 or 100,000 years from now, we could look, sound and behave entirely differently. And exactly what that picture looks like will depend on the actions we take today.

First, to tackle the obvious. It's safe to say that currently we are not an endangered or threatened species. In 2008, humans were officially listed as 'least concern', which is hardly a surprise. I mentioned previously that 99 per cent of all species to have ever existed are now extinct... So, when it comes to talking about human extinction, it's not a question of if, it's a matter of when. As mammals we do have our weaknesses; to paraphrase evolutionary biologist, Nick Longrich, we are warm-blooded and relatively large, which leaves us more likely to be impacted by ecological changes. We have fast metabolisms and need to eat regularly, and that makes us sensitive to periodic food chain destructions. We are also long-lived, with slow reproduction, which makes us less likely to recover quickly from population catastrophes, and we don't have many offspring (comparatively, in the zoological sense), so we are slow at evolving in an environment that is changing quickly.

We are far from untouchable. Scientists vary on their timeline estimates when it comes to human extinction. There are some who believe we have a couple of hundred thousand years left to live on this planet but others, like Frank Fenner (the acclaimed Australian virologist who helped wipe out smallpox), predict that it could happen by the end of the century. Theories of existential crises of course exist; these include possible alien invasions, subjugation by some form of artificial intelligence, future pandemics or self-inflicted annihilation through nuclear war. But what will most likely have a hand in it, if nothing changes, is the climate crisis. Will we be the animals that consciously destroyed the planet as we knew it, or the ones that learned from our mistakes and managed to turn it around at the last second?

The impact that human beings have had on this planet is profound, unlike any other known species before. We have made so many changes that our existence now defines an unofficial unit of geological time. The Anthropocene was first described in 2000 by biologist Eugene Stoermer and chemist Paul Crutzen and represents the significant impact we have made to our climate and ecosystems. From the way we unsustainably manage the land, with intensive farming, fires and draining, to the way we harvest and consume resources, the damage is undeniable. We are causing the sixth mass extinction event. Although scientists predict that humans won't die off any time soon, do you ever wonder – hypothetically – what would happen if we disappeared tomorrow? The answer is quite simple – life would continue. Over time our cities would crumble and fall, new forests would rise where barren fields once lay and the evidence of our existence would be gradually buried as nature took over once more. So when we talk about saving the planet, we should be aware that this is not a fight for life as a whole; that will always persist. This is a fight for life as *we* know it.

I don't know if you've noticed but there is one big subject that I have been purposefully dodging throughout the pages of this book. It's been the elephant in the room, or the climate protesters and petitions gathering on the doorsteps of government buildings… it's there, but keeps getting bypassed. I have written about nineteen wonderful species on the brink of extinction and have discussed the reasons for their disappearance, whether they be disease, persecution or habitat fragmentation, among others. But while each animal (plus one plant) is wildly unique, there is a thread connecting each and every one of them regardless of habitat or classification: climate change. There isn't one species that hasn't felt its punch. As of 2022, our planet has warmed to 1.1 °C more than 1800's levels on average, and current projections predict that temperatures will continue to rise to 2.7 °C or more by the end of the century. At that point, climate breakdown will be irreversible. Global warming has happened mainly in the years since 1975, at a rate of 0.15–0.20 °C per decade. By burning fossil fuels and pumping greenhouse gases into the atmosphere, we have essentially created a planetary hot box full of carbon dioxide, methane, nitrous oxide and fluorinated gases that is forcing environmental change at a rate much faster than the planet and its biodiversity are able to adapt to.

It might seem like an insignificant amount of change; I mean, what damage could a couple of degrees really do? It's a common question from people who are fortunate enough to live in areas that have experienced little change (yet), or from those who are looking for a reason to downplay or ignore its significance. As some yellow-haired former American president once said on Twitter, 'It's really cold outside. Man, we could use a big dose of global warming!' It's quite a shocking statement but it's one that I have heard echoed a thousand times. This idea completely overlooks the difference between weather and climate. Weather refers to short-term atmospheric changes, whereas our climate is the averaged weather of a specific region over a prolonged period of time. It is true that our climate has always had natural fluctuations. For the past one million years, the Earth has experienced cycles of ice ages every 100,000 years or so, which are then followed by a period of warmth. It's driven by a chain reaction that begins due to a slight change in the Earth's orbit, which alters and redistributes the energy from the sun. There are natural changes in temperature and carbon dioxide as a result, but these shifts take thousands of years to happen, and are not responsible for the unprecedented rate at which we are experiencing atmospheric changes today. For example, we are currently releasing 110 million tonnes of carbon dioxide into the atmosphere every single day. In the last sixty years, the annual release rate of atmospheric carbon has become 100 times faster than any previous natural rise that might have occurred in the last 800,000 years. Whatever way you look at it, it's devastating.

As a result of anthropogenic activities, heatwaves are growing hotter and are happening more frequently. The sea level has risen by 8–9 inches and the ocean is 30 per cent more acidic. There is an increased risk of extreme weather events, like flooding, droughts, hurricanes and heavy snow. And the chances are that we will be confronted with more diseases and pandemics along the way – not to mention impending food shortage crises too. Every fraction of an increase in temperature will only intensify the impacts above, pushing us closer to an irreversible tipping point.

I will remember 2022 as the year that filled my news feed up with tips and tricks for staying cool in the 40 °C summer heatwave. It was a temperature never before recorded in the nation. I gave advice on TV and radio on what we could do to help wildlife; I asked people to allow patches of their garden to grow to provide some extra shade for wild visitors, as well as asking them to provide shallow bowls of water and some extra food to help give numbers a boost. It was all over the news – 'keep your curtains closed to keep the sun out', 'put tea towels in the freezer' and 'whatever you do, please don't walk your dogs in the midday heat'. I had hoped that this extreme heat event was going to be the wake-up call we all needed here in the UK, but, once the temperatures returned to normal, it was back to business as usual, as usual.

Prior to that, in 2020 we had the Covid-19 pandemic, resulting in multiple lockdowns. Naturalists, scientists and all other climate-concerned people had hoped that when it was safe, society would return to a 'new normal'. More people than ever had reconnected to nature through time spent in their gardens, watching the birds, the butterflies, the foxes and the bees. For me, it was a time of reflection, and I was full of optimism that when restrictions finally lifted we would be brave enough to change our mindsets and change our ways. Two years on from that moment, I do firmly believe that so many people have done just that. It's not the ordinary people – like you and me – who have forgotten. It's the people in power, who most likely never came to those realisations in the first place, because they either didn't have to lock down or they just carried on partying as usual regardless. The International Energy Agency (IEA) documented that global energy-related carbon emissions rose by 6 per cent in 2021, to 36.3 billion tonnes. It's the highest level ever recorded, and, in their words, 'the world economy rebounded strongly from the Covid-19 crisis and relied heavily on coal to power that growth'. It's not exactly the news we had hoped for as our leaders' obsession with never-ending growth on a finite planet pulled us further into the rabbit hole.

Around the world five million human deaths are linked to abnormal hot or cold temperatures every single year. And that figure doesn't include those who lose their lives due to singular extreme weather events, climate-linked poverty or through increased disease or viral outbreaks. Eleven per cent of the world's human population is already vulnerable to the impacts of severe climate change. But the brunt of the climate crisis is not evenly distributed, and, while it is very much an environmental issue, it is also about social inequality. There will be increasing mass migrations of people trying to escape unliveable conditions as the situation worsens. But there is a chance. The only condition, to put it in the words of Jim Skea, a climate scientist working with the International Panel on Climate Change (IPCC), is that 'it's now or never'. To prevent the future heating above 1.5 °C of pre-industrial levels, greenhouse gas emissions must be halved by 2030 and we must reach net zero by 2050. Otherwise, we won't be able to stop what we've started. In order for that to happen, we as a global population need to work together towards a low-carbon economy. Not tomorrow, but now. A recent report by the IPCC listed the steps our governments need to take to ensure the future for a healthy planet: we must phase out fossil fuels and halt the building of any associated infrastructure, we must cut methane emissions by a third, we must invest in carbon capture and other low-carbon technologies (which are currently about six times lower than they need to be) while supporting all sectors, from transport to food, in their transition to green energy.

I'm pleased to say that it's not all bad news. There are some slivers of hope shining through that give us reasons to be optimistic. While the majority of the population still relies heavily on fossil fuels, renewable energy sources have become the cheapest option in many situations for most of the world. When renewable technologies first came out they were incredibly expensive but, since 2010, the price of solar power has dropped by over 85 per cent. Additionally, the costs of offshore and onshore wind energy have fallen by 48 per cent and 56 per cent respectively. These sources could alter the world's energy supply to favour clean energy by 2030. As much as climate collapse and biodiversity loss should surely be enough of a motivator, low prices make renewables more attractive. In addition to that, the IEA have recently found that more people around the world are employed by clean energy businesses than fossil-fuel ones. Perhaps the tide could be turning after all, even if it is happening at the rate of a sloth's metabolism instead of a wild dog sprint.

In terms of biodiversity, more than 40,000 species are believed to be on the brink of extinction. That number is almost certainly a conservative one as it only accounts for the number of organisms that have been formally assessed. Of all the threats I have discussed within these chapters, there is no doubt that climate change is a huge contributing factor, exacerbating the negative impacts and driving relentless unsustainable habitat destruction. Take the 2019/2020 wild bushfires in Australia as an example: the world watched on as 97,000 square kilometres of the ecosystem was destroyed by intensely raging flames that were more extreme because of climate change. As a result of those fires, it's estimated that the number of threatened species in the area rose by 14 per cent.

We need nature as part of the solution to fix our mess. To have the best chance of saving species on the brink, we must learn to work *with* ecosystems instead of against them. Natural ecosystems and biodiversity play a huge role in maintaining and regulating the climate, as they always have. The concept of nature-based solutions is now widely discussed as a 'win-win' for stopping climate change and biodiversity loss, while also supporting a transition to a more sustainable future. Stored within the world's forests is a huge amount of carbon, an estimated 861 gigatons of the stuff. As the trees are cut down, this carbon is released at rates far higher than previously estimated. Currently, deforestation is responsible for 20 per cent of all global greenhouse gas emission into the atmosphere. If we stopped chopping down the forests and started investing in carbon stores and rewilding initiatives, then there is potential to remove about 30 per cent of the carbon needed by 2030 to keep warming to less than 2 °C. This figure could even be higher in tropical parts of the world. It's not just the forests, of course. It's the peatlands, the mangroves, the salt marshes and so much more. As individuals, we can make the decisions to live as ethically as possible. Each decision we make about how we travel, what we eat and how much we consume is critical, but so is holding our leaders accountable.

We have already damaged our climate and ecosystems to the extent that, inevitably, more species will go extinct in the near future; but how many is up to us. We have this one opportunity now where we can alter the future if we choose to change our behaviour. For the sake of the kakapo, the pangolins, the glow-worms, the hammerhead sharks and for our own survival, too. Life is at its strongest when it's at its most diverse, so, while I've been looking at these species as individuals, it's important to remember that they are all strongly interconnected – from the black-and-white ruffed lemur to the snow leopard, the freshwater pearl mussel to the northern white rhino and the exquisite spike-thumb frog to the white-headed vulture. I don't want this book to become a collection of stories about the species we once knew but tragically lost. Instead I remain optimistic, sincerely hoping that we are on the cusp of a new environmental era.

As long as these species live, then we have a lot left to fight for. Do you remember before when I mentioned that one of the main drivers of human evolution was the development of language and complex communication? Well, that ability gives us the power to shape the future. I often say that the most powerful tool we all have to drive change for wildlife and their habitats is our voice.

We have the fate of the Anthropocene in our hands. The scientists, rangers and conservationists in this book prove that if we are brave enough and loud enough, then we might just be in with a chance to halt extinction rates in their tracks.

Further Reading

Antonelli, Alexandre, *The Hidden Universe: Adventures in Biodiversity*, Ebury, 2022.

Bells, Alice, *Our Biggest Experiment: A History of the Climate Crisis*, Bloomsbury, 2021.

Extinction Rebellion, *This Is Not A Drill: An Extinction Rebellion Handbook* by, Penguin Press, 2019.

Goodall, Jane and Abrams, Douglas, *The Book of Hope: A Survival Guide for an Endangered Planet*, Viking, Penguin, 2021.

Goulson, Dave, *Silent Earth: Adverting the Insect Apocalypse*. Jonathan Cape, Vintage, 2021.

Higgins, Polly, *Eradicating Ecocide: Laws and Governance to Stop the Destruction of the Planet*. Shepheard-Walwyn, 2010.

Johnson, Ayana Elizabeth and Wilkinson, Katharine K., *All We Can Save: Truth, Courage and Solutions for the Climate Crisis*, Random House, 2020.

KATAPULT, *99 Maps to Save the Planet*, The Bodley Head, Vintage, 2021.

Kolbert, Elizabeth, *The Sixth Extinction: An Unnatural History*, Bloomsbury, 2014.

Lack, Bella, *The Children of the Anthropocene: Stories from the Young People at the Heart of the Climate Crisis*, Penguin Life, 2022.

Lymbery, Philip, *Dead Zone: Where the Wild Things Were*, Bloomsbury, 2017.

Pavelle, Sophie, *Forget Me Not: Finding the forgotten species of climate-change Britain,* Bloomsbury, 2022.

Thunberg, Greta, *The Climate Book*, Allen Lane, Penguin Press, 2022.

Wallace-Wells, David, *The Uninhabitable Earth: Life After Warming,* Allen Lane, Penguin Press, 2019.

WWF, "Living Planet Report 2022 – Building a nature positive society", Almond, R.E.A., Grooten, M., Juffe Bignoli, D. & Petersen, T. (Eds). WWF, Gland, Switzerland, 2022. www.livingplanet.panda.org

Acknowledgements

First and foremost, I want to thank all the scientists and rangers who devote their lives to protecting species around the world. It is not an easy job by any means – the conditions, the funding, the hours and the population declines – but it is one that truly makes a difference. I am eternally grateful to those who gave up their time and shared their expertise to tell me about their lives and work. To Dr Ricko Jaya and Lelia Bridgeland-Stephens, Peter Cooper, Connel Bradwell, Dr Christie Sampson, Dr Sara Hamilton, Dr Jonathan Kolby, Dr Louise Lavictoire, Vital Heim, Dr David Shiffman, Anna Jemmett, Dr Kubanych Jumabay uulu, James Mwenda, Professor Cesare Galli, Dr Becky Cliffe, Dr Adriano Garcia Chiarello, Dr Campbell Murn, Dr Andrew Digby, Dr Nicola Hemmings, Dr Erik Patel, Pungky Nanda Pratama, Professor Rosie Woodroffe, Kelsey Prediger and Sharyn Broni. It has been a privilege to listen to your individual experiences and to help raise awareness for your missions. I'd specifically like to thank you all for your transparency, patience and guidance throughout.

Thank you to my childhood dyslexia support teacher, Phil Roseblade, who gave me the confidence to accept my differences and harness my dyslexic mind as a superpower. Lessons that I will never forget.

To my stepdad, Chris, thank you for introducing me to the natural world. You showed me places and wildlife that I could only dream of and never wavered in your belief in me.

To my mum, Jo, for your endless encouragement and support. Thank you for visiting the smelly dead giraffe with me and for allowing me to fill my bedroom with skulls, feathers and living animals.

To my dad, Gordon, for always being the calm in the storm. Thank you for taking me swimming, giving great advice, keeping me grounded and for always delivering the best dad jokes.

To my partner, James, thank you for sharing your infectious enthusiasm about wildlife and for keeping me smiling during the writing process.

To my brother, Mowgli, thank you for your Brobdingnagian contribution and for being the strongest person I know.

To my agent and friend, David Foster, and the team, Gerry Granshaw and Sally McGinn, thank you for all of your assistance and your faith in me.

To my other family and friends, Charlotte Corney, Christine McCubbin, Richard McCubbin, Ayanna Gadsten-Jeffers, Hannah Stitfall, Ruth Tingay, Ruth Peacey, Aaron Evans and Graihagh Guille. Thank you all for inspiring me, for your words of wisdom and for the endless hours of laughter.

Thank you to the talented illustrator Emily Robertson for bringing the book to life with all of the vibrant drawings within its pages!

And last – but certainly not least – thank you to the exceptional team at Two Roads: Kate Hewson, Lauren Howard, Abigail Scruby, Alice Herbert, Jasmine Marsh, Charlotte Robathan and the whole organisation. Your enthusiasm about this book has been wonderful

and your essential edits and advice have been invaluable. Thank
you for your endless patience, kindness and assistance. I would
never have attempted a book without you, and for that, I am
forever grateful.

About the Author

Megan McCubbin is a zoologist, wildlife TV presenter and author. She has studied species around the world and uses her voice to raise awareness for their plights within our changing planet.

Megan co-authored *Back To Nature* with Chris Packham and is a regular presenter for the BBC and other broadcasters. She is one of the faces of the BAFTA award-winning BBC series *Springwatch* and can also be seen on CBBC's *Planet Defenders*, Al Jazeera's *Earthrise*, BBC One's *Animal Park* and ITV's *This Morning*. As a keen wildlife photographer and filmmaker, she uses her skills as a science communicator to empower, enthuse and engage everyone about the natural world.